A Treasure Trove
Of Ideas and Inspiration

Travel & Life

www.TravelTreasureBooks.com

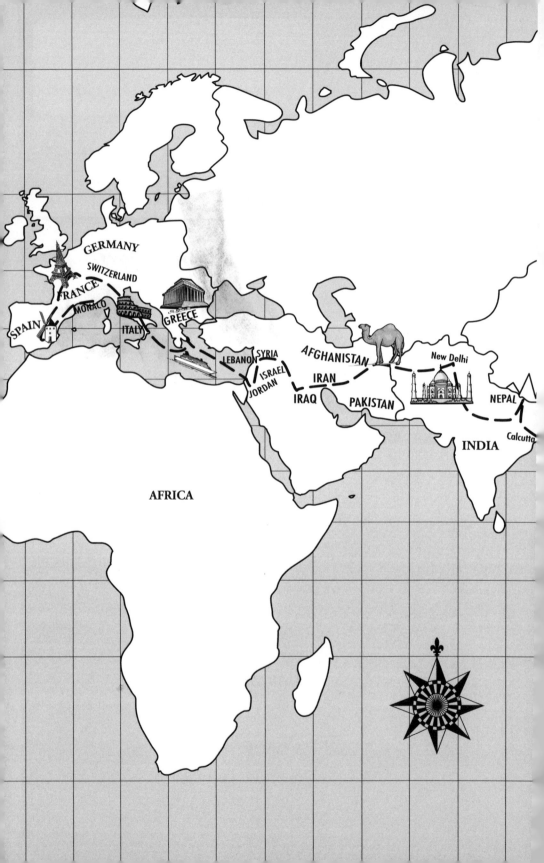

Romancing

THE IMPOSSIBLE

Traveling the World Without Money

Clarke before the Taj Mahal in India.

Romancing THE IMPOSSIBLE

Traveling the World Without Money

CLARKE STRAUGHAN

with Donna Veteto Delvy

TRAVEL TREASURE PUBLISHING
Austin, Texas

Travel Treasure Publishing
6705 Hwy. 290 W.,
Suite 502, Box 130
Austin, Texas 78735

SECOND PRINTING FALL 2009

ISBN 978-0-615-23468-7

LC 2009900724

Printed in the United States of America
at United Graphics, Inc.

Dedication

To my wife Judy,
our daughters Sabrina and Lisa,
and
our grandson Calen,
already an adventurer at five years old

Start by doing what's necessary;

Then do what's possible; and suddenly,

You are doing the impossible.

— Saint Francis of Assisi

Contents

Introduction

I was going to travel! I never had been away
from home and that word "travel" had a
seductive charm for me. I was going to have
all kinds of adventures, and maybe get hanged
or scalped, and have ever such a fine time.
— Mark Twain in *Roughing It*

One seldom has a chance to meet the Beatles, royalty, presidents, movie stars, dine with the rich and famous, and break bread with his fellow paupers. But I did.

My story was written years ago, scripted by my dreams: how I set out against-all-the-odds, with no money, explored the world, had close calls, danced with headhunters, experienced serendipity, dove into adventure, fell into romance, and embraced challenges all along the way—going beyond the horizons of experience.

Telling my story is a chance to give readers a view of the world beyond their own doorsteps—and to encourage them to pursue their dreams.

When I ventured across our globe for seven years, I experienced the majesty and miracle of being alive with a young and eager heart. While this is a personal narrative, I hope readers will be inspired by the fascinating people, places, and cultures I encountered.

Hitchhiking on back roads, sailing on ships across seas, riding trains across continents, ending up in exotic and unexpected places, I traveled anywhere and everywhere in an earlier time. And what a time it was!

How to explain the magic of my travels?

One of the greatest gifts I ever received was a birthday card from my mother on my twenty-first birthday. I took the following inscription from the card to heart. I lived its message!

THE ART OF ADVENTURE

Create mental pictures of your goals, then work to make
those pictures become realities.

Exercise your God-given power to choose your own direction and influence your own destiny and try to decide wisely and well.

Have the daring to open doors to new experiences and to step boldly forth to explore strange horizons.

Be unafraid of new ideas, new theories and new philosophies. Have the curiosity to experiment... to test and try new ways of living and thinking.

Recognize that the only ceiling life has is the one you give it and come to realize that you are surrounded by infinite possibilities for growth and achievement.

Keep your heart young and your expectations high and never allow your dreams to die.

—from *The Art of Living*
by Wilferd A. Peterson

It is a good thing for an uneducated (or educated) man to read books of quotations... The quotations when engraved upon the memory give you good thoughts.

— Winston Churchill

A quotation at the right moment is like bread to the famished.

— The Talmud

The young do not know enough to be prudent, and therefore attempt the impossible—and achieve it.

—Pearl S. Buck

CHAPTER 1

Royalty Comes to Texas

The world is a book and those who do not
travel read only one page.
— St. Augustine

March 2001
Dallas, Texas

*D*reams sweep by: of fragrant flowers; of balmy breezes, un-trodden beaches, and endless waves; of white palaces and faded temples; fallen tablets and unturned stones; of hesitant breaths and love beneath a thousand moons; of lost trails and drifting boats on infinite rivers—flittering dreams like birds settling in the twilight of memory. Now and then they come together as if what has happened happens again, as if once you walk into your dream the door never closes and your life and dream are one....

The feeling was unheralded. It came upon me as I stood there before the stately red brick Georgian structure's five white arches. The feeling enveloped me as the limousines passed like a royal retinue in front of the Meadows Museum and the bushes laden with pink and white buds swayed in the breeze as if bowing to the king and queen.

On the other side of the world from where my adventure began, many years washed away from its shores, I stood watchful, once more serving the King and Queen of Spain, making sure all proceeded as planned. They had come to my home, Texas, to dedicate the museum's grand opening, a festival of a thousand years of Spanish art, an internationally acclaimed collection.

As the official party of royalty and Texas dignitaries assembled inside the entrance hall, museum officials unveiled a bronze portrait of King Juan Carlos by Spanish sculptor Miguel Zapata, then dedicated the entrance hall in honor of his wife, the visiting queen, as the Queen Sofia Room. Afterwards the entourage climbed the sweeping Spanish-style staircase to the second floor to admire the paintings of El Greco, Goya, Murillo, Miro, Picasso, and other great artists.

Following behind, I had no idea if the king and queen would recognize me or even remember me. Discreetly I watched them from a distance, along with others who were privileged to be there. In this distinguished gathering, I ranked at the bottom of the totem pole. In fact, I was not even a part of the totem pole, nor ever had been. But as in years past, my undetectable standing on the social radar had never prevented my entrance into higher realms.

After a private tour of the paintings, sculptures, and artifacts, the royal entourage, the Governor and his wife, and other dignitaries entered the museum's private dining area. Amid the conversational buzz of ninety-four standing guests, the king and queen took their seats and the welcoming remarks began. *How amazing I'm here in this place at this moment,* I thought. The timing was incredible! As the new Director of International Protocol for the State of Texas, I'd been in the position one week and the grand opening was my first assignment. Sitting next to Alfonso Sanz, the Chief of Protocol of the Royal Household, I asked him endless questions throughout the luncheon. What exactly did he do? How did he know what to do in given situations? Did he travel everywhere with the royal couple? I probed his knowledge as much as possible so I could improve my role as a protocol officer. After all my questions, the dessert was placed in front of us and I could wait no longer.

"You know," I began, and then I told my story of how I had to come to know the royal couple. Mr. Sanz's eyes widened, he put down his spoon, and straightened his tie. He said, "As soon as this affair is over, I want you to come with me."

When the luncheon concluded, Mr. Sanz took me by the arm and led me into the hallway. Pointing to a place some twenty feet beyond, he anxiously said, "Stand over there." He then approached the Queen and whispered in her ear. Her eyes moved from person to person until she spotted me.

Within seconds, Queen Sofia stood before me, smiling. "Clarke, after all these years!" Quickly, she caught up with the King and the Governor. She touched King Carlos' shoulder and murmured in his ear. King Juan Carlos turned around and pointed at me with a warm and wide smile on his face. "Thirty nine years!" he exclaimed, and at once our memories flew to decades before, recalling how my seven-year journey around the world had begun.

CHAPTER 2

Dreams Are Born

*Whatever you can do or dream you can, begin
it. Boldness has genius, power and magic in it.*
— Goethe

*Seven-years-old
San Antonio, Texas*

*T*he branches of the giant oak trees that hung over Magnolia Avenue
from both sides of the road appeared to hold hands with each other. They
provided much needed shade in the hot Texas days. From the road, small,
white frame houses peeked out from beyond the sidewalks. Most evenings,
friends and neighbors gathered and sat in wooden chairs on the front porches,
chatting mostly about the major topic of the times: World War II. We didn't
have television yet, so we kids were always outside running and playing, letting our imaginations soar.

Those were simple days. The days of scraped knees and elbows, of picking ourselves up without a whimper and going back to what we were doing.
"You okay?" one of us would ask after a tumble. "Yep!" was always the answer.
Scrapes, bruises, and a little blood never kept us from acting out the adventures we had seen in the movie the week before.

Mrs. Naylon was a kind, older lady who lived across the street from my
best friend Butch's house. When she baked cookies, she would invite Butch
and me over to sample them. I remember a particular afternoon; we had been
playing Tarzan in a vacant lot. "You know what, Mrs. Naylon?" I said, while
munching a cookie.

"What, dear?" she responded.

"When I grow up, I'm going to go on a big ship and adventure all over
the world."

"Clarke, if anyone can do it, you can. You're a good boy, and you have
manners. You'll do fine out in the world," she said.

I never forgot that bit of encouragement.

Kids like us, actually poor by today's standards, received gifts only for

3

Clarke, at 9, as his dream was in full bloom on Magnolia Ave.

Christmas and our birthdays. Toys? Well, we had tons of them! When we were knights, we held up tin garbage can lids in front of our chests as shields and armed ourselves with stick swords. We spent so many summers and after-school hours creating boats, cars, forts, and whatever else we thought of with pieces of wood, cardboard boxes, and old Christmas trees that had been discarded in the alleys for garbage pickup.

The hill at the end of the road—that was our mountain. The creek at the other end of the road was our Amazon River. The vacant lots were the Wild West plains, and the trees and brush at the back of Butch and Milo's yard, our jungle. And when we pushed along on our scooters, we were riding horses or driving chariots—you name it. All we needed then was imagination. And we had plenty of it.

Suppertime was pretty much at six o'clock for everyone in those days. Most moms didn't have jobs and had dinner ready when our dads came home from work. Our favorite feat of swinging from a tree or capturing a renegade was often interrupted by Butch and Milo's dad, a Lieutenant Colonel just back from the war, who let out a shrill whistle calling his kids to come in for dinner. "Phooey!" Milo would say, pulling his lower lip up over his upper lip and sighing deeply. "Well, see ya, Clarke."

The next morning, we were out, swinging from the trees, playing Tarzan again. We never had a problem taking turns being Tarzan. Guess we were all raised with the Golden Rule and on Tarzan movies. From my earliest recollections, I remember sitting on my Grandfather Brown's lap, as he told me, "Whatever you do, and wherever you go, remember the most important thing in life is to treat others as you would have them treat you." It wasn't just words to "Bompie" (the name I had given him when I was a baby). I saw him live the Golden Rule.

During the day he worked as an engineer for the telephone company. On evenings and weekends, he volunteered his time as a Boy Scout Master. From the age of three, Bompie took me in tow to scout meetings, and campouts—my first adventures. Proud of his first grandson, he took me everywhere with him. Bompie was born and raised in Carthage, Missouri. A Mark Twain look-and-act-alike, he played with his mustache as he held me captive with his great wit. A Catholic of Irish descent, he was one of my first great guides in life.

My father's dad, Grandad Straughan, proved to be another man of great character in my life. A self-employed realtor of Scots-Irish descent, he was a Methodist and was known as a good horse-trader. Spending time with my grandfathers was a highlight of my childhood.

As much as we loved our jungle beyond the back fence, we always looked forward to Saturday afternoons. Saturday after Saturday, Butch, 7, his brother Milo, 10, and I tromped four blocks down to the Uptown Theater on Fredericksburg Road. In its front row seats, we entered another world—a world of adventure, daring, and romance.

The Saturday movies were an outlet of hero worship for me. Roy Rogers riding Trigger and saving the Wild West towns from bad guys; brave knights in shining armor; Robin Hood, played by my number one hero, Errol Flynn; and the newsreels of Lowell Thomas traveling to strange and marvelous lands all fired my imagination. (Later in life, I was to have an in-depth, one-on-one conversation with the world famous Mr. Thomas.) When we got back to the neighborhood, we'd immediately do our best to re-enact our film heroes' triumphs we had just seen on the screen.

One Saturday, the marquee of the Uptown read: Errol Flynn in *Captain Blood*. Inside, we watched in awe as Errol Flynn swung from the rigging of a pirate ship. On our walk home, I told the guys, "Some day I'm gonna set sail on my own world adventure."

"Oh, yeah?" Milo said, "Where are you gonna go?"

"I'm going everywhere!" I answered confidently, as though my bags were packed with the tickets inside.

"Gosh!" Butch said; "I'd be scared!"

I didn't feel scared. Somehow I knew my life was going to be as exciting as I wanted it to be.

In those days of childhood, Mrs. Naylon was like a doting aunt to me. Once, when I commented that Butch and my other friends didn't take my wish to see the world seriously, Mrs. Naylon looked at me kindly and said, "Don't let anyone keep you from your dreams." I knew she was serious.

I wanted to take off for strange lands right after high school graduation. My father was a strong disciplinarian and saw it differently. "College is where you're headed next, young man," he told me in a way that defied disagreement. "You need to get your degree, go out and get a job, and settle down like everyone else."

I'm not everyone else, I thought, knowing better than to say it.

My mother took me aside and said, "You are eighteen years old, Clarke. You have a long life ahead of you. Just get your degree, then choose your own path. You can do anything you want to do, sweetheart."

With a scholarship, I set out for Kemper Military School's Junior College program in Booneville, Missouri. Kemper was chosen as an honor military school for over 100 years and was cowboy-humorist Will Roger's alma mater. Kemper's staff ran the school as strictly as West Point.

Being physically fit and having made good grades, I decided to join the Marine Corps Officer Training Program. For two summers during my college career, I attended the Platoon Leaders Class (PLC Program) in Quantico, Virginia. Somehow I endured those two scathingly hot summers of Spartan-tough training along with my fellow officer candidates. Were they trying to kill us? *Just hold on. Nothing lasts forever*, I kept telling myself. *I'll end up stronger for this experience.* Indeed, those "Boot Camps" prepared me well for my coming adventures in the mountains and jungles of exotic, and sometimes dangerous, countries.

After a year at Kemper, homesick for Texas and milder weather, I transferred to Texas A&M University in College Station, Texas.

To make ends meet at A&M, I went to work at the Western Motel, a "one-horse inn" with all of forty rooms. Five evenings a week and Saturdays,

*A bit of role-playing after a hard day of Marine Officer
Training at Quantico. Clarke is in white shirt.*

I wore a multitude of hats. I checked in the guests who arrived on my watch and when the "old-time" switchboard lights flashed, I fumbled with the plugs and answered calls. I also worked as bellboy and maid. I carried luggage, changed sheets, vacuumed, and mopped floors, doing all the things my mom had tried to get me to do when I was growing up. I felt I was ready for anything life threw at me from then on.

But mostly, when I had the chance, I'd talk to the guests. I'd ask them: Where are you from? What do you do there? What has brought you to this part of Texas? As a result, I made many new friends and found I enjoyed the "hotel" business.

While at A&M, I took a course in salesmanship. One day our instructor, Mr. Kenagy, gave out a paperback book to each of us. It was Dale Carnegie's *How to Win Friends and Influence People.* He said, "There will be a test on this book in two weeks." That little book changed my life for the better and still influences me even today. It is basically "how" to live the Golden Rule.

With only months left in college, I spent my spare time reading James Michener's *Hawaii*. He described the islands as an unspoiled paradise with tropical forests, fragrant flowers, and cascading waterfalls. The vision of Diamond Head, the gentle strains of ukuleles, the grace of hula dancers, exquisite beaches, and the soft sands and surf of Waikiki beach, the most famous beach in the world, lured me in. That was it, I decided, Hawaii would be my first adventure destination. It was still an unspoiled paradise at that time.

There was a problem. I had no money and I still needed to complete my Marine Corps military obligation. I decided to work for a year and save up before I started out around the world. I drove up to Dallas, hoping my degree and astounding motel experience in College Station would win me a managerial position at the Love Field Holiday Inn. They weren't impressed. I started out as an assistant night auditor, one of the lowest jobs on the totem pole at $250 a month.

But before the end of the year, our General Manager, Mr. Sweet, introduced me to Randall Davis, the General Manager of the Sheraton Dallas and the president of the American Hotel Association. Mr. Davis said, "I'm told you would like to work at a hotel in Hawaii, Clarke. Mr. Sweet tells me you're not only a hard worker but also good with people. How would you like me to write a letter of introduction you can take with you to Hawaii? That should help open some doors at the Sheraton Hotels there."

I learned quickly that sometimes the right contacts and a friendly personality were more important than a great resume. Mr. Sweet also wrote a strong letter of recommendation for me.

I still needed money. Earlier in the year, a baby blue TR-3 sports car had caught my eye, and I just had to have it. The TR-3 boosted my ego when it was running, but it emptied my wallet when it wasn't. I eventually unloaded it and was nearly broke, again.

Never mind. It was now-or-never, do-or-die. The call of world adventure was totally upon me. Gathering up all my earthly belongings that had any value whatsoever, including my treasured coin collection, I went to a pawnshop on Houston Street in San Antonio and pawned it all for a grand total of $85.40—not quite enough to get me around the world.

But with $200 more, I would have enough money scraped together for the plane fare and $50 when I got off the plane in Hawaii. I had no real credit history at that time, so when I asked my dad if he would co-sign a $200 bank loan for me, his first words were, "Why don't you get a job like everybody else?" But he came through for me, although a bit reluctantly. I was going to start my travels in the hole, with less than "no money."

Later, I overheard him tell Mom, "He'll get this out of his system. Why, he'll be home within six months and settled down in a job."

Mom knew better, but she kept quiet.

After purchasing a one-way plane ticket to Honolulu, I stuffed my small suitcase with a suit, several pair of pants, a pair of blue jeans, four shirts, underwear, several ties and an extra pair of shoes. I thought, *I have no job, no place to stay, only one contact and maybe a week's living expenses.*

Doubts entered my mind. *What if I don't find a job? What if I can't find a cheap place to stay?*" But I knew if I gave into "what ifs," I'd never do anything in my life.

Words from Rudyard Kipling's poem, "If," came to mind:

> *"If you can dream—and not make your dreams your master;*
> *If you can meet with Triumph and Disaster,*
> *And treat those two imposters just the same,*
> *Then yours is the Earth and everything that's in it,*
> *And—which is more—you'll be a Man, my Son!"*

I was 23 years old and I was on my way to a new life of world adventure.

CHAPTER 3

Paradise Found

The poorest man is not he without a cent, but he who is without a dream.

— Anonymous

1961
Honolulu, Hawaii

A watercolor splash of lush green edged by a long dazzlingly white line appeared in the vast blue canvas of the Pacific. Like a child at a candy store, I pressed my face against the window of the plane and spotted the dormant volcano of Diamond Head rising far down the beach.

A flower-scented sea breeze tousled my hair and flapped my clothes as I hurried eagerly down the stairs of the plane and set foot on Hawaii. Thrilled to be taking my first steps in my travels, I never guessed I wouldn't return to the mainland for another seven years. But I was certain of one thing: I was ready for what was to come.

Running up to me was my old high school and Marine Corps buddy, Jimmie, (he was now a lieutenant) and his wife Marty shook my hand and embraced me, welcoming me with flowers and friendship. Our excited chatter about Hawaii and my plans for the future continued to their car. I confessed my uncertainty as to how to finish out my last year of reserve duty with the Marines, but Jimmie reassured me I could finish it at Pearl Harbor.

Jimmie and Marty dropped me off at the Waikiki YMCA where I rented a small room for $2 a day. I remember thinking, *Not many people have been so well-prepared for adventure as me. What with fifty dollars in my pocket, no job, who could want for more?* I was in a truly beautiful paradise.

The next day, Saturday, I wandered around taking in the sights. Everyone greeted me with "Aloha." I recalled Marty saying, "These islanders exude a sweet friendliness like no place you have ever been."

As I walked to the downtown area, I noticed a white banner extending 40 feet across the old YMCA building. It read: "Second-hand Book Sale." Being a book lover, I went to check it out. On the second floor, I found large

10

bins jumbled with books. As I was digging through the bins to see what I might find for fifty cents or less, a moth-eaten book that looked like Marco Polo's original manuscript caught my eye. I carefully opened the faded cover and read, *The Royal Road to Romance* by Richard Halliburton. *This book was waiting for me*, I thought, and went straight to the beach and started reading, immediately connecting with Halliburton's advice:

> *Don't squander the gold of your days, listening to the tedious, or give your life away to the ignorant and the common....*
> *Live! Live the wonderful life that is in you. Be afraid of nothing...*
> *I had youth, the transitory, now, completely and abundantly. Yet what was I going to do with it. Certainly not squander its gold on the commonplace quest for riches and respectability. I wanted freedom to indulge in whatever caprice struck my fancy, freedom to search the farther most corners of the earth for the beautiful, the joyous, and the romantic...to try everything once.*

Halliburton set guidelines for travel, romance, adventure, daring, and the joy of discovering places for yourself. During my year in Hawaii, I drew up my own blueprint for adventure—where I wanted to go and what I wanted to do and achieve for the next five years, all without money or backing of any kind.

On Monday, I put on my only suit and began hunting for a job. Walking from one hotel to another, I left resumes and reference letters. I would be out of money by the end of the week, so there was a great urgency in my step.

On the third day, I approached the grounds of the Royal Hawaiian Hotel, then known as the Pink Palace of the Pacific, one of the most luxurious and famous hotels in the world. Movie stars, royalty, and world dignitaries stayed at the Royal. Standing in the lush lobby, I remembered reading, *This is the hotel where East meets West, the hotel of the famous and the rich.*

"May I help you?" the desk clerk warmly asked me. I showed her my letter from Mr. Davis of the Sheraton Hotel in Dallas.

After making a phone call, the clerk ushered me down a hall of pink walls and marble tables with huge vases of fresh flowers. Howard Donnelly, the hotel's General Manager, a distinguished looking gentleman in his fifties with thinning white hair, greeted me with a firm handshake and had me sit in the rose-colored, brocade-cushioned chair in front of his mahogany desk.

His perfectly-fit, gray silk suit, I learned later, was one of many he'd had tailor-made during his visits to the Far East. While I sat on pins and needles and studied the gold-framed photographs of famous guests on his walls, Mr. Donnelly studied my resume and references.

"Well, Clarke," he began, "you certainly have a fine resume and excellent references. It appears that you would fit into any number of positions here. And I was especially impressed with your vast array of experience at the Western Motel in College Station," he said, tongue-in-cheek.

I thanked him and, smiling, he set my resume and letters aside. Peering over his horn-rimmed reading glasses, he asked me, "How would you like to start work tomorrow as a front desk clerk?"

My heart jumped. Bingo! I hit the jackpot. "That would be wonderful," I said, "What time do you want me to be here, sir?"

Hawaii's blend of cultures was evident in the hotel crew of Japanese, Caucasians, Chinese, Filipinos, and Hawaiians. As I met them, I asked each and everyone about their lives, discovering everyone had a story to tell. Within weeks, the cooks, busboys, waiters, and other Royal Hawaiian employees were asking me to parties, weddings and other family events. Yoshida, one of the cooks, told me, "All people are part of one great family."

As it turned out, a large part of that great family of workers and guests at the Royal Hawaiian were famous people.

When I was a kid, I'd been fascinated by Ava Gardner, a beautiful film actress of the 1940s and 50s. I will never forget her in the title role of the love goddess in *One Touch of Venus*. At nine years old I had a schoolboy crush on her; at 23, standing in her presence, I was blown away by her enduring beauty.

One late evening during her stay at the Royal Hawaiian, curvaceous Ava glided dreamily into the lobby. Shoeless, sandals in hand, the "Barefoot Contessa" sank down into a stuffed chair as if she had a bit too much to drink. Across from her, behind the check-in desk, I wasn't sure what to do or think.

Shaking her head and flinging her hair back, Ms. Gardner's big brown eyes studied me and my fellow desk clerk, Victor, a suave and handsome 30-year-old Mexican, a regular Don Juan. She called him over and said to him, "How would you like to accompany me to my room?" His eyes widened. Was she simply asking him to walk her to her room or was she asking for more? In shock, unable to sort out what was happening, he stuttered, "Uh, ma'am, I would like to accommodate you. However, I'm on duty."

Clarke and other staff at the famous Royal Hawaiian Hotel.

At Waikiki Beach with Royal Hawaiian shown above head.

Her invitation politely turned down, Ava Gardner gracefully glided to the elevator. I suppose her request could have been totally innocent. In all my dealings with Ms. Gardner at the front desk, she was gracious and very unassuming.

One morning, ten months after I'd been working at the front desk, Mr. Donnelly walked up to me and said, "Clarke, I have an assignment for you. The Crown Prince of Spain, Juan Carlos, and his new bride Princess Sofia of Greece have chosen the Royal Hawaiian for their honeymoon. I want you to see that their every need is satisfied from the time they arrive until they leave."

"Yes, sir, I'll make sure they feel completely at home here," I said.

"I know I can count on you, Clarke. You have the finesse for the job," he said. Later that day, Mr. Donnelly brought me a magazine article about the royal couple's wedding, one of the most lavish and publicized in Europe in decades.

For several hours the night before they arrived I had trouble falling asleep. All I could think of was that in a few hours I would be taking care of a prince and princess! What were they like? My grandfather's words came back to me: *Always treat others as you would like to be treated.* The good old Golden Rule. Sleep came easily the rest of the night.

The royal couple arrived the next morning in a limousine. Princess Sofia was a pretty woman in her early twenties and Prince Juan Carlos was a dashing young man not much older. I found them to be two of the most down-to-earth and gracious people I'd ever met. During their stay at the Royal, I assisted with arrangements for them to surf, dine in fine restaurants, and whatever else they wanted during their stay.

One day after surfing, Prince Carlos came into the lobby holding his forehead and wincing. As he approached me, he lifted his hand and I could see a red spot and a lump beginning to form. I walked over to him and asked what happened.

"A run-away surf board hit me!" he answered good-naturedly, still wincing from the pain. But he assured me he was fine and not in need of medical attention. I knew he must have had a whopper of a headache as the same thing had happened to me. Yet, the Prince never complained, nor demanded any more help than anyone else would have.

Another morning, Princess Sofia walked up to the front desk and asked, "Clarke, I wonder if you could do me a favor?"

"Yes, of course. How can I help you?" I asked.

"My brother's judo instructor is from Hawaii. I think he might live in Honolulu. I wonder if I give you his name, could you find him for me? I'd like to see him."

I have always loved a challenge. Three phone calls and two hours later, the judo instructor was walking in the door of the hotel. Princess Sofia was grateful, and never forgot that I helped her find this gentleman. She and Prince Carlos treated me as a friend.

The parade of famous people at the hotel and around the island was endless. The month after Prince Carlos and Princess Sofia were guests, "The King," Elvis Presley, was filming *Blue Hawaii* on Oahu and the other islands. During my off hours, I watched as much of the filming as possible. Elvis and I were about the same age. What was so great, I was living the life he was portraying in the movie. While Elvis didn't stay with us, other celebrities did.

"Front Desk, Clarke speaking," I answered the phone one morning. I heard a deep, rich voice on the other end of the line. *Surely this is the voice of God*, I thought. Actor Charlton Heston, who played biblical roles in the movies, was calling to arrange a game of tennis.

"Yes, sir, Mr. Heston," I said. "I'll reserve a court for 11:00 this morning."

"Thank you, Clarke," Mr. Heston's voice boomed.

Most of the famous people who stayed at the hotel treated the staff with respect, and they called us by our first names. While I was working at the Royal, I had the privilege of meeting, among others, John Wayne, Bing Crosby, Frank Sinatra, Jack Paar, presidents, royalty, prime ministers, and millionaires from all over the world. For a poor boy from Texas, this is what we called "living in high cotton." Since it wasn't the celebrity culture of today, where most famous people are hounded by paparazzi, I got to observe and know them as regular people.

When the summer of 1962 rolled around, I'd been in Hawaii a year. I was 24, I'd lived life to the fullest, doing my share of surfing, dating island beauties, making friends and contacts from all over the world, and acquiring invaluable hotel experience. But it was time to start planning to move on. I was ready for my next adventure, Tahiti, but I needed to save up a total of at least $1,000 to take me as far as that would go.

With Christmas approaching, I found a two-week, part-time job at McInerny's Department Store in the Ala Moana Center, not far from the hotel. On my first day, the personnel associate handed me a time card, pointed to the time clock, and said emphatically as I punched in, "Go over to the men's department and start selling!" The only thing that saved me was that I had worked part-time at J.C. Penney's while in college.

So much for job training!

As I walked into the men's area, I stopped at the chest-high sock counter where a young man about my age stood on the other side. He looked like he needed socks. "May I help you?" I blurted out, just as he said the same thing. We broke up laughing and introduced ourselves. Jim was another part-timer, who like myself, had been thrown onto the sales floor with little training. We became fast friends, and many years later, he was best man at my wedding.

Actually, Jim worked full-time as the first mate on an old-time sailing ship, the *Araner*, owned by John Ford, the movie producer. Legendary movie star John Wayne had sailed on that very yacht in some of his movies. After work that first day, he took me to see the *Araner*. I said, "Wow! Any mementoes left over of John Wayne?"

"As a matter of fact, the ship's log reveals some John Wayne stories," Jim said. "One time, in the late 1930s, he and Ward Bond put in on the African coast and got into a brawl with some of the locals at a bar. Both were thrown in jail."

Jim spent his daytime hours chipping and scraping paint in the hot sun until the captain went home and the ship was then Jim's. Meanwhile, in my coat and tie, I was busy meeting all the pretty girls in the coolness of the Royal Hawaiian. Come evening, Jim had the ship, I knew the girls, and the rest was history.

Jim and I made a great team. In the dark of the middle of the deck, Jim would put on a tape of Tahitian music and retire to the fore deck. There he and his date would watch the stars sparkling in the sky like champagne bubbles. Aft, my date and I danced in the moonlight. Jim and I often wished we actually owned that old-time sailing ship. But for those moments, on those evenings, we did.

Over the next several months, Jim and I talked about exploring the world together. Unfortunately, when I was ready, he wasn't. So when the day came to move on, I was on my own.

Aloha, Hawaii, Tahiti here I come. An exotic, romantic paradise was waiting for me—across the sparkling South Seas of the Pacific.

CHAPTER 4
The Romance of Tahiti

*If one advances confidently in the direction
of his dreams and endeavors to live the life
which he has imagined, he will meet with
success unexpected in common hours.*
— Henry David Thoreau

The first day of my foreign adventures had at last arrived. I had been waiting for this day since I was seven years old and first saw Errol Flynn swinging in the rigging of a pirate ship in *Captain Blood*. Would there be any rigging I could swing from in French Polynesia?

Friends came to see me off at the Honolulu Airport and wished me luck. I needed it. I was about to board an ancient "Gooney Bird," an over-the-hill Lockheed Constellation, a plane first built in 1943. The one I was flying in looked like it was the second one off the assembly line.

The specifications for the "Connie," as it was called, had been laid out by Howard Hughes. Was this huge "Queen of the Sky" going to make it off the ground? I had heard rumors of safety problems with the Connies.

As I walked up the steep stairs to the plane's tomb-like entrance, I asked all my friends to pray for me. So stricken by the sight of the plane, they agreed quickly and I thought they were going to fall to their knees then and there.

Entering the plane, I reminded myself that I was flying on this SPAL (South Pacific Airlines) bird because it was the all-night milk run to Tahiti and the cheapest thing going. But suddenly money didn't seem all that important. Other passengers must have come to the same conclusion: some had a frozen stare on their faces. Some smiled sheepishly, embarrassed by the fact their tightwad ways were going to cause them to die. Then, when the Connie lumbered down the runway, vibrating terribly as if shuddering with fear, I noticed a lady across the aisle fingering a rosary, praying for all she was worth. I almost snatched it from her.

As we lifted uncertainly into the air, what saved me from a nervous breakdown was the person sitting next to me, Jean Charles. A cheerful soul, he was not worried at all, apparently a man of the world. Rich, several years older than me, this young Frenchman knew there was no way he was going to die. Basking in the glow of his positive outlook quickly lessened my apprehension, and the French wine he bought for us lessened it even more. Once we made it into the sky, with no head winds and no worries—and without the Gooney's clumsy, flapping wings falling off—Tahiti again promised to be an exciting experience.

Jean Charles came from a family with a silk business in Calais, France, that was apparently doing superbly. He and I hit it off and talked through most of the night of dreams, plans, and what to do in Tahiti. I kept thinking in the back of my mind, *Here I am sitting next to a real live silk merchant*. But then, sitting next to Jean Charles, I somehow felt rich too. I had $900 to my name, good health, youth, an exuberant spirit, a dream, a do-or-die attitude—which was essential on that particular flight—and a wonderful new friend in this Frenchman.

As the sun rose over the horizon the next morning, a Pacific Shangri-La spread out before us. After safely coming over 2,000 miles of watery emptiness, the vision was a welcome one—Tahiti, the Island of Love, the most famous and romantic island in French Polynesia. Shrouded in legend, I hoped it would play a central part in my travels and romances as it had to so many others in the past.

Among those who had written of these enchanted islands were Jack London, Rupert Brooke in his poem "Tiare Tahiti," James Michener, Robert Louis Stevenson, and Somerset Maugham. Robert Louis Stevenson called the Polynesians, "God's best, at least God's sweetest, work."

Captain James Cook landed on this exotic isle in 1769, and the infamous Captain Bligh of the H.M.S. Bounty landed in 1788. All the early explorers told of a land of spellbinding beauty and enchantment. Although the British were there first, the French later expelled them. In 1842 a French Protectorate was established and Papeete was designated Capital of the Kingdom. Then, in 1957, the area was officially named the Territory of French Polynesia.

In 1961, when Marlon Brando came to film *Mutiny on the Bounty*, Tahiti was still unspoiled. A year later, when I arrived, it was just as magnificently beautiful as it had been for centuries. What a thrill to be there.

When I went through customs, the thrill diminished. After customs authorities inspected my one beat-up old suitcase and carry-on bag, they informed me I had to get a cholera shot. Now, I had already gotten eighty-two shots in Honolulu for every disease known to man. How on earth did they miss cholera?

Luckily, getting a shot was made bearable by the fact that Meelae, a Tahitian beauty, drove me to the local clinic. With her as my gracious escort, I accepted the situation as one of God's many little challenges.

Noticing Meelae was wearing a flower behind her left ear, I asked her about it. I came to find out her flower placement signaled she had a man. A flower behind the right ear meant a woman was still looking. It was important, therefore, to keep a sharp eye out.

As we traveled from the airport, itself unique, having been built on a coral reef, every few blocks disclosed something new to me. Instead of English, the signs in Papeete were in French. The homes and old buildings were of nineteenth century Tahitian and French design. It was almost like going back in time to the late 1800s. There were luxurious banks of flowers glowing in the richest colors, mountains rising majestically into the clouds, and people dressed in all manner of bright clothing.

I breathed the balmy fragrance of hibiscus, gardenia, bougainvillea, bird-of-paradise, ginger, frangipani, jasmine, and dozens of other lovely flowers for which I had no name. Setting all this off was the grand sweep of the ocean, an incredible deep blue expanse surrounding Tahiti that changed to a brilliant, transparent aqua-green near the shore.

As I discovered, it was luxury to sit in the perfumed air and forget there was any world but these enchanted islands, especially while watching the most spectacular sunsets in the world. I learned to call this state of mind Polynesian Paralysis, a way of being transported into a perfect mindless bliss. "And at sunset," I was told, "romance always resurfaces."

Along the waterfront of Papeete, yachts from many countries rocked gently in their moorings, anchor out and stern lines ashore. This was a stirring sight in itself.

Across the street from the colorful yachts of all shapes and sizes, Meelae dropped me right in the middle of town at the aged Stuart Hotel. Probably built in the early 1900s, the hotel had all of 20 rooms. Fortunately, my room had been remodeled and even had a bed in it. Down the way, Jean Charles stayed at a fancy hotel located on a black sand beach.

Hardly anyone I ran into could speak English. I depended on my one-semester of French at the University of Hawaii. Why everyone had such a hard time understanding me I could never figure out.

My first order of business was to walk around the whole town to get my bearings. At a teeming local market, the locals were well represented: Tahitians sold fish, fruit, root crops, and breadfruit; Chinese gardeners sold tomatoes, lettuce, and other vegetables; and both Chinese and French offered meat and bakery products.

To the north of the market were streets lined with two-story Chinese stores built after the great fire of 1884. Notre Dame Cathedral, built in 1875, was located southeast of the market. Then there was the Territorial Assembly building, the Evangelical Church dating back to 1875, and the Catholic Archbishop's Palace, built in 1869, a lonely remnant of the Papeete that Gauguin saw.

Papeete is the kind of place that everyone who has sailed a yacht dreams about. It is the heart of Polynesia, full of swaying palm trees, smells of coconut and fragrant exotic flowers; not to mention, the very best of French Champagne, cold beer, and long loaves of crusty French bread; and, of course, the very friendly Tahitians, especially those long-haired beauties with flowers tucked behind their ears. For a young guy like me, Tahiti was a retreat from a hustling-bustling world, but for the rich like Jean Charles it could be a perpetual playground.

Being a man of means, Jean Charles rented a car. That evening he drove us to the Hotel Taoone, where he was staying. It was our first night out-on-the-town. Soon after we'd finished eating, the wild beat of drums burst forth and six island beauties emerged, along with three Tahitian drummers. The women were performing the phenomenal Tahitian tamure dance, with their hips undulating at machine-gun-like speed.

After they completed their show, it was apparently us greenhorns' turn. Sexy Marta, one of the dancers, picked me out of the crowd. I learned it was my blue eyes that did it. Tahitian women love men with blue eyes. How fortunate for me.

For a sheer beginner, I didn't totally embarrass myself on the dance floor. After the show was over and everyone was getting up to leave, Marta unexpectedly came over to me. In French, she asked, "Would you like to have a drink?" There was nothing I wanted more than a drink with a beautiful Tahitian girl at that juncture.

I soon learned that Tahitian girls laugh at the drop of a coconut. How refreshing!

While having a drink, Marta took my hand, looked me in the eye and said, "I like you. You don't try to impress us. We Tahitians like people for themselves."

That was good because I had nothing to impress her with.

Jean Charles and I hit it off splendidly, the Frenchman and the Texan. We teamed up to take Tahiti by storm. Actually, it was more like a gentle breeze. We toured the island, danced with as many Tahitian girls as a night would allow, ate lavishly (since Jean wanted to treat), swam in the ocean, and relaxed on practically deserted, spotless beaches.

The two of us drank the island into our beings. If, as Paul Gauguin said, "Civilization makes you sick," then Jean Charles and I were on our way to becoming very healthy specimens.

Unfortunately, Jean Charles had to depart after only five days in paradise. But he helped me get off to a first-class start, and become quickly acclimated to the French-Tahitian way of life. Jean Charles was one of the many friends I would make in my travels.

That first week I was paying the princely sum of $7 a night for my "suite" at the ancient Stuart Hotel and I knew I was speeding toward bankruptcy, since I was not allowed to work in French Polynesia.

What I needed was a thatch-roofed hut, one that was in Tahiti when Captain Cook landed, something cheap. The day Jean left, I found it. I rented a thatch-roofed bungalow, without windows or screens, for $100 a month from Monsieur Blanchard. It had a shower, a tiny kitchen, a sitting room with a couch and several dilapidated chairs, and one bedroom. It also came with a brood of chickens that served as a built-in alarm clock in a quaint country setting. I was home! And it was only one country block from the beach.

Next, I found myself a rapid transportation vehicle called a Mobilette. It was a bicycle with a five-horsepower engine above the front wheel. Going downhill, with the wind at my back, I could race along at close to 25 mph. Even though it set me back $35 a month—and that was only after extensive bargaining with the Chinese owner—it was worth it.

One day, shortly after Jean's departure, I literally danced for nearly ten hours straight. The dancing started at 3:00 p.m. and went to 2:00 a.m. in the morning. I ended up making about 40 new friends that day.

It all started when I went to Vaima's, a bamboo-walled, French-Tahitian cafe on the waterfront. After attending a Tahitian church service, where the melodic singing was heavenly, I headed for Vaima's. It was a favorite hangout for foreigners living in Papeete. Its whole setting on the colorful, buzzing waterfront was like something out of the past, like a place out of the "pirate adventure" movies I watched growing up.

After lunch, some of my new friends invited me to go with them to a hotel in the country where everyone went for Sunday dances in the open air. One of the fellows I met was Bob Williams, an affable, fun-loving, and an all-around good guy. Bob was a thirty-two year old pharmacist who, having recently gotten divorced, decided to leave it all behind in California and head straight for paradise.

Bob was looking for a place to stay to conserve his cash. I invited him to share my "mansion in the country" and he moved in the next day. I gained an adventurous buddy and cut my living expenses in half.

Another great friend I made that day was Bruce Turner from Georgia. He was a thirty six year old, balding, pleasant, soft-spoken vagabond. Bruce and I would later stay at the same boarding house in Australia and have many adventures together.

Bob and I had a dandy arrangement. He would get the bedroom one night and I would sleep on the couch, and then the next night we'd switch.

In Tahiti, the philosophy for everything was summed up in one saying: *Why not!* One evening in Vaima's Cafe, while drinking Hinano beer, one of the Tahitian girls said, "Let's go jump off the rigging of the *Dwyn Wynn*, and swim in the moonlit harbor," and everyone shouted, "Why not?" Then all of us rushed to the *Dwyn Wynn*, a look-alike of the old-time sailing ship in the movie *Mutiny on the Bounty*, and dove off the rigging.

That's how we did things.

If someone yelled, "Let's go swim with the sharks." We would all shout back: *Why not!*

"Let's paddle across to the island of Moorea in an outrigger canoe!" *Why not!*

"Let's go climb the mountain and dive off the 300 foot waterfall." *Why not!*

"Let's go dancing at Quinn's bar." *Why not!*

I was seeking adventure. *Why not!*

Movie star Sterling Hayden in his book, *Wanderer,* the name of his old-time sailing ship, writing of his yearlong sailing adventure in the South Pacific, had this to say:

> *To be truly challenging, a voyage, like a life, must rest on a firm foundation of financial unrest. Otherwise, you are doomed to a routine traverse, the kind known to yachtsman who play with their boats at sea…cruising it is called. Voyaging belongs to seamen, and to the wanderers of the world who cannot, or will not, fit in.*

Pictured with a Swedish-Tahitian girl in front of the Wanderer.

I've always wanted to sail to the South Seas, but I can't afford it, these yachtsmen say. What these men can't afford is NOT to go. They are enmeshed in the cancerous discipline of "security." And in the worship of security we fling our lives beneath the wheels of routine—and before we know it our lives are gone.

What does a man need—really need? A few pounds of food each day, heat and shelter, six feet to lie down in—and some form of working activity that will yield a sense of accomplishment.

Otherwise…we end up in a tomb beneath a pyramid of time payments, mortgages, preposterous gadgetry, play things that divert our attention for the sheer idiocy of the charade.

The years thunder by, the dreams of youth grow dim…where, then, lies the answer? In choice. Which shall it be: bankruptcy of purse or bankruptcy of life?

Just to think, I stood on a very firm foundation of financial insecurity, and here I was jumping off the rigging of the old-time sailing ship *Dwyn Wynn*, under a gigantic moon, with the crew and their Tahitian girlfriends. Why not! Wasn't life meant to be lived to its fullest?

Quinn's was one of our favorite hangouts in Papeete, Tahiti.

CHAPTER 5

Sailing to the Magic Isle of Bora Bora

*Twenty years from now, you will be more
disappointed by the things you didn't do than
the ones you did do. So throw off the bow-
lines. Sail away from the safe harbor. Catch
the trade winds in your sails. Explore. Dream.
Discover.*

— Mark Twain

One fine, bright morning, Bob and I decided to go exploring. Off we went on our trusty Mobilettes, zipping along the shore road into an area we had not yet seen. Through the palm trees we saw a beautiful beach and decided to check it out. As we walked toward the beach, we ran into two native Tahitian guys.

They said, "Be careful if you go in the water because we saw several big sharks swimming close to the beach earlier."

Farther down the beach, we came upon an old, two-man outrigger canoe. It was just too hard to resist so we gave it a try. "As long as we are in it, we will be safe," we agreed. We only lacked paddles. We found two old boards and launched into the deep. Slowly we made our way out from the shoreline, gaining expertise and confidence with each stroke.

Thirty yards out, the old outrigger did a sudden flip, and into the shark-infested waters we went. It was my first time to try to walk on water. I came very close to doing so! Looking in all directions to see if any sharks were speeding our way, Bob and I righted the outrigger and scrambled in, our hearts pounding. Gingerly, we headed for shore. We were pleased to discover the sharks weren't hungry for two crazy, raw Americans that day.

Sharks or no sharks, I decided to go surfing. The surf in Tahiti is legendary. The beaches and reef passes are pounded by some of the most awesome surf on earth. I had become a fair surfer in Hawaii, so *why not!* Surfing apparently started with Polynesians using wooden planks. Even today, many in Polynesia argue over who invented the sport, whether it was Hawaiians, Tahitians, or the natives from another island group.

For surfing, the water was incredibly blue and unbelievably clear, and I practically had the waves to myself. And luckily, no sharks crowded in on me. At least none I was aware of. I surfed into the sunset.

Speaking of which, since all the islands comprising French Polynesia are truly breathtaking, their sunsets are exquisite. But in my view the sunsets over the island of Moorea are without equal anywhere in the world. Add to the fantastic sunsets the uplifting sunrises over endless magnificent beaches, with majestic palm trees swaying to the tune of South Sea breezes, and one finds a place on earth where dreams become reality.

One night, having left my racing vehicle at the bungalow, I spent the night in town. But I was up at 6:00 a.m. to watch the sunrise. Sitting at a sidewalk table in front of Vaima's, my usual hangout, no one else in sight, I was sipping my café au lait, waiting for the sun to show its face. With the air sweet with the fragrance of flowers, the palm trees softly swaying in the breeze, and the yachts from all over the world gently rocking along the quay—all was right with the world.

Then this Vespa motor scooter appeared. The fellow on it pulled up and parked in front of Vaima's. He was wearing a T-shirt, cut-offs, and sandals. I said to myself, *My gosh, one side of him is skinned up from head-to-toe. I wonder what happened to him?*

As happened so often on that friendly island, he walked up and asked if he could join me. Of course, I was always happy to make new acquaintants. He said, "My name is Huey." Huey was from New York.

"Pleased to meet you. I'm Clarke."

Huey told me he had sailed in on a yacht a few days earlier. I figured he was another poor adventurer like myself. After chatting over coffee, curiosity got the best of me and I asked him how he got so skinned up. He said, "Well, I rented that Vespa and was going across a bridge when I lost control and almost wiped myself out."

I said, "That's terrible, it's fortunate you only got skinned up."

We talked a little more and developed a good rapport. Finally, I said, "Huey, I need to hitchhike on out to my bungalow in the country."

Huey said, "Come on, I'll give you a ride."

I thought, *Whoa!* Sometimes you're not sure whether to accept an invitation or not. But, I said okay, and prayed every time we crossed a bridge. Happily, we made it in one piece.

As it is in Tahiti, no one went around bragging who they were or what they had. I found out several days later Huey Long, 33, was a highly successful shipbroker, famous in the yachting world for winning many ocean races around the world with his yacht *Ondine*. Though he boasted the same name as the infamous politician of the 1930s, his real name was Sumner Long, known in the 1960s as one of the world's most successful ocean-racing skippers.

Huey and I hit it off well. Several weeks later, he asked me if I would like to sail to Bora Bora with him. From there, he was going to sail on down to Australia and take on the Aussies in their own waters, in the famous Sydney-to-Hobart Yacht Race. What audacity! But as Huey and I believed, *why not*!

Being the seasoned landlubber that I was, I jumped at the opportunity to sail to the magic isle of Bora Bora. I thought, *I hope he can sail better than he maneuvers a motor scooter,* but, there was absolutely no doubt about that! Huey had already proved to be a world-class winner.

It was mid-afternoon and the gentle, rolling sea was calm as Bill Branson steered the sleek, all aluminum, 57-foot racing yawl through the deep blue waters, with only the two of us on deck. Bill said, "Clarke, how would you like to take the wheel?" Wow, what an opportunity! Bill turned it over to me. Within a minute, the sails began flapping and Huey came up out of the cabin like a rocket. My career as a helmsman was over before it began. This yacht was Huey's baby. He could detect the slightest change of any kind. I was reassigned as the new dishwasher.

That night, with a smooth sea running, I was in a dreamy sleep on the front deck under an endless canopy of stars. In the blink of an eye, I was awakened by sheer bedlam. The world was coming to an end! Shouting, pounding, chaos! With my feet pointed toward the bow of the yacht, I tilted my head back to see what was happening. Two feet away, a six-foot barracuda was coming at my head, snapping his jaws, flashing rows of jagged teeth. Well, I did a double somersault, half-twist, back swan dive over the side ropes, holding on for dear life to keep from dropping into the ocean.

My fellow crewmates had pulled this mean fellow in on a trailing line off the back of the boat. He had escaped their clutches and decided to tour the front deck, especially since they were trying to smack him with hammers or whatever else they could get their hands on. Never again did I want to stare a barracuda in the eye. However, I did, along with the rest of the crew, eat that brazen barracuda for breakfast the next morning. Served him right.

Early one morning, as the *Ondine* was moving along smoothly at about five knots, I sighted the awe-inspiring island of Bora Bora, as beautiful as it was when James Michener arrived there in World War II, as magical as it was in *South Pacific* when it was used to portray Bali Hai.

With dramatic peaks soaring above an unbelievable, multi-colored lagoon, seven-million-year-old Bora Bora is made up of a long island, a few smaller islands in the lagoon, and a long ring of reef islets. It is believed it has been inhabited since the year 900 A.D.

In 1962, hardly any tourists visited there. We found it wonderfully virginal, blissfully peaceful, and quiet.

We docked at the one half-decent hotel with all of twenty rooms. Several of us hiked the two miles of dirt road to town. There we found a small school, an infirmary, a dozen or so small houses, and a four-room so-called hotel, actually a bungalow with bamboo partitions ten-feet high.

Being the adventurers we were, one of the guys rented one of the rooms. Several of us snuck in later that night and slept on the concrete floor on straw mats. For light, there was a kerosene lamp. As Bill said, "The beach would have been more comfortable, but, because we didn't pay, we got what we deserved—sore backs."

While on that magic island, I met a captivating Tahitian-Chinese girl. We bicycled all the way around the island and spent many wonderful hours together. In one word, Bora Bora was IDYLLIC. "So stunning, there are no words to describe it," so said James Michener.

CHAPTER 6

Under the Tahitian Moon

Time spent in laughter is well invested.
— *Anonymous*

*N*ot long afterwards, Huey sailed off for Australia and I flew back to Papeete on a seaplane. My money was running low and with no way to make money in Tahiti, I had to leave as soon as I could, even though I desperately wanted to stay. For one thing, I had left something undone. That something was named Henrietta.

Since I first met her, I had had my eye on Henrietta, a Tahitian princess. But though she was something to behold, she played very hard to get.

One night, I arranged a date with her for 10:00 in the evening. We went to a popular little nightspot on the waterfront called Whiskey-A-Gogo's, several blocks away from the other nightspots. At first, Henrietta and I were sitting at the bar, chatting, and getting along fairly well. But that night, Fate had something else in mind.

Out of the blue, in walked Poinette, Moea, and a fellow named Art, whom I did not know. Poinette and I had become good friends, and, though I had met Moea, I had stayed away from her because I heard through the grapevine never to ask her out. It seemed the President of the French Assembly, the most powerful man in Tahiti, was smitten with her. In fact, the story went like this: If anyone even showed the least bit of interest in Moea, they would be summarily deported, cast out of paradise. Well, believe me, deportation was NOT in my plan! But little did I know what was in the cards for me.

Before I knew it, after I started talking with Poinette, I turned around and discovered Henrietta and Art sitting together in a booth across the room. I thought, *Okay, so much for Henrietta*, and was wondering where my evening was headed when, without warning who should enter this den of romance, but the aforementioned President of the French Assembly. Thank goodness I had just pulled Poinette out on the dance floor and wasn't anywhere near the coquettishly stunning Moea.

Over several hours we danced and partied and, when the club closed at midnight, we decided to head out into the countryside for Lafayette's

29

Nightclub, the only night spot that stayed open until 4 a.m. Poinette jumped on the back of my Mobilette and Moea rode with the President in his sleek French car. Henrietta went who knows where.

At the club, things took on a new life. Poinette became very gregarious, chatting with everyone while the rest of us danced, and Moea's wannabe romeo, the President, proceeded to get bombed. It soon was obvious that the President had had so much alcohol, he couldn't see straight, much less walk a straight line. Recognizing opportunity when it staggers in front of me, I summoned up my courage and asked Moea to dance. *Why not!*

Naturally, in no time at all, I became head-over-heels infatuated with this charming 19-year-old French-Tahitian beauty, even though she couldn't speak a word of English. There was only one thing to do. I whispered in her ear, in my now much-improved French, "Would you like to meet me back at Whiskey A Gogo's later?" To my amazement, she said yes, agreeing to ditch the President somehow or other. *Damn the deportation,* I told myself. *Full speed ahead!*

With friends from Tahitian dance group.

Hopping on my trusty Mobilette, I sped off through the deserted countryside toward town. Without a jacket, I shivered as I breezed along into the cold, dark night until I finally neared the club around 2:00. Making my way along the darkened street, the only guiding lights those twinkling in the harbor, I hid behind a high wall next to the club and waited. And waited and waited and waited.

No Moea! Strike two on girls for the night.

In utter frustration, I headed back out to the country to my bungalow. I parked in back and walked around the side. Since it had no windows, just slats that were raised up and hooked overhead, I glanced inside my bedroom as I passed by. Someone was in my bed and it certainly wasn't Bob. Doing a double-take, I stopped dead in my tracks. It was Moea. *Oh my! Now I'll surely be deported. But what a way to go! How on earth did she get here and who brought her?* I could just imagine her saying, "Mr. President, will you drop me off at Clarke's place, *sil vous plait?*"

What explanation Moea gave Le President, I never determined from her mixture of Tahitian and French. It must have been a humdinger. *cést la vie!* Indeed.

There was only one thing to do. I naturally reverted to the philosophy of Tahiti—take it as it comes and be happy. Why not?

The next morning six gendarmes knocked on my bungalow door and said, "From all descriptions, you must be the culprit." I stared at them in disbelief until they vanished into the misty air.

Thank goodness, it was only a dream.

31

CHAPTER 7

Sailing Into the Unknown

*We live in a wonderful world that is full of
beauty, charm, and adventure. There is no
end to the adventures we can have if only we
seek them with our eyes open.*
— Jawaharal Nehru

*K*nowing I was probably a marked man by Le President, and running low on money, the better part of valor told me to hitch up my wagon and move on. The only transportation I could afford anytime soon was the passenger liner *Monterey*, third class, at the bottom of the boat. The price fit my almost empty pocketbook.

I toured this lovely ship the day before she was to set sail. No one aboard appeared to be under eighty years old. I strongly suspected my days of romance were over.

That afternoon some 300 passengers were treated to a tamure dance on the grounds of the Tahiti Village Hotel. Stella, the lead dancer of this top dance group, and I had become friends and dance partners during my stay.

I sat at the edge of the crowd, next to a couple and their most attractive 20-year-old daughter, Dean Anne, and we struck up a friendly conversation. They began talking about the absolutely throbbing pace of the dancers and wondered how anyone could dance that fast. Of course, they took me for just another tourist.

About that time, Stella came over and pulled me out of the crowd into the center of the dance circle. The drums cut loose and so did we. My new friends from the ship were in awe as I rejoined them. Dean Anne even seemed slightly impressed. I was hoping so, because we were soon going to be shipmates.

That evening at Vaima's Cafe, I bid many of my dear and wonderful friends, who had become like family, a fond farewell. Some I invited to the ship for dinner. Among them was Augustine, Tahiti's number one dancer. She kept us laughing all evening with her zany antics.

Many of us ended up at Whiskey-A-Gogo's for final farewells, and then Stella and I headed for the bungalow under a full island moon—palm trees waving us down the road into the indigo night.

32

Clarke, in his one suit, at Captain's cocktail party on voyage from Tahiti to New Zealand.

Heartfelt goodbyes and a 4:30 a.m. departure for the ship came too soon. Stella gave me an exquisite shell lei and a heartfelt, warm send-off. She was one of the kindest, most wonderful people I'd ever known.

It was with a flood of emotion that I sailed at sunrise from that Tahitian paradise. I felt as if I had spent a lifetime there. By that afternoon, I was quite sad, and by evening quite seasick. I sailed on 21 ships in my adventures and got sick 21 times. I was not a sailor. After the first day on board, I gained my sea legs, although one seemed shorter than the other, as the ship rolled along. But at least my stomach was fine. One night at dinner, as the ship was swinging from side to side like a pendulum, I couldn't understand where everyone was. But I enjoyed a hearty meal as I chased my plate back-and-forth across the table.

Several days into the voyage, we reached Raratonga. A group of dancers came on board to do a show. At the Beachcombers Dance that evening, I spotted Dean Anne. I just knew romance was about to bloom.

As we crossed the International Dateline, we skipped November 16 entirely, which was too bad because I thought it had been a pretty good day. No doubt, we all experience lost days in our lives. The key is to make up for them.

Dean Anne and I did a little light courting on the top deck one starry, starry night. I still wonder how her mom and dad knew we were up there. From that time on, I posted guards.

Sail on Captain, and let a new chapter of adventure begin.

As we made our way to the docks in Auckland, New Zealand, the *Monterrey* glided slowly past numerous islands in the early morning sunlight. Some passengers had been banging around since 4:00 a.m., just to get up on deck in the dark of night so they wouldn't miss seeing one tiny island. Sunrise was soon enough for me, especially after a night of revelry aboard ship.

After clearing customs, I walked to the Matson Line office on Queen Street with Barry, a jovial fellow and a Matson employee. He and I had become friends on the voyage. There's nothing like having at least one friend to advise you when you arrive low on money, jobless, and somewhat clueless in a foreign country. A cup of tea at a quaint restaurant put me right.

Barry was first-rate in helping me get my feet on the ground in Auckland, an English-like city stuck in an earlier age. *It looked almost like America did back in World War II,* I thought to myself. The style of clothes seemed out-of-date, the cars from another era, and the buildings very old, but I found the people kind, helpful, and very English in their ways.

New Zealand is about the size of Colorado and also has magnificent scenery. Today it has a population of around four million, including the Maoris, the native people who were once fierce warriors. The Maoris had lived in harmony with the land, respecting it as the property of the gods, and, in the olden-times, they often killed foreigners who set foot on their shores.

The Dutch navigator, Abel Tasman, was the first European to discover these islands in 1642. It was named "Nieuw Zeeland," no doubt after the Dutch island province of Zeeland. In 1769, the British navigator, Captain James Cook landed and proceeded to chart the coastline in great detail. He took possession of "New Zealand" for England.

Missionaries of many denominations spent the early 1800s establishing missions. In 1840, after Auckland was chosen as the capital, colonists began flooding in.

In 1935, New Zealand took up the social welfare banner, which basically meant cradle-to-the-grave care. Perhaps this mentality was what made things seem so behind-the-times and accounted for a slower pace of life, which was not all bad. In 1947, the country claimed full independence.

Fortunately, I did have one contact to look up in Auckland. He was a hotel buddy from Hawaii, Harry Lien. He had arrived weeks earlier. I had his address but no phone number.

I took a bus to the Parnell area. Harry opened the door when I knocked and said in surprise, "I thought you were still swimming with the sharks in Tahiti!" I told him I had outrun the sharks and run out of money at about the same time. We caught up on each other's travels. Just having this one contact in New Zealand was a blessing.

But there was no time to lose! Harry drove me downtown where I hit the streets looking for a job of any kind—manager, sub-manager, bartender, dishwasher, or anything down from there. But that day no one wanted any of my wide array of talents.

Again, one friend led to another. Chris Deans, a friend of Harry's, found an old red brick boarding house where I could stay. The boarding house, a home built in the 1930s, had four rooms that were rented out. I was told the owner was a former madam. At 70-something years old, she exhibited the most flaming red hair I had ever seen in my life.

The Madam was kind and outgoing—of course, she had had a lot of experience along those lines—and I felt right at home. If it hadn't been for Chris, I would never have discovered this special place. My board was three pounds, three shillings a week—about $7.00, an incredible price for a place providing such ambience.

The next morning, the ambience increased ten-fold. I walked down the hallway to the community kitchen breakfast nook. That's where I met Reg, a Cockney from London, a character right out of Dickens.

A 22 year-old "ex-sailor," Reg had recently jumped ship and was using an assumed name so the authorities couldn't find him. He was "on the lam," so to speak.

With his accent, I mused, *the authorities were sure to think he was a German-Danish-Turk, with a lisp, who spoke an unknown dialect of Hindi.* As for me, I couldn't understand anything he said until he had repeated it over four or five times, very slowly. And then I'd figure out about every other word was a cuss word. But we became instant friends, as we were both a couple of young guys full of vim-and-vigor. And like me with his accent, Reg was probably struggling with the Texas drawl I still possessed to some degree.

Discovering we were both looking for jobs, we started walking to town, till one of his Cockney mates came along in a car and gave us a ride. It turned out this new Cockney fellow didn't know anything *but* cuss words. I figured he managed to jump ship with Reg. *At this rate, New Zealand is going to be overrun with Cockneys,* I speculated.

On that beautiful spring day, Reg and I walked all over Auckland. Along the way, he introduced me to the city, as I made some cold calls for a job. I never knew when and where a job might pop up through sheer serendipity. But not that day!

To learn a city, I always planned to spend a day or two just walking all the main streets, and many of the back ones, observing everything closely—the people, their clothes, language, demeanor, pace, as well as the architecture, schools, parks, businesses, entertainment areas, and the whole atmosphere in general. Most likely, a city's residents never saw 50% of what I did.

Chris and Harry had me over for dinner. We talked about travel, future plans, and the ins-and-outs of New Zealand. From all I'd gathered, finding work would be difficult. That was enough to convince me to strike out for Australia soon, while I still had a small amount of money left.

At this point, my contacts in New Zealand consisted of Harry, Chris, and Reg. But the next day, a gorgeous spring morning with flowers bursting forth everywhere, I was walking by the downtown post office when it was my good luck to run into Bruce Wirth whom I had met in Tahiti. We talked briefly and I discovered he was leaving on a bus for the south island. I was disappointed, but he called an Auckland girl named Wendy he wanted me to meet. He had met Wendy in Tahiti. Serendipity strikes once again!

After bumping into Bruce, I made a plane reservation at Quantas Airways and then took a bus tour of the city. Such a tour always covers the main sights in a city, at a reasonable cost.

As I was walking downtown at 5:00 p.m., all of a sudden a great surge of men ran out of a number of buildings. To keep from being run over by this "charge of the light brigade," I pressed myself against a building. *What on earth is going on*? I wondered.

I asked a bloke what the big rush was. He told me that the pubs in Auckland close at 6:00 p.m. "Therefore, it is absolutely essential that you get to the pub quickly to get a front row seat. How else could you get enough beer to drink before closing time?"

I looked at the mad dashers and thought, *Some laws might have the opposite effect intended*. A conclusion confirmed when I spotted several of the pub runners crawling out on all fours at 6:00 p.m.

That evening I called Wendy, met her, and then spent the next several days in her charming company, the highlight of my New Zealand stay. Though beautiful, blonde Wendy had left Tahiti two weeks before I got there, we had a natural fellowship special to those who had lived in that island paradise.

The next day, she and I had lunch with her parents, a quite well-to-do family. After lunch, Wendy played her Tahitian records and we talked about our experiences in Tahiti. Very few women went there to live on their own as she had done.

That afternoon she suggested we hit the beach and go surfing, even though it was a cold, blustery day. After surfing, we lowered our frozen bodies in a hot springs pool near the beach and immediately warmed up.

As we relaxed, she told me a shark's tale. Some lifeguards were training in the waters we surfed when a great white shark appeared. But before it could strike, dolphins raced in to help. Surrounded by the dolphins for 40 minutes in a protective circle, the swimmers made it safely back to the beach. A marine biologist said, "Dolphins like to help the helpless."

What can you say about dolphins except bless them all!

After the beach, it was back across the island to Auckland and a seaside beer garden. The sun came out and all was right with the world.

That evening, Wendy took me to the Gourmet Restaurant for dinner.

We drank German wine and danced to an Italian trio. *Now this is the life, especially for a guy who's way low on funds and has no idea what lay ahead in Australia*, I mused.

On my last night in Maori-land, I walked over to say goodbye to Harry and Chris, thanking them for their gracious assistance. I wondered if I'd ever see Harry again. Among adventure travelers, anything was possible.

The big day finally arrived. Next stop: Australia! Apprehension and excitement held sway over my emotions. I had a migrant's visa, a sea bag, my old suitcase, and ten whole dollars in my pocket. Bring it on.

Clarke with one of his furry friends.

CHAPTER 8

No Job, No Place to Stay, No Money— Welcome To Australia

*The only way to find the limits of the possible
is by going beyond them to the impossible.*

— Arthur C. Clarke

*A*t 1:00 p.m. the Quantas plane made a smooth landing at the Sydney airport.

Reg had seen me off in Auckland. As a result of his fine tutoring, I was now fluent in rudimentary Cockney, complete with the occasional cuss word thrown in.

Not knowing exactly when I would get to Australia, I had no contacts lined up, so I was on my own. But, as always, I was full of optimism, slightly tempered by a touch of apprehension.

The first thing I did was to see if I could find a free ride into downtown Sydney. I started asking at the rental car agencies. Eureka! Margaret at Kay's Car Rental gave me a ride to the main YMCA.

The YMCA building was in a neighborhood of 100 years old, or so I figured. The YMCA, if a city had one, was always the first place I headed when I arrived in a country. I knew that I would find a warm Christian greeting and people willing to lend assistance to an enthusiastic wayfarer. And that was certainly the case in Sydney.

My ten dollars would buy me two whole nights of bed and breakfast. Breakfast consisted of a roll, with butter thrown in, and a cup of coffee. My room was about twice the size of a closet. After this splurge of luxurious living, I would be dead broke, so pulling a rabbit out of a hat seemed my only option.

I spent all of the next day looking for a job, any job, in the downtown area. Fed up with my lack of success, I marched back to the YMCA and went straight to the front desk. I asked the clerk, "Where is the best hotel in Sydney?" She gave me directions to the Chevron Hilton: "Go up the boulevard for about a mile, turn left at Kings Cross, and go about three blocks to Potts Point."

Not having a cent to spare for a bus, I started walking. It was sunset when I entered the lobby of this world-class hotel and ran smack dab into my friends, Huey and the whole crew of the yacht *Ondine*. What a magic hour, seeing my fellow sailors from Papeete-to-Bora Bora re-enter my life!

After warm greetings, they said, "Hey, Clarke, we're getting ready to go to dinner, you want to join us?"

Thanks be to God, I got to eat that night. My spirits were considerably lifted.

After a good meal and warm fellowship, I headed straight to the front desk to see if they might need someone to start work that very evening. "No, but you might want to go up those stairs to the Banquet Office and check with them," the clerk said kindly.

The Banquet Manager happened to be in his office. I introduced myself as the champion banquet waiter of all time. He said, "Leave me your name and number. We may need some extra help this week."

Early the next morning, I charged off to the Commonwealth Employment Office with my migrant's visa in hand. It was two and a half hours before someone saw me. It took them one minute to inform me there was nothing available. Interestingly, there were many poor Greeks and Italians migrating to Australia at the time. I told the interviewer, "I'm half Greek and half Italian," but he only wished me brotherly love as he ushered me out with a brusque "Ciao."

I hit the streets once again for some "cold calling," even though it was 90 degrees and one of the hottest November summer days in several years. I walked a good ten miles that day in search of a job.

The next morning I called the Chevron Hilton Banquet Office out of sheer desperation. They had a serious need for waiters that evening. "Be here at 5:00 p.m.," said the Assistant Banquet Manager. This marvelous news came just in the nick of time! I would at least be able to hold body and soul together a little while longer.

In my neatly starched white jacket, with a black bow tie, I glided across the banquet hall as if I knew what I was doing and only dropped two bottles and one glass during the evening. Not too bad for a first-time waiter. We were serving a stand-up cocktail party with a cadre of waiters that read like a muster of the United Nations representing over twenty countries. One of our waiters, a Scotsman, was taking drinks on the sly every time he got a chance. Finally, he got a bottle and crawled under one of the food tables.

Since the tablecloth reached all the way to the floor, he had become invisible and we only began to miss him after he was totally smashed. "We'll miss Scottie's cheerful presence," we all agreed as we carried him out of the Banquet Hall.

Our headwaiter was a Prussian "Born-to-give-orders" dictator. I should never have sneaked that little bite of Baked Alaska left over in the kitchen, thinking no one was around. As that cold ice cream slid down my throat, I felt hot breath on the back of my neck. "Actung, put dat dessert down now," a voice boomed, and I almost choked in fright. From then on it became us against him. We set up lookouts before we sampled any tasty delights.

After the banquet that evening, the manager said, "Clarke, we can use you almost every day from now on." Now that I had a part-time job and was covered financially, the next day, Wednesday, I called an Australian whom I'd met in Tahiti—Tim Drost. Tim invited me to a party on Friday. He assured me he would get me a date with a good-looking blonde. That sounded promising. I only hoped she wouldn't be expecting a rich Texan.

On Friday, as promised, Tim and I picked up my date, Carol. She was truly a beautiful blonde, five foot, five inches tall with the figure of a model, and a sparkling personality.

We headed for Rushcutters Bay. Frank welcomed us aboard his 47-foot sailing boat. Under twinkling stars, we sang songs from Tahiti, Hawaii, Australia, and everywhere, accompanied by several guitars.

"Our tin voices, out of tune, surely would have driven any sharks completely out of the bay," Tim remarked, alluding to Sydney Harbor's reputation as a breeding grounds for sharks. After Tim's comment, I was determined not to fall overboard or go swimming in these waters. I had read in the newspaper of someone "taken" in one of the bays. Taken! That's such a nice way to put it!

At 3:00 in the morning, we gave up the ship and headed for our respective homes. My first party in Sydney brought new friends. "A friendly lot," as the Aussies say.

Besides Tim, I had one other contact in Sydney, not counting Huey and his crew. I'd met the Boyces, a couple in their forties, when they stayed at the Royal Hawaiian Hotel, and had called them a few days earlier. They invited me to spend the following Saturday at their home, and though I had no idea what to expect, I was surprised when they picked me up at the YMCA at nine o'clock in the morning in a large, beautiful car. Then as we drove out into the suburbs and the homes got bigger and bigger, we drove into their driveway

With friends at famous Bondi Beach in Sydney, Australia.

through a huge stone gate complete with an arch over the top and a twelve-foot high stonewall surrounding the grounds. Before me was an enchanting castle, "The Hermitage," a famous Australian landmark that sat on a high point overlooking all of Sydney Harbor. There were tennis courts, a swimming pool, a sleek cabin cruiser at the dock, and two Great Danes bounding across the manicured grounds.

Here I was, a young adventurer, with only a couple of bucks to my name, getting ready to spend the day with some very important, highly successful Australians. It was only my sixth day in this great land.

We boarded the *Murray*, a 60-foot cabin cruiser, for a cruise along the Sydney shoreline. Among the distinguished guests was the Chief Justice of the Supreme Court of the State of New South Wales.

For lunch we anchored in a fantastic little cove. Then came the announcement—it was time for a swim. This was my first chance to swim with the Sydney sharks and my resolution from the night before, not to immerse myself in these waters, evaporated. *Was I, a Texan and Marine, afraid to swim with those little old sharks? No, not me!* I encouraged myself. There always has to be a first time and a last time for everything. I prayed this wasn't my last swim.

I survived the sharks and, after a lovely day of indulgence, the Chief Justice shuttled me to the Y. As I went to sleep, I realized I was going to love Australia.

It was early Sunday morning when I checked out of the venerable YMCA and took a cab to my new abode. All I could think was, "Bless Tim!" We had only met briefly in Tahiti but had become friends here, and now he had invited me to use his spare downstairs bedroom until I could find a full-time job. A go-getter manager of a downtown travel agency, he had a small two-story flat on the side of a hill overlooking Ruchcutters Bay. *Now I'd be able to afford bacon and eggs once a week*, I thought.

After I stowed my stuff, I hurried down to the beach. I'd heard so much about the famous Bondi Beach I couldn't help myself. The 10-foot waves were daunting, as was the idea of bodysurfing with sharks. Anything to enjoy this amazing beach, jam-packed with people, half of them incredibly gorgeous birds—girls that is. My, was Australia looking better by the minute, or what?

One Sunday evening, I went to the Methodist Mission, one of the largest churches in downtown Sydney. Afterwards, I was invited to attend the single young adult group meeting. Rev. Ted Noffs, a wonderful bloke (guy), made it his custom to bring up on stage anyone there from another country. So before I knew it, I, along with two others was standing on stage like a celebrity. I had already learned it's important, no matter where you may live in the world, in order to make friends it is helpful to seek out worthwhile and friendly groups of people like this church group. With a friendly and open attitude, all kinds of good things happen. That night I walked away with many new friends from all walks of life. Glory be! This group became one of my many homes away from home. So elated was I, I indulged myself and rode the bus the three miles to my new home by the bay, instead of walking to save the five cents.

Monday, my eighth day in Australia, I applied for a front desk position at the Chevron Hilton. Mr. Christy, the General Manager, greeted me, "Well, Clarke, I hear you have set a record for dropping trays, breaking glasses and dishes, and stealing desserts, as a waiter."

I confessed, "Yes sir, but I hope I did it with flair and style."

"To save dishes and money, we need to get you out of banquets and on the front desk right away," he said. I was all for that. The excellent letters of recommendation I had from three managers of the Royal Hawaiian Hotel must have mattered, too.

I was down to eleven pounds to my name ($25 U.S), which actually to me was true wealth. I had only $10 when I arrived and I was proud I had more than doubled my money in one week.

CHAPTER 9

Ghost Ship Appears

Ideals are like the stars, we never reach them,
but like the mariners of the sea, we chart our
course by them.

— Carl Schwig

Since it was the middle of December and the warm summer weather was prevailing, I dropped by to say hello to my friends on the yacht *Ondine*. Their preparations for the Sydney-Hobart Yacht Race were coming along well. The race was just ten days away and it appeared they were ready to go for victory. An attitude that made the Aussies bristle. Their sentiment seemed to be, "That American has the audacity to think he can take us on in our own waters. Who does he think he is?" Besides that, the *Ondine* was thought to be tender at sea, which meant it did not sail well in rough seas. It was the first time for an American yacht to challenge the Aussies in their own waters.

The race took the utmost in skill, guts, determination, and luck, and the Aussies must have been concerned about the 57-foot American yawl because it was a highly tuned racing machine. In the Sydney newspaper, a headline read, "Spies Watch Glamour Yacht *Ondine*." The copy read, "Four men equipped with binoculars trailed the American Yacht *Ondine* when she had her first Australian sea trial. The men followed the yacht along the coast in a car to watch her progress."

My first day of work at the front desk of the Chevron Hilton arrived. The front office manager, a cross between Woody Allen and Mickey Rooney, briefed me on my duties. "There's the front desk and if you have any questions, ask one of the other clerks," he said. Now, all I had to worry about was a guest asking me a question.

Russell Ryan, one of the clerks, was short, had a medium build, red hair, freckles, and was about as friendly a chap as one could meet. He took me under his wing, reassuring me, "Don't worry about Mr. 'Bouncy,' we hardly ever see him."

However, the hotel's front office manager bounced in every now and then to make sure everyone was properly criticized and then bounced off. "I think he bounces to make himself look taller than his 5'5", I told a coworker. Despite the manager's busybody ways, I couldn't help liking him.

Huey standing by his world class racing yacht Ondine *at the Yacht Club of Australia.*

The doorman, on the other hand, was a character beyond belief. Irish, with a thick accent, he was tall, fit, and most congenial. Born in Casablanca, his language abilities were limited to Irish, Arabic, French, Italian, and "Australian." All thrown together, those languages made for an unusual accent. I can still hear him in my head. Every day as I approached the hotel, Jack would say, "Whistle a little Irish tune and you will be all right." I've been whistling that little tune ever since, and it has worked, Jack my boy. It has worked.

One day, Jack forgot to take his own advice. In back of the hotel, a huge hole, four stories deep, had been dug for a second hotel tower before the money ran out. Jack would back cars up to three feet of that hole when parking them. One day he put a car in gear, gave it the gas and went sailing into thin air backward, without benefit of a parachute or seat belt.

Jack's training as a paratrooper and wrestler came into immediate play. No one else could have survived that crash. Talk about tough! But though he wasn't hurt seriously, he afterwards always wore a parachute when parking cars.

Meanwhile, safe at the front desk, I was fascinated by the stream of interesting people passing before me: Louis "Satchmo" Armstrong; a Spaniard from Madrid; the President of Jack Daniels Liquor; J.C. Penney and his wife; movie star Maime Van Doren; the singer Vicki Carr; Chubby Checker; a wealthy family from the Philippines; an Italian silk merchant; a Japanese magnate; a South African diamond dealer; the great pianist Carmen Cavallero; and publishers, movie stars, tennis pros, scientists, professors, bishops, crocodile hunters, and so on.

Over the next few days, friends turned up unexpectedly—Bruce from Tahiti, Harry from New Zealand, and Dean Anne from the ship *Monterrey*. It was like old home week. And throughout December, different members of the *Ondine* crew, including Huey, would drop by the front desk and say hello.

The Boyces, and their two young boys, John and Peter, also adopted me into their family at "The Hermitage." How lucky can one person be?

On December 23, we went cruising on their yacht with everyone singing Christmas carols, and then they graciously had me over for Christmas dinner—each member of their family had a present for me.

On weekends, Frank's yacht became party headquarters. It was docked just two blocks from the flat. When I arrived one evening, Eric and his jazz band were playing away on the forward deck. One of my favorite people came to be Manoa, a Fijian. He could play the guitar and sing like few people I have ever known, besides having a loving spirit about him. We became fast friends.

The day after Christmas was gray and windy. Called Boxing Day, it was the start of the great ocean race from Sydney to Hobart. I was aboard the Boyces' cabin cruiser, *Murray*, anchored not far from the imaginary starting line for the race.

Forty-two racing yachts were circling in the harbor, poised to charge ahead at the sound of the gun. In a dramatic move, the *Ondine* broke out of the pack toward the starting line. I held my breath. *She was going to cross it too soon*, I thought. But no! Just as the *Ondine*'s point was an inch from the imaginary line, the gun sounded. Huey and crew exhibited precision timing and magnificent sailing skills!

The *Ondine* was out front and away. Proud of my former shipmates, I, of course, went on to explain to everyone on board the *Murray* how it had been done, as if I had a clue. But after all, I *had* sailed on the *Ondine*.

This renowned yachting challenge was initiated in 1945. It ran from Sydney Harbor to Hobart Harbor on the island of Tasmania. Between these two points, 630-nautical-miles, mean seas could erupt. In fact, cyclones were known to strike the area. Would this be one of those times? Imagine sailing in 100-mph winds.

In 1962, Huey's *Ondine* was considered the world's ultimate racing yacht of the time. Could this "upstart" win in these often-dangerous waters? "No way," many said, "she was a light weather craft and tender at sea." As if in response, the December 23 *Sunday Mirror* reported that, "Long was out to take down some gloomy Sydney yachting critics."

As I remember hearing on the news the next day, the *Ondine* was nowhere to be found. She had apparently disappeared into thin air. For several days, the mystery continued. Then as the lead Australian yacht was bearing down on Hobart Harbor, the *Ondine* appeared from out of the mist. From reports, the *Ondine* went farther out to sea to catch beneficial winds and currents. Another of Huey's brilliant racing strategies, no doubt.

On December 30, the *Sunday Telegraph* headline read: "HOBART RACE SHOCK, Ghost ship wins for U.S." And in the *Sunday Mirror* was, "ONE-MINUTE WIN, The American Yawl *Ondine* snatched a breathtaking victory." Simply put, a sensational victory.

It was the closest finish in the 17-year running of the race. Huey and his crew had pulled off a miracle, being first-timers in these seas. They had smashed by 15 hours, 44 minutes, and 23 seconds, the 1957 record set by *Kurrewa IV*. "Good on ya, mate!" as the popular Aussie saying goes.

Another newspaper stated, "*Ondine* ghosted across the finish line only a minute ahead of the yacht *Astor*." All agreed, it was the most thrilling finish ever. Huey said the race compared with the toughest in the world. And he certainly had the credentials to know what he was talking about.

I was one very proud American that day, along with the whole crew of the *Ondine*, my buddies.

CHAPTER 10

Going Walkabout—Never Knowing What Each Day Will Bring

A journey of a thousand miles begins with a single step.

— Lao Tzu

The day the great ocean race started, I had been *down under* exactly one month. I'd kept from starving and had stayed out of the poorhouse, while at the same time making many new friends.

A week after the *Ondine's* stunning victory, I was invited to a party. As a Texan and American, party invitations started flowing in and I met Aussie birds (girls) who told me, "I just love your Texas accent." *Hmmm,* I thought. *There's gold in this here accent.* So, after another girl's comment, it seemed my accent quickly grew more pronounced.

Soon after, the pretty blond I had had a date with when I first arrived called and told me, "My parents have a room for rent that just became available." Because my friend Tim had decided to move to Tahiti, it came at just the right time. The Brittliffs on Waratah Street rented out rooms in their cozy white stucco house. All of a sudden, I became a part of their family. If ever there were an award presented for "the nicest person in the world," Carol's mother, Betty, would have easily reached the finals. And by that time, Carol and I had become just friends, as she had a fairly steady boyfriend. Darn it!

The famous King's Cross area was now only a few blocks from where I lived and worked. More than anything else, the Cross was a focal point for nightlife in Sydney. It had a cosmopolitan atmosphere, with many shops and restaurants either owned or staffed by European immigrants. One minute you felt as if you were in the middle of Greece; the next, Italy. It was a most interesting place to stroll through, day or night, have a continental meal, or just people-watch. It was a fun place to go when one wanted a change of pace.

The Chevron Hilton had the best supper club in Sydney, the Silver Spade Room. Many of the top entertainers in the world appeared there, and I was able to see them for free. Nat King Cole was my favorite, one of the smoothest entertainers I ever saw perform. Mesmerizing was the only way to describe him.

Meanwhile at the front desk, I checked in Trevor Howard. He was in town to attend the premiere of the movie *Mutiny on the Bounty*, in which he starred along with Marlon Brando.

One warm, sunny afternoon, my pretty and shapely buddy, Carol, asked me to wash her hair using the garden hose in the backyard. Maybe it was the bikini she had on that made me drop the hose three or four times. It was a totally disconcerting, but nevertheless pleasant, task.

I had no complaints about my boarding house, and Mrs. Britliff fixed a great breakfast every morning as part of the rent. *This is the life*, I thought. *How I love Australia and its people!*

Almost every weekend, I was at the Boyce's "castle" for tennis, swimming in the pool, water-skiing with the sharks in the harbor, yachting, and meeting many new and prominent people. Often we boarded the cabin cruiser, *Serenade*, and headed for Quarantine Cove. Anchoring there, we dined on board, danced, and sang songs.

To make a little extra money, I became a part-time dance instructor at a studio downtown. One Saturday evening, I dragged my friend, Bruce, an Alabaman, along to the Trocadero Club, the city's showplace of ballroom dancing. There I met a real doll by the name of Rhonda. She was 5'2", part Spanish, full of fire, and had a vivacious personality. I danced with no one else the whole evening. Bruce, being the shy type, sat on the sidelines taking it all in.

When the Trocadero closed, Rhonda and I went to the Sound Lounge and danced until 4:00 a.m. Afterwards, we had coffee in the famed King's Cross. Her favorite saying was, "That's for sure." She was an Australian doll, that's for sure.

Wanting to become financially independent, I had invested a small amount in a stock some time ago. My first dividend check came to a whopping $.83. I wasn't sure whether to buy a yacht or Rolls Royce with it, but finally settled on a hot dog. At least, I was doing a little investing.

One Sunday, Carol, Bruce, and I went to Domain Park. Soap box orators ranted away "for and against" such topics as socialism, Jesus, Catholicism, youth gangs, and opposing newspapers. I came very close to mounting one of those boxes to tell everyone how underpaid I was as a front desk clerk. Fortunately, Bruce and Carol held me back. In actual fact, I was more than grateful just to have a job.

It was time to be bold. At the beginning of March, with autumn weather setting in, I decided it was time to take off around Australia. I had saved up some money and started planning my trip.

My four months in Sydney had been fabulous. There's no way I could ever repay the Boyces and the Brittliffs for all the kind and wonderful things they did for me. There are many people in this world who are special, but I would call these folks "extra" special.

As the Aussies say, "A beaut time it was."

It was early morning, April 28, when I hit the road hitchhiking. The key to my success was the sign I had put on the side of my small, battered, leather suitcase. In bright yellow tape, it read, in big letters, TEXAS, and in smaller letters underneath, USA. It worked like magic in getting rides. Texas seems to have a mystique for many people.

I rolled into Canberra, the capital city, around 1:00 p.m. The brightly colored autumn leaves were a cheerful sight. The city was laid out magnificently. The grand lake and bridges were all in the process of being built, reminding me of the paintings of the early days of Washington, D.C.

Having nowhere lined up to stay, I called the Accommodation Center. All the hotels were completely booked. I couldn't afford any of them anyway. As was my usual style, low on funds, I played it by ear.

Mrs. Thompson put me up at her bed-and-breakfast for 30 shillings a night, a situation allowing me to get to know some more Aussies first hand.

The next day I walked the city from one end to the other.

As the sun was setting, I decided to walk across the long, long bridge being built over what was to be the huge lake near the Parliament building. As I started across the uncompleted bridge, I could see several men, about two blocks in the distance, working on the bridge. I thought, *surely they will tell me to get off*, but I proceeded anyway.

As I approached the first man, I said, "Good day," the general form of greeting in Aussie Land. He smiled and said the same back. I asked him a few questions about the bridge, which he cheerfully answered. Lo-and-behold, he was the concrete foreman for the project. This was how I became friends with Tom Gaffney, an Irishman straight from the old country, with an accent to match.

It ended up that Tom invited me to his home to have dinner with him, his wife, Nora, and their two little girls, Marie and Elizabeth. After dinner, we had a few drinks, lit the wood fire, and sang Irish songs.

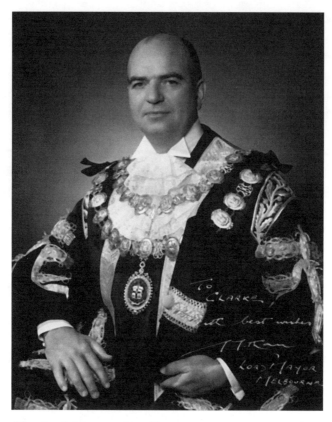

The Lord Mayor of Melbourne, Sir Maurice Nathan, wrote in the front of the beautifully illustrated picture book he presented to me: "To Clarke, with best wishes and the best of luck to a man with a mission and the ability to win out."

It was a grand evening. When I left that night, I felt we had been friends for twenty years. And to think, I would never have met Tom and his lovely family if I had not crossed that bridge for fear someone might tell me to get off. It's marvelous what happens sometimes when one proceeds forward, instead of hesitating or retreating.

Early the next morning, I started hitchhiking from the outskirts of Canberra. Tom Butler gave me a ride to Yass. Two blokes my age, David and John, got me to Gundagai. In a tiny town six miles past the Wagga turnoff, I got a ride in a huge diesel truck. Alex, the driver, was an Italian who had been in

Australia for twelve years. We went through Albury, Wondonga, Wangaratta, Benalla, and Seymour before arriving in Melbourne.

The roads weren't the best. Riding in the truck cab could be compared to riding a pile driver. *I'll take a horse any day*, I thought. Averaging only 35 mph, it took us nine hours to go 300 miles. In all, thirteen hours on the road to make it to mellow Melbourne, an English-like city. God bless Alex for letting me join him on his long-haul journey.

It was 10:00 p.m. I called Rita and her son Russell. They had been expecting me a bit earlier. When I got to know them in Sydney, they invited me to stay in their home. I was grateful for being able to sleep on their couch.

The next morning I took a tram downtown. Rita introduced me to the staff throughout the film studio where she worked. One of the directors wanted to put me on a TV show the following week. *What a lark that would be! I'm still trying to discover what talents I may have*, I thought. *Maybe he can help*.

That following morning, I was ushered into the office of the Lord Mayor of Melbourne, Sir Maurice Nathan. Lady Nathan had invited me to call them when she had stayed at the Royal Hawaiian.

The Lord Mayor and I talked for one-and-a-half hours about Australia's political parties, knighthood, the Queen's visit to Melbourne the month before, the duties of the Lord Mayor, my adventures and plans, and other interesting topics of the day. A few days before, I had watched the proceedings of Parliament. The Speaker wore a big white wig, just as they did in England.

That evening I had a date with Pam, whom I had met in Sydney. Of all the possible movies available, we went to see *The Alamo*. Since I had been visiting the Alamo in San Antonio from the time I could walk, the movie made me feel at right home.

On the third day in town, Russell drove me around to see all the sights. That evening, the Dixons had Lord Mayor and Lady Nathan, other friends, and the hitchhiker over for drinks at their impressive home. A fire was roaring in the fireplace to counter the nippy weather outside. Then we went to Maxim's for dinner, the finest restaurant in this splendid city. What that dinner cost could have gotten me by for a year. But who was I to complain about such kind, awe-inspiring hospitality?

At 7:00 the next morning, Mr. Crisp, who worked for the Lord Mayor's furniture company, picked me up at Rita's house. It was a foggy morning with the temperature a cold 39 degrees. He was giving me a ride as far as Horsham, but we ran out of gas eight miles short. *Take it as it comes, and all will be right,* I reminded myself.

After lunch in Horsham, a Mr. Stanway gave me a ride to the Adelaide highway. An English bloke named Terry gave me a ride the 20 miles to the next small town; Dennis O'Day took me another 20 miles to Nihl; and John McRae, a traveling salesman, got me to Adelaide. It had been 12 hours since I left Melbourne.

John offered me a free night of sleep in the twin room at the motel where he always stayed. After we had dinner, too tired to go out, I hit the sack early. I had a big day ahead of me. *It was going to be another fun adventure,* I speculated. *No telling what was going to happen.*

The Australian family that adopted me in the outback—Brian, Glenys and their fine young sons. We are still in touch.

CHAPTER 11

The Admiral and the Hitchhiker

The trail is the thing, not the end of the trail. Travel too fast and you miss all you are traveling for.

— Louis L'Amour

*T*he next morning, I ventured into the small Australian American Association office wearing my blue jeans, t-shirt, and tennis shoes, and asked, "Is there anything a young American might do in this most pleasant city?"

I was told, "You will be one of our honored guests tonight at the Coral Sea Week Celebration Dinner."

"What is that?" I asked, ignorant of the history of the celebration.

So, along with Admiral Sides, Commander of the U.S. Pacific Fleet, I was one of the honored guests at the dinner. Timing is everything! "It was a most unlikely combination, the Admiral and the hitchhiker."

I'd learn from these benefactors that each year there was a Coral Sea Battle Celebration held in almost every large port in Australia, with dinners, parades, and commemoration services. I just happened to walk right into the middle of this one. In that unprecedented battle of WW II, the American fleet literally stopped the Japanese fleet in its tracks—saving Australia from invasion.

A lady journalist at the dinner heard of my quest for adventure. She came over to ask if she could do a story on me in the *Adelaide Advertiser* newspaper the next day. "I'd be honored," I said. Naturally, I was flattered that I had such an opportunity, having just rolled into town the previous night, not knowing a soul.

The next morning, on the way up the inside stairs at the *Adelaide Advertiser,* I asked a striking young lady for directions. I ended up taking Cheryl to lunch and then to a movie that evening. I'll have to take the stairs more often. We double-dated with my new friend, Jeff, and his girlfriend, Fritz.

A U.S. Navy Band and a Marine Corps Drum & Bugle Corps marched down Main Street to the Centopath at 11:00 a.m. Semper Fi! It was a stirring Coral Sea Battle Memorial Service.

I attended a reception afterward for honored guests, including my pal, Admiral Sides. Amazing!

John Quay had kindly let me share his room for two nights at the Sunny South Motel. At around 8:00 the next morning, he dropped me off at Adelaide's city limits on the road to Port Augusta.

Within about five minutes, a police car stopped in front of me. An officer questioned me, thinking I was a navy deserter. Apparently, several sailors couldn't contain themselves when they sailed in and saw all the pretty Aussie girls waiting to greet them. Actually, I was highly offended that the police thought I was a sailor when it was perfectly obvious I was a Marine.

They were about to take me in when John drove up. He had gone up the road to turn around and saw the police getting ready to haul me away. For a guy who'd been hobnobbing with the Admiral the past two days, this was sinking very low. John was my life preserver, "Hey, this guy is the brokest Texan you'll ever see, but he ain't a deserter. Call the Admiral. He'll tell ya, mate."

I didn't know it but I was on the "Road to Heaven." The police were just for starters. It would be a day of short rides. One mile, three miles, five miles, eighteen miles—which put me out in the middle of nowhere—with one horse for company. This was the real *outback*.

After about half an hour, along came a Russian-born house painter. Ivan had fought against the Nazis as a member of the Russian Army in WWII, and then, somehow, deserted to Australia to escape Communism. He dropped me forty miles down the road, again in the middle of nowhere. He turned right on to a narrow dirt road and I watched his car disappear over a rise ten minutes later.

Two hours passed and not one car appeared on the narrow, two-lane, asphalt road. And this was one of the busier roads in South Central Australia.

Naturally, I was beginning to give up hope of ever getting a ride again. Then, I heard the low roar of an engine in the far distance from where I had come. To my right, no car was visible. All of a sudden, a white blur appeared over the horizon several miles away. A Ferrari? No. A Massaratti? No, it was an Australian Holden, bearing down on me going at least 90 mph. Did I dare stick my thumb out to this hell-bent-for-leather driver? I figured if he tried to stop, he'd probably kill us both.

Well, he didn't give me so much as a glance as he raced by, the speedometer, no doubt, approaching 100 mph. Almost bowled over by the rush of air, I dropped my upright thumb to my side, wondering how much longer before I got a ride. I was standing at the low point of the road. To my right and left, the road gradually inclined up into the distance. It wasn't five minutes later when I heard an engine roar coming from my left. It was the same guy. *What in the hell was going on here? Should I jump the fence and run for it?* was my first thought. He was coming at the same high rate of speed. About twenty yards before he got to me, he slammed on his brakes, laying rubber eighty feet down the road. As he slid past me, I stood there in awe with my mouth agape, dumbstruck and goggle-eyed. He whirled the car around and pulled up to me. He appeared sane enough, a slightly bald man in his forties, wearing glasses.

He leaned across with his hand outstretched and said, "Want a Lifesaver?" I needed a lot more than a candy Lifesaver, but I took one and said, "Thanks."

He asked, "Where are you headed?"

"Port Augusta," I said.

He told me to throw my suitcase in the back seat and hop in. As I got in the car, I could see he had seat belts around his waist, crisscrossing his chest and a few more for good measure.

He looked over at me and said, "Buckle up!"

Gladly, I thought, *do you have crash bags*?

Satisfied I was strapped in, he said, "Hold on!" and floor-boarded the gas pedal, exerting 100 Gs of pressure, or somewhere in that neighborhood. We were off to the races! Literally!

As we raced down that desolate stretch of road, he asked me, "What are you doing out here in the middle of nowhere?" I told him my story. Then, without taking his eyes off the road, which was good, he reached in his shirt pocket and handed me a card. It read, *Reverend John Smith, Minister of the Gospel,* such-and-such church, Port Augusta. Saints preserve us! I later gave a number of speeches on this hair-raising ride entitled, *On the Road to Heaven*, because it looked as if he was trying to get there right away, taking me with him.

Even though we were cruising at Mach One, in the middle of nowhere, Australian law required cars to stop at railroad tracks. We could easily see down the tracks for 100 miles each way and there was no train in sight. But he slammed on the brakes. As we came to an abrupt stop, he yanked a chart off the dashboard, checked his watch, and wrote down the time and again blasted off.

He explained, "I make this trip to Adelaide about once a week. Each trip, I try to better my time." Of course, he would handicap his time by stopping to pick me up. What an all out, wacky ride! But I might have had to stay in the wilderness for the night, if it had not been for him and the loss of one inch of rubber from his tires.

We took every shortcut known to man. As we were coming into a little town, he said, "Watch this!" and made a sliding right turn into an alley, scattering several cats in the process. He saved 23 seconds on that adroit maneuver, he told me. The lifesavers ran out and that left only prayer, as we flew down the last lap of the Australian 200—his best time on this run—2 hours, 46 minutes, and 17 seconds. Glory be and the saints be praised! I made it to dusty Port Augusta—alive and very grateful to John, a man of God (but mostly thankful to God for saving me from this man).

Though frazzled, I rather enjoyed the novelty of being scared out my wits on what would have been otherwise a routine trip. I thanked the reverend kindly for what was to me "the ride of the century," because I was never taking another ride like that one again.

Atop rocks. Playing scout in the dead center of Australia.

CHAPTER 12
Way Back in the Outback

*Life isn't about how to survive the storm, but
how to dance in the rain.*

— Anonymous

Since it was sunset and time to find a room, the Reverend pointed out a small building they called a hotel. It was half a block away on a corner. Bag in hand and worn down, I stumbled through the swinging doors of the old, saloon-like pub. It was just like the Wild West. I expected a bunch of cowboys to come riding up any minute. I put a foot on the brass rail around the bottom of the bar and ordered a much-needed beer.

A bloke standing a few feet away said, "Where ya from, mate?" I told him Texas. I was so tired I could have sworn he said, "My name is Crocodile Dundee." But, he actually said, "Brian," and I introduced myself. As we began to talk, it was as if we were old friends.

Brian invited me to stay at his house, so I escaped having to pay for a hotel room out of my dwindling funds. Glenys, Brian's sweet and kindly wife, fixed us Whiting, a fish caught right there in the Gulf for dinner. After dinner, they took me to a dance at the Central Football Club. Brian was singing and playing in the band. I felt right at home in Port Augusta.

Brian worked as a clerk for the railroad. The next morning I filled out forms for a job as a "fettler" (laborer on the tracks). I needed to build up my cash reserves. Later on, we went to the pub where he placed his usual weekly bet on the horses, along with everyone else in Port Augusta who all seemed to use the same bookie.

Brian and his wife had three little boys—Peter, 4, Paul, 3, and Allan, 1. Peter and Paul started calling me Uncle Clarke, and copied everything I did at breakfast. My manners improved immediately. In a few short days, I'd come to love this wonderful family.

Port Augusta is on the edge of where the Australian Outback takes over. Because little rain falls in this area, water was brought in by pipeline. No wonder it seemed a bit dusty.

My first day as a laborer on the railroad started at 6:30 a.m. As part of the yard gang, I was assigned to work with two aborigines. Both were easygoing and talkative. Most of the morning was spent loading sleepers on a small push rail car. Sleepers are large wood railroad ties that the steel tracks lay on.

That afternoon I was introduced to laying sleepers. Two men work as a team. While one digs a trench out to the side of the track, the other pulls the spikes out of the old sleeper with a crow-bar-like tool. The old sleeper was pulled out with a pick and a new one put in its place.

I learned a very valuable lesson that day from those aborigines. There was an art to laying track. They worked easily at the job as if there was nothing to it. There I was: young, strong and tough, and yet, by mid-afternoon, my hands were bleeding and every muscle in my body ached. I thought I was tough. Not so, because I was not used to the "art."

I've always believed there is an art to everything and one can learn something from everyone they meet. Once the aborigines began teaching me their art, things went much smoother. It was the hardest day of physical work I had ever done. Now I know how John Henry felt. "Where is the closest pub?" I asked my coworkers at the end of the day.

If I thought the first day was tough, the second day was a real topper. I was put on what was called the "special gang." It was my first time to be a gang member.

At 7:30 in the morning our gang—five aborigines, our Italian foreman who spoke no English and I—boarded a bus. One mile out of town, the road turned from asphalt to graded red dirt. Twenty miles later, we turned onto a small, winding dirt road that runs through saltbush. The driver let us off at some tracks, an isolated spot on the Nullabor Plain.

Welcome to camel country, mates, I thought to myself. Camels were introduced into the Outback in 1860, along with Afghan camel drivers. These Afghans played a significant part in the opening up of Australia. "The Ghan," short for Afghan, was the name given to the train from Adelaide to Alice Springs and the trail was still known by that name. Here in the desert, rock supported the tracks, not dirt. The old pick and shovel did not take to the rock easily. Covered in flies, sweating profusely under the hot desert sun, we labored on, with our foreman waving his arms and urging us on in Italian. I had finally found my place in life—a chain gang without chains.

It rained all afternoon. The rain started and it looked like it would never quit. Something like 40 days and 40 nights came to mind. By quitting time,

I looked like a red man: I was covered with red mud from head to foot. The heavy rain took its toll. For the first time in years, a number of bridges and some tracks were washed away.

Notwithstanding Brian and Glenys' marvelous hospitality, Port Augusta was not an exciting place to be in, especially for a soon-to-turn 25-year-old "rootin', tootin', son-of-a-gun from Texas," as the old song goes. But then that night I went to the South Football Club dance where Brian was playing in the band, and things started to look up.

My date was Denise, who taught me two of the Aussies' favorite dances, the barn dance and the military two-step. Of course, I had been dancing in barns since I was six, so I mastered that one fairly quickly.

On May 18, while staying as a guest, treated like family, in Brian and Glenys' home, I turned 25 years old. The entire family came into my room to wake me up and sing "Happy Birthday." Glenys was carrying a cake she had baked with 25 candles on it. Tears came to my eyes. I was so moved, I could barely blow out the candles, much less speak.

Every morning when we sat down for breakfast, little Peter and Paul would copy everything I did. If I used cold milk on my cereal, then they had to do the same and so on. "Look Uncle Clarke, I'm using the milk just like you," Peter said. It is remarkable how young children learn. They are great mimics.

Winter was coming on and it was still flooding to the north of us. On May 21, the tracks were repaired well enough for the train to depart for Alice Springs, the dead center of Australia. I bid my Port Augusta family a fond farewell, thanking them profusely for their unbelievable kindness to this wayfaring vagabond. I still keep in touch with them after all these years.

At the town of Maree, we had to change trains. Would you believe that as each state in Australia was formed, some states chose a different gauge of railroad track? I shook my head. *Someone must have been asleep at the switch.*

On this interesting train journey, across tracks repaired after flood damage, I had the dubious distinction of working as a *silver boy*. That meant helping to set silver on the tables in the dining car, pouring coffee and tea, slicing bread, and washing dishes. It sure beat laying track.

I shared a two-berth compartment with Max, my new friend and a pantry man. Max was the kitchen man; Jim and Johnny the cooks; Tony the other *silver boy*; Marty, Otto, Aspro, and Malcom the conductors; and Jimmy and Mike the waiters. There were three sittings for meals, after which our crew ate. We worked straight through for 15 hours, until 7:30 p.m.

By that time, I was buggered, or worn-out in proper English. The train stopped or slowed down many times during the day, due to the quick and temporary repairs. The scenery didn't change much in the whole 1,000 miles. It was mostly flat, red sand, rocky country. I could have been on Mars.

As I remember, there were few paved roads on this long, remote trek, mostly dirt tracks left by big trucks. That would be like no paved roads from the Texas-Mexican border to Kansas City. The railroad from Adelaide to Alice Springs was completed in 1929.

At 6:30 in the morning, we steamed into Alice Springs, located in what was called the Northern Territory. Alice was basically an oasis in the desert, mainly because of an artesian water basin only seven feet beneath the city. No camels were in sight, though they were somewhere about, roaming the vast reaches of the Nullabor Plain and the Great Victoria and Gibson Deserts.

Carrying my now two bags—I had moved up in the world—I walked the four blocks to the small Stewart Arms Hotel. I offered the manager my services as a dishwasher for a week, but the Aborigines had beat me to it. There was no opening, so, jobless, I stayed at the railroad workers' lodge that night.

I had one contact someone had given me. It was Ben Usher at the United Church Hostel. With Ben's help, I checked into the Church of England's hostel. That afternoon he took me on a motorcycle tour of the whole area—a great way to see it!

After breakfast with Brother George and his staff, it was *walkabout* time. The Macdonnel ranges were looming up several miles to the south of Alice, so off I started walking toward them. Along the way, I walked with a very old, barefooted aborigine man. I could only understand about half of what he said, but he was as friendly and happy as they come. He wore a handkerchief over his head, his large stomach stuck out from the bottom of his shirt, and he carried a burlap bag, full of who knows what.

Walking across bush country toward Mt. Gillen, the highest mountain around, I ran across a man and his wife, aborigines, who lived in a "whirly" there in the desert. A whirly was a shelter made of sticks, leaves, and whatever, kind of an igloo-like affair.

It took me several hours to get to the base of the mountains. It was then a steep, hard climb up over a lot of loose rock. Of course, there was not another soul around, no one else being crazy enough to attempt such a thing. Halfway up, I discovered an ancient, square-box Brownie camera, just like my Grand-dad used to own in the 1940s. Since I had not brought my camera with me,

An aborigine couple at home in the outback.

Hoisting one of the Devil's Marbles in the far outback.

I started snapping pictures with this one, probably lost ten years before. The pictures of the mountains turned out perfectly. Unbelievable!

The view from the top was nothing short of fantastic. I came to understand how really vast Australia was, standing at the very center of it on the highest mountain.

In the evening, Brother George took me as his guest to the Memorial Club dance. I danced with Gwen and Velda as long as my legs held out, especially after such a hard day of hiking and climbing.

My room at the hostel was setting me back 1 pound a night, about $2 U.S., with cereal for breakfast, an apple for lunch, and perhaps a can of Irish stew for dinner.

After two days in Alice, I went out to the narrow highway going north. After three hours of trying to hitch a ride, I gave up. There were hardly any cars or trucks on the road. From Alice north, there was no railroad.

In the evening, a fellow at the hostel told me of a fellow going by car to Mt. Isa in two days. The next day, Sunday, Lilly and Ben Usher had me for breakfast, to church, then lunch, and dinner. What great people there are in this world!

Harry Holla and I started sharing a room at the hostel, since I would be riding with him. On the morning of departure, we had breakfast with the Arch Deacon of Darwin and a Father from Brisbane. We needed all the blessings we could get for the coming trek through the Northern Territory.

The road from Alice to Tennant Creek was 300 miles of lonely, rugged dry country. Along the way, we stopped to take pictures of the Devil's Marbles, which are gigantic boulders. When we got to Tennant Creek, on a winter day, it was 96 degrees. Flies were swarming everywhere, around my face and landing in droves on my back—a lovely place to visit. Never had I had such a welcome.

Brother Matthew of the Church of England put us up at his place for the night. He was a saint to live there. His order was known as the Brothers of the Good Shepherd. May the Good Lord keep the flies from multiplying any further, for everyone's sake.

Harry and I took off to Mt. Isa, 400 miles to the north. Going 80 mph, the right back tire blew out just short of the small town of Fruvena. Brother Matthew's blessing paid off and Harry was able to keep the car on the road and from rolling over. With flies swarming us, we got the tire fixed quickly.

At one of the few rivers we crossed, we stopped for a lunch of canned meat and canned peaches. I got too close to the water and sank in mud to above my ankles.

Harry dropped me off in Mt. Isa, and we bid each other farewell. Where to stay cheap? That was the question. I parked my two small bags at a hotel and walked the town. About sundown, I saw an old deserted church hall with no windows in it. Next to the hall was a small frame house with a sign showing it was a minister's residence. Hopefully, donations would pick up and he would be able to get windows for the church.

I knocked on the door and introduced myself to the minister and his wife and said, "Do you know of anyplace I could stay for the night that would be reasonable?" He was a pious and generous man. "You can sleep in the deteriorating, holey, warping, windowless, unpainted church hall, if you like," he said.

And so, I slept on the cold floor of the church hall, using old newspapers for a pillow and as a blanket. It had to be one of the most miserable nights of my life, waking up at least ten times with cold feet. I'd done enough penance for my sins, I hoped.

The next morning I walked to the Cloncurry Highway. Two hours went by trying to hitch a ride with no success. I gave in and bought a train ticket through to Cairns on the northeastern coast. It cost me about $15 U.S. I was never happy spending money for travel on this adventure. Nevertheless, what I made working on the train to Alice covered the fare, so I was even.

CHAPTER 13

The Night Horror, Great Barrier Reef, and Fantasy Island

*Life is not measured by the number of breaths
we take but by the places and moments that
take our breath away.*

— Anonymous

On the train, I sat across from John McIntyre, who was just back from a two-year "working holiday" around the world. As always with fellow adventurers, we swapped stories and knowledge about "roughing it." I picked up some good pointers on other countries from him.

There were three, deliriously drunk Aussies in our car singing songs in excruciating voices. An Italian immigrant apparently took exception to the butchering of a song by this mini-opera company. It was a dandy fight. Opera was quite dull compared to the performance they put on. At the next stop, they were all put off. One thing about riding on Australian trains: the entertainment was hard to beat.

Even though I spent the night trying to sleep in 100 different positions in the hard train seats, it sure was an improvement over the cold, drafty, rotting wood floor of the church.

The train pulled into Townsville on the coast at 5:00 p.m. That gave me seven hours to do the grand tour of the sights. I met a girl I recognized from the train. We had coffee together, and I learned she was from Brisbane. She promised to show me around when I got there.

To pass the time, I stumbled onto a dance going on. I paid a few bob (coins) to get in and went to dancing.

At midnight, the slow, steam-engine goods train, dubbed "The Night Horror," lurched off in creaks and spurts. We were off like a turtle!

What a joy I had a decent place to sleep. This time on a wooden seat on a railroad car built in the 1890s from the looks of it. Thick black smoke and cinders poured in the open windows. By morning, I looked as though I had fallen into a coal mine.

The first order of business on reaching the coastal town of Cairns was to find an ultra-cheap boarding house. The one I found was so cheap that everyone washed their clothes in a huge black kettle in the backyard. Shades of Mark Twain! A wood fire roared underneath the kettle to warm the water.

My few clothes needed all the help they could get, being an interesting combination of red from the desert dirt and black from the train smoke and cinders.

My roommate was Gerard from New Zealand. The fine establishment we were boarded in was owned by a friendly Polish fellow.

The next day I went out to Green Island, on a boat with 70 others, to the Great Barrier Reef. It took one and a half hours to go the sixteen miles. On the way, I met three cute girls from Melbourne. Jill and I ended up walking all the way around the island together.

The Great Barrier Reef is one of the wonders of the natural world. It is known for a combination of glorious weather, a pristine rain forest, white sandy beaches, and an ocean varying in hue from blue to green to turquoise. The reef system consists of more than 3,000 reefs and 600 beautiful islands.

It was time to move on, so the next morning I caught a bus to the outskirts of the city and started to hitchhike. Within five minutes, I got my first ride.

After three rides, I was 100 miles down the coast road. A Swedish fellow then took me as far as Ayr, where I checked into a cheap motel. The score—300 miles for the day in nine hours over poor roads. Not bad for a day's work.

At 8:00 the next morning, I was back on the road and got two rides right away for a total of seven miles. I had no idea where I would end up on that day. There was a lull for an hour. Things were not looking promising when unbelievable luck struck. Larry Foley, the chief publicity man for the People of the North Campaign, picked me up. It just so happened he was on his way to Hayman Island, one of Australia's most famous resorts, to write a story.

Larry asked me to come along to this paradise island as a guest of the Proserpine Shire Council. Along with eight Councilors, we set out from Shoot Harbor in a 50-foot launch. We arrived at Hayman Island just as the sun disappeared into the sea and the curtain on the island "play" was about to rise. This was a fantasy on a Fantasy Island.

After dinner, there was a dance. The place was suddenly filled with pretty single girls from all over Australia, most around my age. *What on earth did I do to deserve this?* I wondered. I discovered that hitchhiking does have its gigantic surprises.

I got acquainted with many of the singles. When the dance ended, a group of them invited me to come along to a little bar down the beach called

Hernando's Hideaway. At Hernando's I got acquainted with George Stefanoff. He and I began scheming as to how I could remain on the island free for several extra days. My treasury was now down to about $13.50 U.S. George seemed like a friend I had known for years and we became buddies for life. After a while, both of us decided to take in the sights at Hernando's. I paired up with a wonderful girl from Sydney by the name of Jan and went for a stroll with her. As we walked down a gorgeous beach under a full moon, we heard an ominous sound: something was in the jungle foliage. All of a sudden out popped a baby kangaroo. As it stood there eating grass, we petted it for quite some time.

I had heard stories of kangaroos such as Big Reds in the Outback. One such story was of a rancher surprising one in his barn and being cut in half by the giant claws on the Red's two bottom feet. I just hoped this little fellow's mom and dad weren't around.

At the dock early in the morning, I bid a fond farewell to and thanked Larry and the Council. And my new day began with a whole set of great new friends. I went to the general manager of the resort to let him know I was a hotel guy, too. He said, "Clarke, you are welcome to stay for free as long as you like."

What a fine day I awoke to the next morning! I paddled on a surfboard out to the reef, then joined a barbeque luncheon on the beach. Next, it was a walk in the sand with pretty Jan, dinner, a talent show, and the usual nightly dance. All my new friends then threw a party in my honor and started calling me "Tex." They had never met a "rich" Texan before.

Three wonderful days later, we all departed on a launch at 10:00 p.m. A full moon bathed everything in its magic light as Bill Denton played his ukulele. We sang all the way to the mainland.

At 1:00 in the morning I arrived at the Railway Court Hotel in Proserpine. Doug Virtue had let the lady know I was coming, but the hotel was completely dark. I turned on the hall lights and started trying doors quietly until I found an empty room upstairs. There were no sheets on the bed but I was too tired to care.

I woke up at 8:30 the next morning. Not a soul was stirring upstairs or downstairs. It was as if this place was a ghost hotel and I was the head ghost.

With my two small bags in hand, I walked to the edge of this small town. My luck was amazing at times! Almost immediately, a big semi stopped to pick me up. Ray was going straight through to Brisbane 900 miles away. A bloke of about 40, Ray had a friendly, humorous personality and enjoyed having people ride with him. If I had to drive long runs over narrow, rough

The joys of a Hayman Island beach.

Caught in a moment of contemplation or confusion on "Fantasy Island." Usually, it was a bit of both.

roads, I'd want some company, too.

After five hours of being bounced, jolted, and shaken (not stirred), we stopped at a creek crossing for some tucker (food). We built a fire and fried sausages. To go with it, we had fresh tomatoes, bread and butter, fresh pineapple and, naturally, a cup of tea. Food never tasted better.

We were back on the road quickly and drove through the night. With nearly 21 hours of straight driving, we pulled into Brisbane around 8:00 in the morning. Not only was I shaken *and* stirred, I was also homogenized.

I called Rita as soon as we rolled in. Rita and her father picked me up, took me to their home, and fed me a fabulous breakfast of four eggs, six pieces of bacon, toast and coffee. As I discovered, "we" truckers are big eaters!

There are so many kind people in the world. Rita and I had just met and talked for an hour in Townsville. Yet, there I was in their home being treated like a prince. Their family migrated to Australia from Germany in 1949.

Rita was a fourth-year psychology student at Queensland University. As she drove me around to all the sights in Brisbane, I thought back to my Uncle Millet sailing into Brisbane in 1941, as his artillery battalion was getting ready to battle the Japanese.

That evening after supper, Rita and I went to a movie and then a coffee house to discuss the affairs of the world.

The next morning Rita fixed another super breakfast for me. She walked with me to the tram stop to see me off. I thanked her to no end and said, "I hope you can come to Sydney so I can try and repay just some of your generous and kind hospitality."

On the outskirts, it was thumb out once again to the adventure of the open road. Within minutes, Les, a swell bloke, gave me a ride to Surfers' Paradise, 50 miles away. I left my bags at the Chevron Hotel and headed for the beach to get some sun and check out the birds in bikinis.

Two hours later, I went back to the road. In a few short minutes, an English couple took me seven miles; Ken, a traveling salesman, carried me to Bryon Bay; and at the last glimmer of twilight, Father Scanlon, a priest of Irish descent, took me along to Lismore. For the equivalent of $2 U.S., I checked into a boarding house for the night. I wouldn't be able to afford these expensive places much longer.

Looking back on the day, I had thought of trying something a bit bold and fun at the same time. My plan was to stride into the Chevron Hotel in my blue jeans and white t-shirt, carrying my two beat-up bags. I figured the staff wouldn't immediately sense from my swagger, just who I was. That seemed to happen frequently.

As I boldly entered, I would ask to see the manager. When he approached, I would introduce myself, stating, "I am a hotelman and am in hopes you would extend me the courtesy of a comp room for the night, so that I may enjoy the full delights of Surfers' Paradise." What did happen was, I talked to the Beverage Manager first about getting a comp room. He seemed quite unable to cope with the question, so he got the manager. The manager didn't know whether to be nice or treat me as a con man. He had to call regional headquarters to get an answer. They passed it on to international headquarters to check out my hotel credentials. While this important decision was being debated across the length and breadth of Australia, I went to the beach.

When I returned to the hotel, a final decision had been reached. NO! A pity. They blew their chance to further peace and harmony in the world. It would have cost them a lot less just to give me a room for the night. My philosophy was, *It never hurts to ask. One never knows what miracles may come of it.*

God bless Father Scanlon. We resumed our journey the next morning. We arrived at Taree, 300 miles south at 5:00 p.m. with me on the verge of joining the priesthood.

Along the way, we had to stop at a checkpoint to make sure we weren't toting a passel of ticks somewhere in the car.

Eight cars were waiting in line to be checked. When the old Aussie making the check got to us, we were the third car, and he said, "I hope this line doesn't ever go as far back as the pub. If it does, I'll get in there and won't come out the rest of the day." The Aussies love their beer. That's for sure!

From Taree, I got a ride quickly. And I mean quickly. Like a log in a sluice, we raced to Newcastle, a 100 miles of curves in the rain.

My two new buddies from Hayman Island were waiting for me. George and Geoff picked me up on the road and Geoff's mother welcomed me into their home at around 8:00 p.m. She fixed dinner for me, since I hadn't had a chance to eat.

The next morning Geoff took me to the outskirts of Newcastle. Two rides got me to Hornsby. With rain pouring down, I used the last of the money I had with me and took the train to good old Sydney town.

I was home. Mrs. Brittliff, my Australian mom, invited me to have tea (dinner) with the family. I gave them a blow-by-blow account of my rambles around Australia. I had been on the road for one and a half months.

CHAPTER 14

Snowy Mountain Hideaway

No longer forward nor behind
Do I look in hope or fear;
But, grateful, take the good I find,
The best of now and here.

— John Greenleaf Whittier

Once again, I had come face-to-face with the inevitable—the shadow that often dogged my footsteps—the specter of money. It was getting low and I hit the ground running to prevent abject poverty.

My first stop was to have coffee with my Greek travel agent friend, Angelo. There were still prospects of working on a Greek freighter to Japan. Any nationality of freighter would do, as long as it was free. I thought I'd have to row to Japan.

After a number of job interviews, the light came on. I was hired to sell light bulbs door-to-door. That lasted three days before that career burnt out. I was down to eating my evening meals out of cans to preserve what funds I had left.

Not wanting to leave one stone unturned, I registered at the Casual Workers Bureau. Right after that, Mr. Rix, with Ampol Oil, called me to come in for a second job interview. I was hired and started to work two days later. All was right with the world again.

Working as an oil accounting clerk, from 9 to 5, was flat boring. All day I shuffled and marked paper—non-adventure at its best. However, it allowed me to eat, which was not a bad trade off.

As far as transportation went, I figured I probably wouldn't have a car for another four or five years, so moving around would have to be by foot, bus, hitchhiking, subway, train, horse-drawn cart, camel, boat, and other assorted modes of transport. By this time, all my friends in Texas probably had a house, two cars, and assorted playthings. Yet though I had nothing, I couldn't have been happier.

From my perspective, having things wasn't what it was all about. Give me freedom to roam, walk along virgin rivers and pristine beaches, hike through peaceful meadows and across mountains, and plunge into the wonders of nature, and I was happy. Throughout my travels, I would go out exploring on my own whenever an opportunity presented itself: many times I just sat and took nature in—in all its glory. It was refreshment for my soul.

My big break in TV finally came. Twenty of us were selected as the audience for a fencing match for a Rothman's cigarette commercial. For three hours of sitting, I got paid the equivalent of $14 U.S. I had finished number one in my college fencing class, so I would have preferred being one of the fencers making fifty times as much.

To break the monotony of my dull office job, I was spurred on to sign up for fencing at the Academy of Swordsmen, where I promptly got cut to ribbons by real fencers. Good thing foils lack sharp points or I'd have been in real trouble.

With only three more weeks to go before my temporary job at Ampol ended, nothing was happening on my goal to get to Japan. My desires and alternatives were: work at a ski resort in the Snowy Mountains, work on a station (ranch) in the Outback, get a job on a ship for several voyages, or take anything I could get.

I finally decided to head for the Snowy Mountains, in the southeastern part of Australia, and get any kind of job I could at a ski resort. From mid-June to October, this region is affectionately known as the Snowies and offers Australia's best snow sports. It could be considered the rooftop of Australia.

The snowfield resorts there offer exhilaration and spectacular scenery by day and after dark warm fires and lively nightspots—and it has always been a mecca for snow bunnies.

I left Ampol on August 30. The next day, unemployed, I wrote a letter to Harry Lien, my old friend from Hawaii and New Zealand. He just happened to be working at the Thredbo Ski Resort in the Snowies.

Next, I contacted Mr. Franklin at the New South Wales Government Tourist Bureau. I'd heard he might be able to arrange for me to visit some sheep stations in the Outback. Ever since seeing the movie *The Sundowner*, starring Robert Mitchum, I'd always wanted to have a go at shearing sheep.

Four days after leaving Ampol, I set off hitchhiking for the Snowy Mountains. My first ride was in a Shell Oil truck. It took me twenty miles. After several more rides, I arrived in Canberra. My Irish friend I'd met on the bridge several months before, Tom Gaffney, and his wife Nora, put me up for the night. It was a joy to see them again.

My "James Bond" friend, Robin, and me with our faithful companion at the ski resort in the Snowy Mountains of Australia—an abundance of snow was on the mountains.

The next morning, Tom gave me a ride out to the Cooma Highway. Jeff, a traveling salesman, got me 70 miles down the road, then a family of six got me to Jendabyne on the edge of the Snowy Mountains. The Clarke family took me the last 23 miles to Thredbo Alpine Village.

It was a glorious day to be alive and to be in Thredbo, a snowy mountain hideaway. I found my friend Harry in the Bistro having coffee. He introduced me to the manager of the ski lodge hotel, Mr. Forass, who said, "Clarke, we have no jobs. Sorry." Hearing those words had become S.O.P. (standard operating procedure) for me. Later in the day, Mr. Forass came up to me and said, "I fired the night porter. Can you start tomorrow?" He didn't realize he was talking to the night porter of all night porters—me. Be confident.

Exulting in the mountains around me, I climbed up the first slope to look around. Tall pines and an out-of-this-world view were my reward. I literally felt as if I were on top of the world. On the way down, I found a lost ski. When I went to turn it in at the ski shop, I got a wonderful surprise. There was Alex, whom I had met, along with his mother Mrs. Stanley, in Sydney at the Royal Golf Club. Amazing how these things happen.

Alex and I had dinner together to talk over our plans. After that, everyone from the lodge and the ski lodges all around started gathering at the huge Bistro. Warmed by a roaring fire and a number of hot buttered rums, we danced and made merry with all the girls until 2:00 a.m.—closing time. Harry put me up in a sleeping bag on the floor in his small room. When the day dawned, I would have a job in ski paradise.

How many people have changed jobs in one hour flat? Not many. I was supposed to start work at Coach House Inn at noon. That morning I met Mrs. Hughes from the Silver Brumby Ski Lodge. She offered me a much better deal and I started to work there at 1:00 that afternoon. Two jobs to choose from on the day after my arrival were beyond my imagination.

I went to Mr. Forass to thank him and to apologize for bowing out of the job he'd offered me. He wasn't happy, but then again he'd told me yesterday there were no jobs open, period. So I became the new dishwasher, maid, and handyman at the Silver Brumby Lodge.

But to help out Mr. Forass, I went on and worked the all-night shift since he was short staffed. I gained a friend.

The Silver Brumby was up the mountain from the Inn. It was two stories high, had twenty guest rooms, a large living-dining area with a huge rock fireplace, a big kitchen, and a basement for skis, doing laundry, and playing ping pong. The Hughes, from England, had built the lodge. They had two children, Robin and Ceila. Robin, 20, looked like Pierce Brosnan and had every girl in the resort chasing him.

I later learned that in the 1990s, an avalanche on the mountain swept away many of the lodges with a considerable loss of life. One never knows when something that looks permanent, not dangerous, and safe—*isn't*. When I look back at all the truly dangerous situations I got myself into, it's a wonder I survived. The blessing was that I lived—and how I lived!

My first day of work consisted of chopping logs, making a fire, helping prepare meals, setting tables, waiting on them, and then the *coup de grace*, washing dishes. Washing and drying dishes had never been so much fun. With lively music going full blast, all hands were singing, dancing, and cutting up as we went about our chores.

We were a crazy crew, if ever there was one. Mr. Hughes was a bit stern and above the fray. But Mrs. Hughes, her son and daughter, David from England,

75

Rae, an Aussie, and the Texan were a part of the musical melee. We made quite a glorious opera!

We finished up the day's work at 10:00 p.m. and headed down to the Bistro to the nightly dance. I met Leisha soon after we walked upon the scene. We hit it off and danced until 2:00 a.m. She was of Hungarian-Chinese-Javanese descent, as beautiful a combination as I had ever seen.

I went to bed at 3:00 a.m. and got up at 7:00 in the morning. We started work at 7:30 a.m. and worked through until 10:00 p.m. with one hour off in the afternoon. *What had I gotten myself into?* I wondered. Thank God for that one-hour off. I'd go hiking in the woods and along mountain streams.

My first time on skis was a disaster. David, 28, the English bloke I worked with, took me to the top of the mountain where there was a ski basin for beginners. Beginners, heck! I was just trying to keep upright on my skis. As I teetered one way and tottered another, David said, "Follow me." He suddenly disappeared from sight.

The next thing I knew I was at the lip of the mountain, looking almost straight down. I turned my skis sideways to keep from falling six miles through thin air, my arms churning, my body twisting trying desperately to stop. *Really funny, David, just wait till you see all I have in store for you. If I live,* was my last frantic thought.

And over the precipice I went! Luckily, I didn't fall, and turned my skis sideways and dug into the steep slope. I'm sure there were many asking, "What is that guy at the top of the mountain doing going sideways across the steepest ski run? He must be nuts!" No, he was in sheer panic and praying he wouldn't fall and go tumbling 3,000 feet down the mountain.

That night, while David was sleeping soundly, I yelled, "Fire!" and threw a bucket of ice-cold water on him. He woke up with a start. *After all*, I thought, *one good turn deserves another.*

As our crew put in one long workday after another, I picked up this saying from Rae—*It's character building.* She and I became great friends through it all. Although the work was hard, the walks in the mountains, skiing, the comradeship, dancing, roaring fires, reading, wine, girls from everywhere, and fun events, like costume contests, made it an exhilarating time.

I got a letter from Mr. Kong, from where else—Hong Kong. I'd met him while working at the Chevron Hilton. He was trying to help me with a job there.

My good buddy, Harry Lien, was getting ready to shove off. He would be taking a ship from Sydney to Italy, and then from there to Austria. Harry had seen me off in Hawaii, welcomed me in New Zealand, caught up with me in Sydney, and then I had joined him in Thredbo. Perhaps our paths would cross again in Europe. He had been a true friend.

My skiing talents were far from developed. One bright sunny day as I was going down a steep slope, I lost my balance and fell. I didn't think I would ever stop sliding. Having on only athletic shorts and no shirt, it was a cold and scary tumble. Of course, I set a new all-time record for getting downhill with that cool move.

Later, sunning on the veranda, I was trying to warm up after that smart ski maneuver, when the next thing I knew, a bucket of cold water hit me four-square on the chest. Good old David had thrown it from the window above. *Wait till tonight*, I thought, as I fought my way back from cardiac arrest.

As the ski season was winding down, I got ready to leave this beaut (an Australian term for great) place. I washed all my dirty clothes by hand in the bathtub and hung them up to dry on the back slope. Then, wearing only sport shorts, I was off with the gang to ski one last time. I had become quite tan skiing with no shirt.

I had loved every minute of my month there. Truly, one of the best months of my life! Our "working family" had a last dinner together, wine and all. Then I ironed my shirts.

CHAPTER 15

On the Outback Road Again

*Stop worrying about the potholes in the road
and celebrate the journey.*

— Fitzhugh Mullan

*T*he next morning Rae and I said goodbye to everyone and drove away in her car. She dropped me off four miles out from Cooma at a country crossroads. A few minutes later, I caught a ride to Adaminaby, thirty miles away. My theme song could well have been "On the Road Again."

Hardly any cars traveled this road. It was an hour before I got another ride. I made 250 miles hitching, not having any idea where I would end up that day.

Thanks to Mr. Franklin at the NSW Tourist Bureau I would be visiting a number of sheep and cattle stations (ranches). When I arrived at Yandilla Station, a one-day-old lamb was the first to run up and greet me. He was a sweet little boy.

The Yandilla was owned by the Caldwells. Mrs. Caldwell and her two daughters, Margo and Judy, came out to welcome me.

Margo, 22, took me down to the shearing shed to meet Mr. Caldwell and his son, Don, 20. Later Mr. Caldwell took me over to Netherby Station, owned by the Hines family, where I got my first look at sheep shearing.

Yandilla Station consisted of 1,600 acres of rich pasture land, 3,200 acres of other land, and 14,000 sheep on the combined properties. Added to that were 600 acres of wheat, 200 shorthorn cattle, four horses, and five Kelpie sheep dogs. An impressive spread.

The next day, Margo and I rode horses over to see the Dixons at the Branshott Station. I later helped Bob plow 15 acres to kill weeds so oats could be planted in April.

In three days, I had had an opportunity to get a look at five stations and try my hand at shearing sheep. I was a miserable failure at shearing, as those buggers did not want to cooperate! Another promising career bit the dust.

On Monday, I was back on the road. I met Tina McFarland in the township of Young at noon in front of Town Hall. We met at Thredbo and this Aussie

78

beauty invited me to come see her and meet her family. They owned Milli Milli Station. It consisted of 2,000 acres with 16,000 Merino sheep. The other stations I visited raised Corridales sheep.

My first job at Milli Milli was to help push a mob of sheep through a dip to kill any parasites or diseases they might have. The dip nearly killed me too, but at least I was free of parasites and every other disease known to man. It was the first real bath I had had in a week.

Next, on horseback, we drove 100 rams to a new paddock. After a delicious dinner of lamb, we sat around the fire and talked. They ate a lot of lamb in the Outback.

Tina woke me up at 6:30 the next morning. We rounded up a group of cows before breakfast. Then it was back to dipping sheep. Getting that mob through the foul smelling stuff was not my idea of a good time. I was ready to retire.

Tina kindly dropped me on the highway leading out of Young at noon. A Scotsman gave me a ride to Bathhurst. At 2:30 p.m. I walked into the Civic Center and introduced myself to Gordon Bullock. He was the town's Public Relations Officer and had been waiting for me to show up.

Gordon's first order of business was to call John Dudley, a reporter for the *Western Advocate*, who came over and did a story on all of my travel shenanigans. That night I gave a talk to the Rotary Club.

Gordon and his wife put me up for the night. Sue Ellen, their eight-year-old daughter, had never seen an American, so she was quite excited about my visit.

During my world travels, I was often the only American who many folks ever met. So, in a way, I was an unofficial ambassador for my country. What's more, I was just an average guy working, living, and traveling the world, making friends as I went.

The headline in the next day's paper read, "Texan in Bathhurst." I visited the Silver Lea Station and had another go at sheep shearing. I figured in another year or so I would be able to make those buggers toe the line. Harley, a sheep shearer, took pity on me and took me to his club that evening for a game of pool and a beer.

I resumed hitchhiking, and two rides later, I was 70 miles down the road in Cumnock. Terry Woods picked me up in his truck. He was wearing a pair of old trousers, a shirt with rips and tears in it, and a wide-brimmed, rotting, Aussie hat that had to be close to sixty years old. Again, shades of Robert Mitchum in the movie *The Sundowners*.

*Me on "Trigger," riding on an Outback property (ranch),
mainly helping to round up cattle.*

When we got to Wansey Station, Bob Young came out to welcome me. Bob was like a hero right out of the movies; tall, strongly-built, handsome, suntanned, with a rich and deep voice. He and Terry provided a distinct contrast, but both were great blokes.

After the shearing stopped at 5:00 p.m., Bob and I went up to his house on the hill. We sat on the front porch, had a pleasant conversation, a beer, and then dinner at his niece's house. Peggy welcomed me warmly.

"Your arrival in the area is well known," Peggy said. "They have been broadcasting it on the radio all day." This was truly amazing. Finally, I'd reached celebrity status. Now all I lacked was the money to go with it.

Many of the homesteads on these stations were built as far back as the 1880s. Most had old wood Z-burning fireplaces in the kitchens.

Individualism reigned supreme here in the Outback, along with warmth and friendliness. It reminded me a lot of my native Texas.

At the general store the next morning, we asked if anyone was going my way. Mr. Hawkins, a jam salesman of thirty years, got me to Wellington. Ron, a toy salesman, took me all the way to Narromine and right out to Nundah Station where I was going to stay.

Peter Perry, a red-headed bloke about my age, met me at the door. His folks were off on a trip to the Orient. He showed me around their 6,000 acres with 10,000 sheep, 70 head of cattle and 600 acres of beautiful, tall wheat. A magnificent property!

The next day it was back to the road, getting rides to Dubbo, Gilgandra, Coonabarabran, and two hours of waiting before Bernard Cook took me to the front door of Kirkbright Station.

Des Malcahy greeted me with enthusiasm. He introduced me to his wife, their six children, and Jack and Helen who worked for him. It was a dinner of lamb, as usual. It was getting to the point where I was ready to swear off lamb for life.

Des spent most of the evening telling me about his three years in a Japanese prison camp, because of my deep interest in what he had gone through. My Uncle Millet had spent the same amount of time in a similar camp.

Des gave me a tour of his extensive property before we drove into the town of Malalley. There was one service station, one pub with lots of dinkey-dye shearers inside enjoying themselves, and one small general store. He then drove me into Gunnedah.

There we met Ron Heath. Ron and his two sons ran a stock and station agents' business and they also owned Hartfell Station. Ron asked me a lot of questions on various subjects, and I asked him a lot, too. Robert, his son, was curious to know how the game of American football was played.

Hartfell consisted of 3,500 acres with 1,000 of them planted in wheat. This was apparently one of the best wheat producing areas in Australia.

Mr. and Mrs. Tweedie gave me a ride to Quirindi. Peter Coote, the town clerk, received me cordially when I presented him a letter of introduction from Mr. Franklin.

Peter would soon be going to Tahiti on holiday and was most interested to know all about those lovely islands. Over a cup of tea, I filled him in.

Peter drove me seven miles out to the home of my new hosts, the Uppertons. Again, I was asked to be a guest speaker at the Rotary Club. I spoke about my travels up to date. As always, the hospitality was superb.

Mr. Upperton gave me a ride out to the Sydney highway. I was missing the beaches, the bikinis, movies, friends, and my "home" at the Brittliffs. However, I wouldn't take anything in exchange for the rich experiences I'd had in visiting the stations. Among those experiences, my favorite was earning a beginners merit badge in giving haircuts to sheep. The sheep were cheering, "Thank our lucky stars he's out of here."

As I stuck out my thumb, a truck with two blokes pulled up to me. Seeing "Texas" in big, yellow-taped letters written across my small suitcase, one of them asked me, "Where are you from in Texas?" I said, "San Antone," the way a lot of us Texans say it.

He said, "I was in jail in Galveston."

I asked, "What for?"

He said, "For murder, mayhem, robbery and setting fires to buildings."

I said, "That's all?"

He laughed and said, "Just kidding. It was for being drunk and disorderly."

Well that was a relief! I stood there on the side of the road and listened to the whole story of all his experiences in Texas. My mom always taught me to be a good listener, and did I get an earful.

Next to come along was Mr. Magoo's twin brother, right out of the cartoons. He kindly took me all the way in to Sydney. Home again, after three weeks on the road. *Now what?* I wondered.

CHAPTER 16
Someday My Ship Will Come

Only those who will risk going too far can
possibly find out how far one can go.
— T.S. Eliot

If your ship doesn't come in, swim out to it.
— Jonathan Winters

*T*here was a Travel Lodge on the bay, just down from my boarding house, with the Chesterford Restaurant at the top. When I walked in through the glass doors in the late afternoon, the only person there was the hostess who was preparing for the dinner crowd.

Nancy's looks and figure took my breath away. It was like Rita Hayworth, the movie star, had just appeared in the scene. Awed by her beauty, I mumbled sheepishly, "Is there a manager here by any chance?"

Her smile was radiant. "Let me check if he has time to see you." The manager came out, and I gave him a short pitch on my experience as a chief cook, bottle washer, maid, drink waiter, dishwasher, and other various and assorted specialties. A Hungarian, and not too impressed, he said, "Maybe I can use you part-time starting next week."

To celebrate, I went to the steel-netted pool in the bay for a swim. Hopefully, no holes had opened up in the net since the last time I swam there, which would allow the sharks to cruise in on me.

The next day, the Hungarian restaurant manager at the Travel Lodge called and asked if I could start as a drink waiter/dishwasher right away. As the only drink waiter, I brought drinks out to the tables for four waitresses. Boy, did I look spiffy in my white shirt and black bow tie.

Having never been a real drink waiter before, I found myself in one uncomfortable situation after another. Like the time I poured wine in a gentleman's glass, he tasted it, and then I forgot to give him any more wine. Then after opening a bottle of wine at another table, expertly I thought, I proceeded to pour half the cork in a lady's glass. It was just flat out embarrassing.

Two redeeming things about that first night were I did not get fired and I got to know Nancy. She was 30 years old and I was 25. Was there any hope for romance? No way. She was a mature woman and a model of sophistication.

For four hours of work, I made four pounds ($8 U.S.) and got a free steak dinner. And another plus was that the hotel was just a half a block from where I lived.

In November, late one night, I decided I should put all my energies into getting to Hong Kong, one way or the other. So I started scheming and dreaming in earnest.

One evening at closing time, I was in the small, dark room off the kitchen, minding my own business, washing all the dirty glasses in the sink. Out of nowhere, Nancy came up behind me, wrapped her arms around my waist, kissed my neck and said, "I can't keep my hands off you any longer." Do dreams come true? Yes, they do!

Now there was a switch—the model-like hostess falling for the dishwasher. Of course, I fell just as hard. A torrid romance bloomed.

To keep in shape, everyday I ran three miles around a nearby track, and did a whole lot of situps and pushups. Plus I swam, water skied, bodysurfed at Bondi Beach, and played tennis whenever I got a chance. Except for maybe when I went through Marine Corps Officer "Boot Training," I was about as fit as I had ever been.

A new manager took over the restaurant and let four of us go in one fell swoop, which was a shame because I was just getting the hang of pouring wine into a glass without pieces of cork floating in it. There's an art to everything.

I went back to job hunting. I called almost everyone I knew. I landed a job at the Menzies Hotel working a banquet and the Chevron Hilton banquet manager said I could work straight through to Christmas from December 9. A huge relief! It allowed me to earn money to move on.

"Hong Kong, here I come!" I shouted. I started filling out travel papers. I got a ticket from P&O Lines to cover the Singapore to Hong Kong part of the voyage. The bad part was I also had to pay for the passage from Hong Kong back to Sydney—in case the Hong Kong authorities kicked me out. At Sitmar Lines, I bought a passage from Sydney to Singapore on the *Castel Felice*. Lastly, I got a re-entry visa for Australia, just in case they shipped me back. The dice had been rolled, the die had been cast and fate awaited me.

As a casual waiter, I worked one of the largest banquets of the year at the Menzies Hotel. It was a celebration of the twenty-seventh anniversary of the Australian-American Association. The speaker was none other than the

Governor-General of Australia, Lord D'Lisle. I managed to create the most excitement of the evening.

In the middle of Lord D'Lisle's address, I dropped a tray full of glasses, ice and drinks. There was a resounding crash that echoed through the huge banquet hall. Fortunately, the bloke I dropped it on took pity on me since I was an American. The Menzies banned me from ever working there again. I live on in the annals of that hotel, no doubt.

I was more than short of money to go to H.K. Having to pay for a passage back from there to Australia almost did me in. With only four days to go before I sailed, my passport arrived with my visa in it.

My going away party was a beaut. Nancy and about twenty others came. I had gained a host of wonderful friends in this wonderful country.

Two days before I was to leave, I had my last round of shots. I felt bad all afternoon. Having cholera and typhoid at the same time is no fun but I would have been lost without my cholera shot. It seemed that every time I arrived or departed a country, I needed a cholera shot. It was getting ridiculous.

Christmas Day was one of the hottest days on record for Sydney. It got up to ninety-seven degrees. The gracious Boyce family once again had me over for Christmas dinner. They and other friends came to see me off to new adventures.

At 8:00 p.m. the ship Castel Felice set sail from Pyrmont, Wharf 20, for Singapore. Finally, after many months of trying, making contacts, dreaming, and persevering, I was sailing west to a new life in the Far East. Would my luck hold?

CHAPTER 17
A Cruise to End All Cruises

For the resolute and determined—there is
time and opportunity.
— Ralph Waldo Emerson

*T*his was going to be a tough voyage with many hardships. The girls outnumbered the guys five to one. Most of the single girls were headed to London on holiday or to work. Love boat indeed!

Chris was a congenial tablemate and my cabin mate was Peter, a twenty-three year old "comedian" from Tasmania. He kept me laughing all the time. Peter and I just happened to be the only ones in a four-berth cabin.

"Let's offer the other two berths to any girls who are not happy with their cabin mates," Peter recommended.

With some of our ship's gang on deck
of the Castel Felice.

"Great idea, Peter," I said. "I'm sure there will be a rush to take us up on such a generous offer."

The first day out the bikini-clad girls were so thick I almost went blind and Peter came close to having a stroke.

It was great weather and smooth sailing. We danced into the night and sang songs on deck until 3:00 a.m. Each day we met new people as our circle of friends grew. On the fourth night, I danced with every good-looking girl in sight that I hadn't met before. They all seemed happy with their cabin mates, much to Peter's and my regrets.

On December 31st, it was a high celebration on the high seas. At our table were twelve girls and six guys. At the stroke of midnight, I must have kissed twenty girls. As the band played *Auld Ange Syne*, everyone gathered on the dance floor, hand-in-hand, and sang along.

When the band gave up at 1:30 a.m. we all went out on deck and danced Scottish reels to the music of an accordion and a harmonica. When those two musicians retired, we sang songs for two more hours.

At 5:00 a.m., after I had walked Angie to her cabin, I found my room-mate, Peter, sitting at the bottom of the stairs near our cabin. He was amazed when he saw me at the top of the stairs. "Peter, what are you doing sitting out here?" I said. "When I found the key gone and our door locked, I thought you were inside with a girl," he sleepily said. He had patiently been waiting for three hours for me to come out. What a noble soul.

On January 2nd, we sailed past the Indonesian Island of Timor at 11:00 a.m.; but the really big show took place that afternoon. I was sunning by the pool when this young guy jumped in with all his clothes on. *That's weird*, I thought. The guy then got out of the pool, strolled over to the railing, climbed the railing, and jumped overboard—from five stories high. Such a jump would kill most people. It was bizarre. At the time, we were plowing through the Java Sea at full steam ahead when he hit the water. The ship immediately went into a hard left turn with the emergency horn blaring, as a rescue boat was lowered. We could see the daredevil in the distance lazily doing the backstroke. It was a wonder he could swim at all after such a long fall. He must have been on drugs, drunk, or just plain crazy. No doubt he was out for a pleasant afternoon swim in the shark-infested ocean. They threw him in the brig once they got him back on board. At least the ship didn't lack for entertainment, I told Peter.

When we docked in Singapore on January 6th, the monsoon season had arrived in all its glory. I had never seen it rain buckets before.

Celebrating a glorious New Year's Eve in the Java Sea.

Singapore has an interesting history. One of the earliest references to it was found in Javanese writings in 1365. It was called Sea Town. By the end of the 14th century, it was called Singapura, which means Lion City. The British who were extending their dominion over India saw the need for a port-of-call in the region to refit and to protect their merchant fleet. In 1819, they established a trading post there.

Singapore proved to be a prized settlement for the British. By 1860, the population had grown to around 80,000. The peace and prosperity ended when Japanese aircraft bombed the sleeping city on December 8, 1941.

At the gate to the docks, armed guards checked my passport, as well as the taxi driver's license. With Indonesia's confrontation policy toward Malaysia, and its strong communist leanings, it basically amounted to an undeclared war. Security precautions were strict. I was told that not many tourists were coming to Singapore at the time.

I checked into the cheapest room at the old Strand Hotel. It had a high ceiling with a blade fan, right out of an old movie. At the Peking Night Club, some of us from the ship danced until midnight. From then until 2:00 a.m., Abdul, our Malaysian taxi driver, gave us a tour of the city.

To get to Singapore, we had sailed along the Great Barrier Reef of Australia, through the Arafura Sea, Flores Sea, Java Sea, South China Sea, and the Singapore Straits. I was approaching the status of becoming an "old salt."

After one night in the hotel, I checked into the Chinese YMCA at less than half the cost of the hotel. I then set out on foot to explore Singapore. That evening Anna Lou, who I met on the ship, and some of her friends showed me the Singapore of the natives.

The next day, my new friends from the YMCA, Gordon Parker from London, Kerry Wanda from Australia, and I hired a sampan for $7 Malaysian. We then took a tour of the harbor. I had now literally covered the waterfront.

On the morning of the third day, a young student by the name of Chris approached me as I was exploring deep within the city and asked, "Where are you from, sir?" He was interested in practicing his English and became my unofficial guide for the rest of the day. He helped bring alive the inner workings and cultures of the city.

On January 10th, I set sail for Hong Kong on an English ship, the *S.S. Chusan*. Compared to the *Castel Felice*, it was the difference between day and night and going from excitement, romance and revelry to dull, duller and dead. But I had learned that every experience has its rewards.

Will I be able to survive in Hong Kong, having no job lined up? I wondered. I was excited but apprehensive. *Will this be the place where my adventures came to an end*? I knew I was taking a path that few others had taken. I could see the headlines, "Texan sent packing."

I had one friend in Hong Kong, John Moore, and hoped that he would be able to assist me. For months, I had been informed many times by many people that Americans could not work in Hong Kong. Being a firm believer in the saying, *Destiny is not a matter of chance, it is a matter of choice,* I moved forward.

Until disembarking, I would enjoy the luxury of having a four-berth cabin to myself, even though I had paid the cheapest fare. There was plenty of room to spread out my few belongings that I had crammed into my one suitcase and old seabag. *Take advantage of luxury when you have it*, I told myself.

I drew several interesting tablemates. My Kazemi, a most learned man from Iran, had been an Ambassador to fourteen countries. Eva, a sexy blonde from Norway, spiced up what was to be an otherwise dull voyage.

Watch out for blondes from Norway! a little voice in my head said, but I ignored it. Whoever was handling the table seating arrangements knew what they were doing.

Ninety-nine percent of the passengers seemed to be in their late seventies. For most, mealtimes were the peak of activity each day it seemed.

I soon met Dave Calvert, an Australian skydiver and adventurer about my age and we became fast friends. Every year at Christmas time, Dave would take off on an adventure trip some place in the world and this was his year to see Hong Kong. We agreed to get together soon after we arrived.

CHAPTER 18

Starting Off with a Bang and Broke in Hong Kong

Do not go where the path may lead, go instead where there is no path and leave a trail.
— Ralph Waldo Emerson

*A*ll we could see from ship's deck was a heavy fog. Then, as if by magic, there was the crown jewel of Hong Kong rising out of the oriental mists. It was a dramatic entrance into a new and uncertain world.

A letter was delivered to my cabin even before we docked. It was from my good friend, John, whom I had gotten to know in Sydney. He wrote, "A newspaper reporter and photographer will be meeting you as soon as you dock. They want to do a story on your adventurous life and how you travel without any money. I'll see you at the YMCA at 6:00 p.m. Welcome to the British Crown Colony, my friend." What a wonderful surprise. John just happened to be working for the *South China Morning Post* newspaper. He was a generous and thoughtful person.

After the surprise newspaper interview, I checked into the YMCA. As at all YMCAs that had rooms available, I received a warm and friendly reception. And, it was the cheapest place to stay in Hong Kong. Counting my money, I found I would be able to hold out a week before sinking into poverty.

While I was sailing to this one-of-a-kind city, I read up on its history. In 1276, the Southern Song Dynasty court fled Mongol invaders to the region that is now Hong Kong. In 1279, the Song army was defeated in its last battle with the Mongols.

The first contacts between the West and Hong Kong came during the Mong Dynasty. In 1517, a Portuguese merchant met with Chinese officials through an interpreter at the Pearl River estuary to negotiate trade with Canton. There was a waterfall on the island where foreign ships got fresh water. Nearby was a village called Hong Kong Village. The name stuck.

In 1699, the British East India Company made its first successful sea venture to China. Hong Kong's trade with British merchants soon developed. In 1711, the company started a trading post in Canton, now called Guangzhou.

The British occupied Hong Kong Island on January 20, 1841 after a series of Chinese defeats. The Island was ceded to Britain in 1842. With a base in Hong Kong, British traders, opium dealers, and merchants launched the city that would become the "free trade" center of the East.

In 1898, Britain executed a 99-year lease on the New Territories to make sure Hong Kong could be defended. Although nearly a century seemed like a long time, on July 1, 1997, Hong Kong ceased to be a British Crown Colony and became a Special Administrative Region of the Peoples' Republic of China. As a result, many residents who opposed the handover immigrated to other countries.

What an intriguing place was this Hong Kong of 1964. I read a story in the *South China Morning Post* announcing that, for the first time, more than 10,000 ships had visited the harbor within a year.

The whole colony was less than twenty miles across before one ran into the Bamboo Curtain of China, a 17-mile border fence. A British Officer told me, "One word from Mao and the Red Chinese could march straight into Hong Kong with no problem."

But the Communist Chinese were not as completely tucked safely away behind the Bamboo Curtain as I thought. They owned a skyscraper right smack in the center of Hong Kong. The building resembled a fortress and was said to be full of spies. It was their headquarters in the Western world.

Hong Kong had become a very important location for American intelligence operations according to Lombardo's *A Mission of Espionage, Intelligence, and Psychological Operations: The American Consulate in Hong Kong, 1949-64.* There was no telling how many Russian KGB agents were roaming the streets at the time, but surely there were dozens of them.

The Cold War was totally red hot. All kinds of movies were being made about it—many in Hong Kong. To top it off, the Hong Kong Chinese were enamored with James Bond-type films. I had landed in a playground for spies, spying, and spy movies.

As I arrived in Hong Kong in January 1964, all seemed calm but unbeknownst to me, there was trouble brewing in Harbor City.

When John and I met for dinner at the Kingfisher Restaurant that first night, he gave me a rundown on hotels to check out for a job. Of course, the rule was Americans couldn't work in Hong Kong, unless there were special circumstances involved. For me it was work or starve.

John had preceded me to Hong Kong by several months and had already made a lot of important contacts. It could almost be said that my fate was in his hands. Without him, as we say in Texas, *I would've been up a creek without a paddle.* The day after I arrived, there was my picture and story in the number one newspaper of the Crown Colony. Miracles do happen. I was pleased to observe that I had not been exposed as a pauper. There was still ample opportunity for that to be revealed.

As I took my first Star Ferry ride across the harbor from Kowloon to Hong Kong Island, I thought of the movie *The World of Susie Wong.* It was on this famous ferry system that the two lovers met. Unfortunately, I didn't meet a beautiful Chinese girl on that trip but I saw dozens of them I would have liked to meet. All were in their colorful, tight fitting, slit-to-the-thighs dresses called cheongsams.

Besides the newspaper interview, I had my first radio interview the next day. Barry Haig of Commercial Radio interviewed me about my travels, thanks to John.

Then, Mike Bullmer of Radio Hong Kong interviewed me. It took place in the evening at the Hong Kong Cricket Club. Mike bought me a beer and three vodkas during the process. I had no idea what I said. I knew one thing for certain, I was going to hire John as my Public Relations man. He had literally opened up the news media in Hong Kong to me.

I wasn't real steady when I boarded the Star Ferry for the fourth time that eventful day. I had no job but everyone in Hong Kong knew I had arrived. Word still hadn't leaked that I was the brokest guy in the colony. *So far, so good*, I thought.

Over three days, I was turned down by fifteen hotels. It was always the same story, "Americans can't work in Hong Kong, only British subjects with special passports." John had done everything he could do, so it was now do or die for me.

On the fourth day, someone on Hong Kong Island mentioned that the new President Hotel in Kowloon was getting ready to open soon. It was 8:00 p.m. when I heard this news. There was no time to spare as I was down to my last three dollars. I went back across the harbor to test my luck. I walked up one block from the ferry terminal along Nathan Road. There sat the President Hotel covering an entire square block. It was completely dark except for lights in the lobby.

Surely, no one is there and the doors are locked, I thought. I tried the glass door and it opened. It was as if I had entered a Chinese Emperor's palace.

There was only one person in sight in the gigantic lobby. She was behind the front desk. Very humbly, I asked, "Is there a manager in?" She replied, "Just a moment," and went through a swinging door behind the desk. As she came back out, a Caucasian gentleman followed her. I speculated, *He's got to be British and I am going to starve to death in Hong Kong. This is it.*

I introduced myself and with hat in hand, so to speak, I asked, "Could you possibly use an experienced hotelman?" To sum it up, he grabbed my hand, shook it vigorously and said, "Boy, can I use an experienced hotel hand. You're a godsend." As my luck would have it, he was desperate. That made two of us.

Mr. Friscia, an American and the General Manager, hired me on the spot as the front office manager of the newest and biggest hotel in the British Crown Colony. My beginning salary was $1,000 U.S. a month, a fortune in Hong Kong. A splendid room in the hotel, all my dry cleaning, laundry, meals, drinks, and entertainment were all thrown in for free. In a flash, I went from rags to riches.

One week after my arrival, I entered this in my diary, "I have to be one of the luckiest and most fortunate people on God's earth." The Immigration Department had just approved my work visa.

Several weeks later, the Grand Opening of the hotel burst forth, literally. It is a Chinese custom to set off firecrackers for the opening of a new building. There was a thick string of firecrackers that hung from the roof seventeen floors above down to the street. We opened the hotel with a colossal bang, and the best news was, I was no longer a near pauper. In fact, I had ended up in the lap of luxury.

CHAPTER 19
Dazzling City, Hidden Intrigue

*Plunge boldly into the thick of life, and seize
it where you will, it is always interesting.*
— Johann Wolfgang Von Goethe

*I*t could be said that Hong Kong was near its zenith at the time of my arrival. Business and tourism were booming, people seemed well dressed and well fed, optimism was in the air, new hotels and buildings were being constructed, and on the surface, peace reigned.

The fabled "Pearl of the Orient" was my new home. In the mid-1960s, it was a remarkable world uniquely situated between East and West. There were 3.5 million people living in the colony, many were refugees from China, which made the city feel overcrowded.

However, tens of thousands of boat people preferred the water to the land, or had no choice. Chinese junks of all shapes and sizes could be seen plying the waters of the harbor. Countless others lived in tightly clustered communities of squatter shacks without running water.

Without a doubt, it was the most dazzling and fascinating city I had ever seen to date. The lights at night changed in to a seeming fairyland. One big problem was that the status of the colony's water supply frequently made headline news. There were only two sources of water—rainfall and China, with whom Hong Kong had negotiated for fixed quantities of water that was piped in. Before typhoons replenished reservoirs, there could be serious water shortages. I experienced six of the water giving typhoons.

During several periods of drought, and when China would cut off the water pipeline to spite the British, the local water authority turned on the spigot only a few hours every fourth day. Everyone had to fill buckets, bathtubs, or whatever they had and that water had to last for four days.

Fortunately, the Chinese brothers who had built our hotel thought ahead. They had a huge water reservoir constructed under the hotel. Many tourists chose the President because we never lacked for water. I was everyone's friend who wanted to take a bath, so I started selling tickets.

During the first ten days of October in Hong Kong, times were always tense. Political loyalties became overt and occasionally clashed. The Communists celebrated October 1 as Red China's National Day, and on October 10 the Chinese Nationalists celebrated the founding of the Republic of China.

The flags of the two countries would be flown from certain buildings. Hong Kong authorities were nervous, especially with the display of Nationalist Chinese flags in areas where pockets of former Nationalist troops lived. And there was no telling how many Chinese had escaped to Hong Kong to get away from the brutal Chinese Communist regime.

At the time, Hong Kong was the closest Americans could get to arch enemy "Red China." British and American ships of war used to dot the harbor. Nothing was for certain and there was a two-mile wide no-man's land before the actual Hong Kong-China border.

In 1964, the infamous Cultural Revolution was revving up, but few people outside China understood this at the time. Hong Kong had more than its share of spies and intelligence resources involved in their machinations. Clavell, in his book *Noble House*, provided some insight into the hidden world of Hong Kong. The spy services searched for useful informants among the stream of refugees reaching the colony.

I had the advantage of being an innocent, young American, going forth in the world as if all was peaceful. No telling how many spies I bumped into or encountered or how many natives thought I was a spy. I imagined myself a James Bond type—as I had some intriguing conversations over tea and crumpets with some interesting people.

Soon after I arrived, I contacted Mrs. Stanley—one of the grand dames of the colony. I'd had the privilege of meeting her and her son, Alex, in Australia. Major and Mrs. Stanley invited me for tea in their lovely flat on the Peak. The Peak was where the cream of Hong Kong society lived because there was a spectacular view of the breathtaking harbor.

Major Stanley, the Director of the Hong Kong Tourist Association, cut a dashing figure right out of British lore, while Mrs. Stanley was a warm and gracious lady. I learned over tea that Mrs. Stanley was a leader in Hong Kong refugee work.

The next thing I knew, Mrs. Stanley signed me up to tutor a sixteen-year-old Chinese boy by the English name of Roderick. The next day I went with her to Reclamation Street. There I met Roderick's family who slept on the sidewalk. The father was blind, the mother in poor health, and all the children underfed. We left a message for Roderick. It was an eye-opening introduction to the back streets of Hong Kong.

Several days later, I started tutoring Roderick. Even though he was 16, he was skinny and looked more like he was twelve. I had never met anyone who was more interested in education than this young boy. Not only was he polite, but he spoke English fairly well.

It was a reminder and a valuable lesson for me as I got to know Roderick. If one thinks they are disadvantaged, they need to meet someone like this boy who lived on a back street sidewalk. I am not sure what happened to him, but my guess is that he became successful. All he needed was a little help.

With little to eat each day, Roderick would get up at 6:00 a.m., do his family chores, walk wherever he had to go, come home from school at 5:00 p.m. and do more chores, eat whatever was available for dinner, and then study until 1:00 or 2:00 a.m.

It was rewarding for me, over the next year, to become one of his teachers. I'm the one who learned the most from the experience. My belief is that every human being has great potential so long as they have a willingness to learn and someone to teach, encourage, and support them. With this, there is no telling what they can accomplish in life.

As Front Office Manager, I had fifty-three people on my staff. This included three shifts of room clerks, bell captains and bellboys. Just making out work schedules was a Herculean task. For example, Joe was off on Monday but wanted to switch days off with Paul. Paul was sick on Monday but got Dorothy to fill in for him, so Joe had to work on Dorothy's usual day off. And so the merry-go-round continued until nobody came to work.

My Chinese front desk group was an interesting crew. Dorothy was quiet, polite, thoughtful, serious, a lady, and very efficient. Joe had a million-dollar smile and a personality to go with it, but he put work second. Paul was easy-going, humorous, lazy, and looked like what I thought a Chinese gangster looked like. David was Mr. Personality, a go-get-em, party man; Jimmy was reserved, short, efficient and a good worker; and Tommy was a warm, hard-working, sincere, natural leader. I liked them all.

The male crew took me out for dinner a month after I started and then introduced me to the Savoy Nightclub. Nightlife was always booming there. Many of the bands in the clubs were from the Philippines. I found the Filipinos to be great musicians.

For reasons unknown, Mr. Friscia was replaced as General Manager by Mr.

Souers, also an American. Mr. Souers was fat, jovial, and, from all reports, one of the best hotelmen in the world. He had his work cut out for him working for a group of eight Chinese brothers, only one of who spoke English. It was going to be a roller coaster ride.

After the official grand opening cocktail party, my Chinese staff insisted I have a sumptuous Chinese dinner with them at the White House Restaurant. Afterwards, I went to the Firecracker Bar for drinks and dancing with John Moore, his girlfriend, who was one of Hong Kong's top models, and others. Hong Kong was fast growing on me.

Since I had only one suit, I got measured for my first custom-made suit at Chainrais Tailors. I'm sure people were beginning to think that I slept in that one suit. Maybe so, but I never admitted it.

My Australian skydiving friend from the ship, Dave Calvert, and I began checking out the fascinating harbor city together. Every two or three days, we would walk different routes "off the beaten path." We often thought people walking down the street were yelling at each other, and then they would suddenly start laughing uproariously. That was because the Cantonese dialect had the appearance of an argument, we soon learned.

To get a feel for what Hong Kong was like in those heady days, I recommend people see the film *The World of Susie Wong*, starring William Holden and Nancy Kwan. Nancy Kwan was one of the most alluring women I had ever seen. In fact, Miss Kwan came into the President Hotel quite often and I was able to visit with her on one occasion. She always generated titillating excitement as she strode across the lobby in her high-slit cheongsam.

On my one day off, Jimmy the desk clerk took me for my first look at the renowned Tiger Balm Mansion and Gardens. Little did I know, at that moment, that I'd be staying at the mansion in the future. Two Chinese brothers patented the famous Tiger Balm oil medicine and became wealthy. They started their first newspaper in Singapore in 1929. In 1935, Tiger Balm Gardens was built in Hong Kong, and in 1937, the one in Singapore was built. It was one of the brothers, Aw Boon Haw, who lent his name—meaning Tiger—to the remedy. The tiger is synonymous in the East with strength and vitality, so the name seemed the obvious association for such a pain reliever.

Even today, Tiger Balm is known as the essence of the gods and good for everything, including a foot rub, backrub, sore throat, stuffy nose, or whatever. It cures what ails you. Devotees of the product say, "I use it for everything; I bought it for my Grandmother and she found it really helped with her arthritis pains in her knees; I have a bulging disc; the Tiger Balm pain patches give me immense relief and it helps relieve my sinus problems at the same time; I am a Tiger Balm junkie; I use it for muscle aches, headaches, sinuses and inflamed joints." It appeared to work better than the snake oil we have in Texas.

According to these tales of balmy bliss, one does not want to go home or leave home without it, no matter what your ailment. No wonder the Aw brothers made such a fortune.

One fine spring weekend, Teresa, who worked at the YMCA, invited me to take a train with her to Fanling. This small Chinese village is 20 miles from Red China and it was my first venture into the New Territories.

Mrs. Cablao, Teresa's aunt, lived there. We spent a wonderful day walking around the village and countryside. It was an agricultural scene right out of ancient China with black-clad Hakka women working in the fields.

Mrs. Cablao and her family would become like family to me during my stay in the colony. I ended up getting her oldest daughter, Helena, a job at the *H.K. Tiger Standard* newspaper when she graduated from high school.

I think Hong Kong at that time had to be one of the most fascinating cities in the world: It was ruled by the British; tourists poured in from countries across the globe and well-built Chinese girls in their tight cheongsams were everywhere; there was a thriving Chinese movie industry and famous people kept popping up everywhere; there were spies galore, hawkers, pedi-cabs, ferries, sampans, junks, and ships filling the harbor; mountainous beauty; businesses of every shape, size and form; a booming economy; night life like no other place; the din of Cantonese being spoken; wheeling-and-dealing going on at every level on every corner; unbelievable bargains; opium traffic; and me, a young Texan, in the big middle of it all. It was quite a life to be living—and it was only beginning.

CHAPTER 20

Coffin from Hong Kong

*A large volume of adventures may be grasped
within this little span of life by him who interests his heart in everything.*
— Lawrence Sterne

One never knows exactly what is going to turn up in life. My philosophy has always been to make the best of it, dead or alive.

Not long after I started working at the hotel, two of Germany's top movie stars came to stay with us. Heinz Drache and Elga Andersen were a congenial pair. One day they asked me if I would like a part in *Coffin from Hong Kong*, the movie they were in the process of making. I asked, "What role would I play?" Heinz said, "You will be in the coffin." I could tell right away that they had tremendous confidence in my acting potential.

The next morning, I went with them by taxi to the Chinese movie studio in the country. There were so many Chinese beauties assembled there I could hardly believe my eyes.

The next day it was back to the movie set to continue my work as a budding movie star. The Chinese actresses were helping me learn to speak Chinese when we were on break from filming.

As it turned out, I was an extra in a nightclub scene, dancing with a gorgeous Chinese actress. I felt like I had died and gone to heaven. It sure beat being in the coffin!

There was one actress I was especially attracted to. Her English name was Flora. She did not speak a word of English but somehow that didn't matter. I ended up with the girl—just like in the movies. A true friendship developed between us.

About this time, some Chinese friends decided to give me a Chinese name. It was Sown Ching. I hoped it stood for something special, but I soon discovered it meant "sowing one's wild oats." How did they ever come up with a name like that?

Repulse Bay is a special place in Hong Kong and to me. In 1841, the bay was used as a base by pirates. The pirates who attacked merchant ships were

Actress friend from the movie Coffin *from*
Hong Kong.

subsequently repulsed by the British fleet, hence the name Repulse Bay. In 1920, the famous Repulse Bay Hotel was built. The Verandah Restaurant at the hotel became the setting for classic English afternoon tea—where I whiled away some pleasant hours.

It was wintertime. Surprisingly, not a soul was on Repulse Beach on this particular Sunday morning. The weather was sunny, but nippy, like a fall day back in Texas. Being my only day of the week off, I needed to relax after having taken care of four large Japanese tour groups.

I took off my polo shirt and tennis shoes and laid back in my blue jeans on the sand to soak up the sun's rays. Finally, I had found a beautiful peacefulness in crowded Hong Kong. This was too good to be true. I drifted off to sleep.

All of a sudden, I was awakened by shouting in Chinese. I looked up. The sun was in my eyes. I could faintly see three figures twenty yards away throwing a football around. An American football! This couldn't be. Immediately, I jumped up and asked if I could throw it around with the guys. Luckily, they spoke English. Fred Aw, the one who owned the football, and I hit it off right away.

You never know whom you'll meet on a deserted Chinese beach in wintertime. Once again, fate seemed to have had a way of bringing certain people together. And why a football on this particular beach? I had played quarterback in school for seven years, so it got my attention.

Fred was a Stanford graduate, thus, the football. He lived, of all places, in the mansion at Tiger Balm Gardens. He was the eye of the tiger and a part owner of the Hong Kong Tiger Standard newspaper. Being the same age, we had a lot in common. Several days later, I showed Fred around our new hotel. It was the beginning of a great friendship. As I had heard it said before, "chance is the providence of adventurers."

The hotel business was a fascinating world. Each department was filled with diverse personalities. In Hong Kong, it was on a magnified scale, given the intrigue, British control, the threat from Red China, tourists from all over the world, and an 800-person Chinese staff, many of whom did not understand English at all.

At the top of the pyramid were the eight Chinese brothers who owned the hotel, only one of whom could speak English. As anyone with a lick of sense could see, this meant chaos. The setting of policy sailed forth like a rudderless ship in one of Hong Kong's many typhoons. *Yes! No! Maybe! Never! Do this today! Forget what we said yesterday!* The challenges to the managers were vast and this didn't even take into account the guests' needs.

Then there were some of the desk clerks and bellboys running their own businesses on the side, such as running girls and touting their friends' businesses.

One of my room clerks, I discovered, had been arranging contacts with our hotel guests for a local vendor. As a guest would get to their room, the so-called vendor would call and state, "I represent the travel agency and I am to be your guide in Hong Kong." If the guest was a man, "Would you like a lady escort?" If a guest fell for it, the vendor would then take the guest to all his friends' stores where he got commissions out of the whole business. My room clerk promoted himself right out of a job.

Our famous Firecracker Bar had three beautiful hostesses. Apparently, one of them had the reputation as the Dragon Lady of Hong Kong. No telling what that meant. All I knew was that she could have doubled for a Chinese movie queen.

Our English housekeeper, an old maid, felt sure she was born to run the hotel with an iron hand. Pay no mind to what the general manager said. I had my share of run-ins with her. One day, she decided she was going to show me her authority by taking away my room and giving me a rollaway bed in a broom closet. It led to all out war, but I got used to the broom closet.

I had three outstanding Chinese bell captains on my staff. Freeman Ho and I would eat out together from time to time, and he gave me insights into how the Chinese think. Wong had escaped Red China by paddling an inner tube for miles at night through shark-infested waters to gain freedom. Yao was soft-spoken and a man of character.

Our new Assistant General Manager from Mexico, who had a fiery temper, went after our Chinese American personnel manager one day. When we rushed to the personnel manager's office, the Mexican had him by the throat with both hands on top of the desk. Mr. M. was turning blue. It took several of us to save him.

On every floor a room boy was present 24 hours a day. He sat in a small office beside the elevators. Actually, I believe they were spies for the owner-brothers. "Yes sir, Clarke brought a Chinese girl to his room at 12:03 a.m. She was wearing a blue cheongsam, black high heels, walked with a limp, had on a gold necklace, was 5'6" tall, weighed 116 pounds, had measurements of 34-22-34, and had a beauty mark on her left cheek. No sir, they did not have free drinks from the Firecracker Bar in their hands."

I really blew the room boy's mind one night when I took six Chinese girls to my room. I did it just to test his powers of observation. "Well, sir, I think one was short, one was tall, one had no shoes, I think they were all Chinese, however, one could have been Eurasian. No sir, I think only two had earrings on." That night the brothers' intelligence operations went to hell in a hand basket. And they hadn't seen anything yet.

The chef, Manfred, was German. He had everyone in his kitchen marching or at attention. His staff had a hard enough time with English but they were rapidly catching on to German. That is, if they knew what was good for them.

Every morning I went to the coffee shop for breakfast. Only one time in a year did I get what I ordered. I always had better luck with the lottery.

Every day in Hong Kong was a revelation. As a manager in the newest and largest hotel, invitations of all kinds were constantly flowing my way. Every businessman in the colony was eager to have tourists visit their establishment. Tourists were their lifeblood.

No matter what restaurant or club I entered, the owner or manager would greet me by name and say, "Mr. Straughan, right this way please. I have a table right in front for you." Life was good for a guy who had only three dollars in his pocket when he started to work.

How things had changed.

CHAPTER 21

Mysterious Macao

*A man practices the art of adventure when he
breaks the chain of routine and renews his life
through reading new books, traveling to new
places, making new friends...*
— Wilferd Peterson

*M*y friend, Tom Russell, and I were hitting the nightclubs almost every night. I was not only burning the candle at both ends, but in the middle, too. I resolved to change my wayward ways at a later time.

After a cocktail party for the famous Italian actress, Gina Lollobrigida, Tom and I, on the spur of the moment, decided to investigate Macao. We had heard many intriguing stories about that Portuguese bastion on the Chinese mainland. That galvanized our adventurous spirits into action. We boarded the midnight ferry, in a scene reminiscent in an old movie, for Macao. It was a foggy night. We awakened that morning to find the vintage ferry had docked.

I learned the Portuguese founded this colony some sixty years after Columbus discovered America. It is the oldest European settlement in the Far East and indeed a meeting place of *two different worlds.*

There was a seamy side to Macao's history. Through the centuries, many girls were sent there by Chinese families to become domestic workers or prostitutes. In the early decades of the 20th century, Macao was one of the "cities of sin" (De Leeuw 1934). It was rife with gambling, drugs, crime, prostitution, contraband, and racketeering. Tom and I felt right at home.

Gambling still existed as one of the central pillars of the economy, although, on the surface it appeared as a peaceful, colonial town with beautiful tree-lined streets. Some gambling took place on boats tied up to the docks.

It was not only a fascinating place at the time, but Macao supplied its share of danger. It was known as a den of sex, sin and spies.

It has been reported in current times, that since the Chinese Nationalists fled from China to Taiwan in 1949, over 3,000 Taiwanese spies have been captured or disappeared in their espionage activities against the Chinese mainland. Therefore, it was always a difficult job for the Taiwanese to establish a network of special agents in Macao.

After the Taiwanese spy network was sold out by a turncoat, speedy measures were taken to shift all their exposed spy agencies in Hong Kong and Macao. Many of their undiscovered spies were still in hiding.

Tom and I got off the vintage ferry and hopped in a pedi-cab peddled by one Lam Kow. No telling whom Lam might be spying for. We were the perfect picture of two low-spending CIA agents. Lam brought us safely to Rivera Villa on a small Portuguese-looking side street. Agent 008 checked us in. The rooms were clean and comfortable.

It needs to be noted that two years after our visit, Communist-organized riots shook the colony, resulting in the capitulation by the Portuguese to Chinese demands to bar entry to refugees and prohibit all anti-communist activities. Subjugation was on its way.

On-the-lam, our suspected spy pedi-cab driver, wheeled us all around and through the small, quaint and colorful city. Much of it resembled Portugal in architectural design, with houses of every color.

In the evening, we took two Chinese beauties, Mae Ling and Monica Ho, probably spies, dancing at the Macao Palace. We decided to leave our trench coats and sunglasses at the hotel.

The Palace was a floating restaurant and gambling casino. Most likely, owned by the KGB. It would not be proper to leave any spy agency out of the picture.

The next morning we had breakfast and talked with Mr. Chueng, the hotel's General Manager, and Mr. Loo, the Manager. Being a hotelman of sorts myself, I developed a good rapport with them. Contacts and friendships make such a difference wherever one goes.

Mr. Loo drove us around to show us some interesting areas we had missed on the pedi-cab tour. The colony moved at a leisurely pace compared to the hectic, traffic clogged city of today.

At 11:30 a.m., the seaplane rose from the ocean off Macao. John, the Australian pilot, and I had met previously at the hotel where I worked. Another coincidence! It was only my second ride in a seaplane.

Macao, one of the oldest and most intriguing colonial territories of the West, reverted to Chinese sovereignty at midnight on December 19, 1999, 442 years after its founding.

The world came knocking on my hotel door or I went knocking on new doors, every day. Doors of opportunity and friendship opened up constantly.

One day, for example, I met Mr. Halleck Rose, the Director of the International Refugee Center, and Mr. Eu, Director of the Hotel Singapura in Singapore. There were always distinguished and successful people such as this coming into the hotel. And it would not be long before "the sensation of the whole world" would be arriving at my doorstep.

The parade of movie stars, adventurers, millionaires, scientists, entertainers, statesmen, businessmen was impressive. The movie stars John Derek and Ursula Andress created quite a stir as they strolled through the lobby.

In the meantime, it was live life to the hilt. One of my bell captains drove me all around the new territories; I invested in 200 shares of an Australian Timber Company (the forest then burned down); volunteered to teach at the hotel training school; attended a fashion show with the Hong Kong Hilton owner's daughter; took Teresa dancing at our Firecracker Bar; taught English to movie actress Flora Ho, and helped poor-but-bright Roderick with his studies.

One night, I was showing eight VIPs our fantastic Starlight Restaurant on top of the hotel. As we got ready to head back down to the lobby, the six elevators decided not to work properly. Rushing from one to another, we finally caught one before the doors closed. I told them we kept parachutes on the roof for just such occasions. I never saw any of those folks again.

Annabelle, the lovely English lass I had met upon arrival in Hong Kong, invited me to a splendid ball at the Mandarin Hotel. We had drinks at the private Hong Kong Club before dancing the night away.

Sometimes the days were long and hard. One day, we went from 8:00 a.m. until 8:00 p.m., as we checked in over 400 people who had arrived by ship.

I had a favorite quiet place to take a break and get away from the maddening crowds. It was the roof garden of the YMCA. Unbelievably, the peaceful view of the harbor was the best-kept secret in the Colony.

On a more down-to-earth note, my friend Flora and I went exploring country villages in the New Territories. I learned from a Hakka woman in the fields that a Chinese girl at the age of six becomes old enough to assume responsibilities for running a household. This would include caring for a baby, cooking, washing, and sewing.

In March, I joined Toastmasters International to learn to become a good speaker. I had read about the club in the newspaper. It was made up of Chinese, Indian, and American men and women, along with the South African Trade Commissioner and some British army officers. I could tell immediately that this experience was going to corrupt my Texas accent.

Delivering a speech at the Hong Kong Hilton Hotel.

Margaret, our head hostess at the Firecracker Bar, took me to Happy Valley to see my first horse race. The Chinese are known gamblers. That became very evident at the racetrack.

When I had been in Macao, I had seen frantic Chinese gamblers swarming around the gaming tables. In later years, according to rumor, many Red Chinese government officials gambled with public money that had been entrusted to them.

I came to understand that some Chinese high rollers, including officials, did not bat an eyelid while dropping $1 million U.S. dollars on a turn of the cards. And that was at the same time I was dropping a Hong Kong dollar into the slot machine. Everything is a matter of scale.

CHAPTER 22

Chumming With the Beatles

You must do the things you think you cannot do… The future belongs to those who believe in the beauty of their dreams.
— Eleanor Roosevelt

*D*ick, a young American, started work part-time at the hotel. He was well connected and his father was a military attaché at the U.S. Consulate—most likely involved in the spy business. It just so happened Dick and I had both attended Kemper Military School in Missouri. It was the beginning of a good friendship.

Dick lived in a huge Chinese mansion on the Peak. It included a tennis court and extravagant swimming pool. Every now and then, he would throw one heck of a party. I'm sure there was not a finer mansion in all Hong Kong and no finer parties anywhere.

The famous singer, Frankie Laine, was one of the top entertainers that came to appear in our Nine Dragons Supper Club. I escorted a vivacious Chinese girl by the name of Irene to the show. Getting to know famous people I'd heard about all my life was always exciting—especially when it was free.

I was always getting invitations to dinner. Grateful though I was, I never seemed to have enough time to be outdoors, to exercise, or just be quite and contemplate life. I believe it is so important to find balance in one's life and mine was wobbling a bit.

Remus, a name I associated with the song *Zippity Do Da*, was one of our Chinese room boys. He worked on the floor I lived on and I thought of him as one of the friendly spies. He kindly invited me to go along with his family to the Tin Hau Festival in Yuen Long. This festival celebrated the birthday of the Goddess of Heaven, her 985th. It was always a privilege to be invited to such Chinese functions. Almost without fail, I was the only Caucasian in attendance.

The Beatles are coming! The Beatles are coming! They happened to be the sensation of the world in 1964.

Our General Manager came up to me one morning and said, "Clarke, block off the entire 15th Floor for the Beatles." This was to make sure no one

109

Meet the Beatles

To Claire
John Lennon

George Harrison

— Thanks.

Paul McCartney

I was assigned as the Beatles' personal assistant at Hong Kong's
President Hotel during their first world tour.

could get to them without an escort. I was assigned to baby sit them once they arrived. What an opportunity it would be for me to get to know them first-hand!

At 5:00 p.m. on June 8, Hong Kong came to a boiling point. There must have been 50,000 screaming Chinese teenage girls surrounding the hotel. I suspected there were close to 800 Hong Kong Chinese policemen trying to hold them off and out of the hotel. It was the grandest melee I had ever seen.

As the Beatles appeared, pandemonium ruled. Chinese teenagers were invading every entrance, passageway, and stairwell. I escorted the boys up to their huge suite after their welcome by our general manager. They seemed like regular guys.

Their manager, Brian Epstein, was with them. He and I went over all the arrangements for their stay at the hotel. Everyone I knew was asking me to get them an autograph. Running short of money, I offered a bargain basement price of only $100 an autograph. My popularity had skyrocketed. Actually, I did manage a few autographs for friends and myself!

Most of the next day was taken up with assuring that the Beatles had all their needs met. I went up early that morning when I got a call from their manager. The boys were all running around in their underwear when who should appear, none other than the "housekeeper of the hour," on her broomstick. She took one look at clothes scattered everywhere and said, "Boys, you know better than to make such a mess. I want this all picked up right now." One would have thought she was their mother. But with her stern, authoritative tone, the boys got busy picking up after themselves. It was an interesting start to "Beatles Day" in Hong Kong.

In the annals of show business, no other group has ever had such a phenomenal rise to success as the Beatles. If George Harrison and Paul McCartney hadn't been in school together in Liverpool, the Beatles might never have been formed. They met John Lennon in 1956 and played together as a group under numerous names before becoming world famous.

In 1961, they met Brian Epstein, who became their manager. In 1962, Ringo Starr, a school days friend, joined the group, and they recorded their first nationwide hit, "Love Me Do," in London.

They started off their first world tour in 1964 when 5,000 fans welcomed them in America. Their American appearances were a sellout success. They were watched by a total of 70 million people on *The Ed Sullivan Show*. And now here they were in Hong Kong on their first world tour.

On the second night the Beatles were at the President Hotel, they asked me if they could come down to our supper club and jam with our hotel band around midnight. "Of course," I said, "I'll set that up right away." They came down and had a great time—surprising and delighting everyone present.

In 1964, the Beatles' first movie, *A Hard Day's Night*, was released. Their press reception was at our hotel on their way home from their Australian and Asian tours. The lads were tired but jubilant and their connection to the place was to be immortalized.

Their CD, *Beatles Tapes IV: Hong Kong 1964*, was recorded at the President Hotel in Hong Kong on June 8, 1964. They performed two concerts at the Princess Theater in Kowloon during their stay in Hong Kong.

It was my privilege and joy to be a part of it all. Ringo had to miss Hong Kong due to tonsillitis but I got to know him at a later date in Rome.

During the Beatles' stay, we also had five Thai fashion models in the hotel for their own show. Here I was living the dream. Mine had come true and was in full bloom. Why? More than anything else, I believe it was because I had dared to venture into the wide world—against all the odds.

My brushes with the famous continued. I was about to meet one of the stars of the classic movie *The Wizard of Oz*. The movie was made when I was one year old, in 1939, and starred Judy Garland. It soon became a classic and a rite of passage for everyone, and is reported to have been seen by more people than any other motion picture. I first saw it when I was five years old. It was magical experience for a kid.

It was June 12 when I boarded the luxury liner, *SS President Roosevelt*, with my friend, Dong Kingman, Jr., a reporter for the *Hong Kong Tiger Standard*. He had invited me to accompany him to interview Judy Garland on board. Over drinks, I got to know this famous lady whom I had watched on the silver screen since I was a small boy. I found her to be a gracious person indeed. I was elated at an opportunity to meet a living legend.

I had been in Hong Kong five glorious months, but it was time to start looking beyond the rainbow to either the Philippines or Japan. It all depended on what opportunities might come my way. I recalled the words of one of Judy Garland's songs in the *Wizard of Oz*: "Somewhere over the rainbow, skies are blue, and the dreams that you dare to dream, really do come true."

Before leaving Hong Kong, I had the opportunity to return to Macao. I decided to take in the Grand Prix race, having never seen one before. The only place I could find to lay down on the midnight ferry was on one of the side decks. It was cold, uncomfortable, and windy. During the three-hour trip, I battled to get some sleep. A free ticket had been given to me, so I couldn't complain. Upon arrival, I took a pedi-cab to the Rainbow Villa, my favorite small hotel. The sleepy eyed bellboy answered my 4:00 a.m. knock. A free room had been arranged for me.

I rented a bicycle and headed for the first day of racing of the Macao Grand Prix. I peddled around the entire racing circuit to get a feel for this exciting event as the cars raced past. After the race finished, I peddled all the way around Macao. Another adventure realized—a Grand Prix.

Not all of my experiences were glamorous. One evening late, I got a call in my room from the hotel nurse. Apparently, a guest had threatened suicide in his room. When I entered the room, Alex, a British soldier, was lying on his bed smoking a cigarette. We talked for half an hour about his problems, which were numerous. I listened and asked questions when appropriate. I then pulled the Gideon Bible out of the bedside drawer. We took turns reading from it. He had begun calling me Doctor at that point.

Alex finally seemed to take heart. He agreed to call his commanding officer and was later taken to the British Army Hospital. I felt like a doctor, preacher, and psychologist all rolled into one after that draining session. One never knows when one might make a positive difference in another person's life.

On my 26th birthday, Jim Leavell, an American friend, and I took a ferry across to Hong Kong Island, a bus to Nai Chung Gap, and started hiking the mountains at 9:00 a.m. Along the way, we saw a number of concrete blockhouses used in World War II in fighting the Japanese.

Once on top of Mount Parker, we hiked across some other mountains and down to the beach at Sheko. It was a peaceful, pleasant outing with no one else crazy enough to be on the mountain peaks. At Sheko, we jumped into the ocean for a cool swim.

That evening Margaret, the *Tiger Lady*, took me for a lovely birthday dinner at the Carlton Hotel overlooking all of Hong Kong. She seemed to know all the key Chinese in Hong Kong—and I was on my way to meeting many of them.

CHAPTER 23

An Exotic Port Beckons

No vision and you perish; No ideal, and
you're lost; your heart must ever cherish faith
at any cost. Some hope, some dream, to cling
to some rainbow in the sky.

— Harriet Du Autermont

As I began contemplating my next port of adventure, typhoon Viola struck. She was a mean one. One man was killed right across from the hotel when a huge sign came crashing down on top of him. It was my first typhoon. I eventually weathered six of them in Hong Kong. A typhoon is a tropical cyclone or hurricane of the Western Pacific area and the China seas.

At 3:00 in the afternoon, storm signal #7 was hoisted for Viola. When #9 went up, that meant we were in the center of the typhoon. My English friend, Mike, and I braved the storm to go see a Japanese movie. Not too smart with pieces of tin, signs, and debris flying around at over 100 m.p.h. Maybe it was the storm or maybe it was just my wanderlust but I was ready to travel again to experience new places. My plan was to spend several more months in the colony. Responsibility I found rewarding but restrictive at this exciting time in my life. There was still so much to see, do, and learn.

Every night I wrote down my experiences, joys, and the trials and tribulations of the day. Someday I hoped to write a book on my adventures and misadventures. *Mark Twain had nothing on me in his own seven years of adventure while broke and unknown.* His book *Roughing It*, came out of those experiences which beagan exactly one hundred years before my travels—an ironic coincidence if ever there was one.

For encouragement, I started reading *Marco Polo*. And I learned he wasn't a writer either. When he returned from his travels in China, he was thrown into jail with a writer. Thus, one of the greatest travel books ever written was produced. If I'm ever tossed in jail, I pray a writer will be present.

Mrs. Cablao, the Filipino lady whose family had virtually adopted me, introduced me to Izzy. Izzy was 45, 4'9" tall, 130 lbs., and was a small businessman in more ways than one. He was a true character, if ever there was one.

Izzy told me how he met the Pope, Rock Hudson, President Kennedy, and other famous people—and I believed him. Not long after we met, he came up to the desk at he hotel to let me know his friends, the Magsaysay family from the Philippines, were coming to Hong Kong. Mrs. Magsaysay was a former First Lady of that country. President Magsaysay had died in a plane crash in 1954, while still President.

At Izzy's request, I made reservations for the Magsaysays. They were to become one of my families in the Philippines.

I developed a saying, "Izzy does it." The little guy seemed to be able to produce small miracles at the drop of a hat. I had learned, on a number of occasions, never to underestimate anyone, especially Izzy.

I had started writing letters to contacts in Japan and the Philippines about a job. Anything from a manager to sub-desk clerk was an option.

It was August. I began a concentrated effort to line up a job in Manila for a December start time. Shortly thereafter, the Magsaysays arrived in Hong Kong—Mrs. Luz Magsaysay, the former First Lady of the Philippines, and her two daughters, Terrisita and Mila. Her son, Ramon, Jr., did not accompany them. Izzy arranged for us to all get together for dinner.

What wonderful people. They gave me the book *Magsaysay of the Philippines*. Ramon Magsaysay had been a true hero and man of the people. He was the Teddy Roosevelt of his country, in my mind.

Ramon and Luz were married in 1930. When the Japanese invaded the Philippines in 1941, Ramon became a guerrilla leader responsible for 10,000 Filipino fighters. His prowess as a military commander became well known and resulted in the Japanese placing a 100,000 peso bounty on his life.

MacArthur appointed Major Magsaysay the military governor of Zambales Province due to his honesty, integrity, and ability. In that role, Ramon became the outspoken champion for veteran rights. He impressed the local population with his dedication to improving their life.

President Roxas asked Magsaysay to run for Congress but he refused. He relented when he was presented a petition signed by 11,000 of his men asking him to run. He was elected to Congress in 1947, receiving the largest popular margin in Zambales history. It is a great story of leadership and true service.

In 1950, Magsaysay became Secretary of National Defense. It was a page right out of Teddy Roosevelt's life, when he became Police Commissioner of New York. Ramon shook up the corrupt Philippine military from top to bottom.

Magsaysay set the example. He refused special treatment and lived on his government salary. He began to clean house. He traveled extensively on unannounced field trips and wiped out favoritism and corruption.

Magsaysay's surprise inspections were so numerous and effective, leaders throughout the military began to improve the condition of their units. No commander, even in the most isolated outpost, could go to bed at night sure that he would not be awakened at dawn by an irate Secretary of National Defense.

Magsaysay almost single-handedly put down the Communist HUK rebellion. As a result of the love, gratitude, and respect of his people, in 1953 he was elected President. More than 2 million people attended his inauguration.

Unfortunately, Magsaysay died in a plane crash on Mt. Manunggal on the island of Cebu. Again, two million showed their love for him by attending his burial. His son, Ramon, Jr., who was to become my friend, was later elected Congressman and then Senator, carrying on his father's crusade for honest, efficient, responsive, and open government.

As Mrs. Magsaysay was leaving, she said she would see what she could do to help me get a start in the Philippines. I couldn't ask for a better offer than that.

Several days later, I received an invitation from Barbara Black, the daughter of the Governor General of Hong Kong, for a sailing party on the 60-foot cabin cruiser *Senorita*. An appropriate name to make a Texan feel right at home.

We anchored at Lamma Island where everyone went swimming and water skiing. A staff of Chinese men served dinner and drinks. My date was Betty, a vivacious Chinese girl. We danced for several hours to a collection of great records.

It was a splendid evening right out of a movie set. We returned to Queen's Pier in the Harbor of Fragrant Waters at midnight. The lights of Hong Kong provided an atmosphere of a fairyland to the whole evening.

All I can say is, "This is the life. Hong Kong is everything I thought it would be, and more." Thank goodness I didn't listen to all those voices over a period of a year who said, "Americans can't work in Hong Kong. Forget about it." Determination, perseverance, and a goal are always the keys, even if you have only three dollars in your pocket.

Don Del Rosario, a Filipino businessman, took me to lunch to meet an American businessman friend of his, Mr. Scheff, who lived in Manila. It would later prove to be a superb contact. Many times, it was my experience that one good thing led to another. Having read *How to Win Friends and Influence People,* I applied its lessons on a daily basis. As a result, at times, magic happened.

Another special contact from Manila came along in the person of Bill Andrews. He and I talked in the hotel's Chin Chin Bar from midnight until 2:00 a.m. It appeared my trip to the Philippines was shaping up.

Kim Hong from Singapore, whom I befriended when he checked into the hotel, was another key contact. He was a big exporter of rice and corn. He told me, "Clarke, when you get to Manila, I want to offer you the services of my company office there."

Typhoons #4 and #5 hit us within a one-week span. They could be compared to the hurricanes Katrina and Rita that hit the Gulf Coast states in a period of one month. I had never experienced a hurricane or typhoon before Hong Kong. The poor Chinese living on the mountainsides in tin shacks suffered most.

I wrote a letter to the owner of the Manila Hotel asking for a job. It was considered "The Hotel." When General Douglas MacArthur went to the Philippines in the 1930s, he took up residence there.

At this pivotal point in my life, I had been traveling for two years. I worked out an estimate of how much longer I wanted to be adventuring the world. It added up to six more years: three months for the Philippines, one year for Japan, nine months through Taiwan, Thailand, Cambodia, Burma, India, Arabia, Israel, Turkey, Greece, two years in Europe, and two years for South America, the Caribbean, and Central America.

Getting geared up for Manila, I made calls to prominent acquaintances to see if they could help me work my way across the China Sea on a ship. No luck there.

My prospects for Japan had faded into oblivion. Then I met Matthew Emoto, a small businessman living in Hong Kong, who was from the Land of the Rising Sun. It would later prove to be one of the most important contacts of my life.

The "big break off" at the hotel finally came. The Chinese owners fired the general manager, two assistant managers, the food and beverage manager, and the housekeeper. I thought we never would get rid of the fiery-tempered, unpleasant housekeeper. She had been trying to run the hotel and everyone since the opening.

Only the Executive Manager, Mr. Escalante, and I survived the purge. He would try to break his contract as soon as he could. My fate remained open.

The Chinese owners, eight brothers, only one of which could speak English, knew little about running a hotel. With most of the management staff gone, all guest complaints were channeled straight to them. The Chinese fire drill was about to begin.

The brother who spoke English gave me a lecture one evening on how to run the hotel. He said, "I have learned more in two weeks running the hotel than you have learned in five years in the hotel business." He had to be one of the smartest men that has ever lived. I'd never met such a fast learner who was so full of himself. The hotel was definitely on its way down.

The hotel owners pulled another disaster off. They cut the salaries of the bell staff in half. The entire bell staff walked out. Yes indeed, they certainly knew how to run a hotel—into the ground.

One morning I had breakfast with an Australian who lived in Manila. He told me just about everyone living there carries a gun or knife. I contemplated going out that day and buying a six-shooter and a knife. "None of this just-one-or-the-other business for me," I rationalized. It sounded like there was much adventure in store for me in the Philippines and I was looking forward to it.

All my Chinese staff showered me with going-away gifts. These were kind surprises I did not expect. My good friend Dong Kingman, Jr. gave me a going-away party. I might note that his father was a world famous artist.

Not long before my departure date, I met a vivacious Thai princess who was in training to be an airline stewardess. When I first saw Chim, it was like love at first sight. She had a shy charm about her. My friend, Fred from the Tiger Balm Mansion, and I took Chim and her friend, Yupa, swimming at Repulse Bay on our first date. Chim could easily have been a pin-up girl the way she looked in her swimsuit.

I ended up being with Chim every night before I shipped out for Manila a week later. It could be said, "I was head-over heels."

The day after I met Chim, I received a cable from Mrs. Magsaysay in Manila. She had arranged a free passage on a ship for me. It was the Philippine cargo ship *President Osmena* and would be sailing for Manila in six days.

The next day I got my visa, bought an aluminum trunk, took my passport to C.F. Sharp & Co., bought a thank you card for Mrs. Magsaysay, and met with Emoto-san about future possibilities in Japan. I was wired and ready.

At Chartered Bank, I withdrew my $3,753 H.K. in savings. That was $657 U.S. Wealthy by my standards, considering I had $3 U.S. when I went to work at the President Hotel.

I knew I would miss all the wonderful friends I had made in Hong Kong. Dong, as a newspaper reporter, had put a clip in the *Tiger Standard* about me, stating in part, "One of the giants of the British Crown Colony is leaving." It was in jest, of course, but I had had the opportunity to be in the middle of everything going on in Hong Kong during the past ten and a half months, including The Beatles, Judy Garland, and all.

Mrs. Cablao, one of the kindest people I have ever known, also gave me a going-away party. The next day Izzy, my hotel staff, and many others waved me off as I set sail for Manila Bay.

With the Estrada kids in Manila. The little one on my shoulders knew every Beatles song by heart!

CHAPTER 24

Forward to Adventure

To achieve great things we must live as if we were never going to die.
— Marquis de Vauvenargues

*T*he *Philippine President Osmena* was a cargo ship and I was part of the cargo. About half way to Manila the South China Sea turned mean and ugly.

Never had I been so seasick. The ship was rocking so far from one side to the other that I knew it was going to roll over. Holding on for dear life, I did everything I could to keep from being tossed out of my bunk. I vowed I would never eat again when one of the cooks brought down greasy eggs and bacon to me. No, thank you.

I had been expecting a smooth passage across. I thought back to what happened to Richard Halliburton, the famous young American adventurer of the 1920s and 30s. He sailed from Hong Kong on a Chinese junk and was never seen again. I was praying we would not join him at the bottom of the sea in Davy Jones' locker.

Adventure sailing is fine as long as the ship doesn't rock. I had sailed on a number of ships before this and had been seasick every time. Now I had experienced the ultimate in seasickness and fear. I would not have been a pirate worthy of his grog.

It was noon the next day before the ship stopped rocking and rolling. At 4:00 p.m. on December 1st, we entered Manila Bay. There was the famous island of Corregider visible through the haze. It was nightfall before we docked at Pier 5.

I immediately called Mrs. Magsaysay and other Filipino friends I'd made in Hong Kong. Lulu Lejano and four of her friends picked me up and took me on a tour of Manila. It was an old city with many charms and many dangers. That night I slept like a baby on the ship with no pitching and rocking going on.

After all the stories I'd heard about thieves and gangsters in Manila, I was holding my breath as I went through customs next day. The lady who went through my bags was about as friendly as a hungry tiger.

With some trepidation, I climbed into a cab. The cabbie dropped me off at Tessie Reyes' Gift Shop. Tessie then had her driver take me to the apartment where I would be staying. I would have been even more apprehensive had I arrived in this bustling city with no contacts or friends.

Mr. Scheff, the American businessman I had met in Hong Kong, had offered a comfortable apartment for me to stay in at no cost. How fortunate could one be? It was located in a pleasant downtown area on U.N. Avenue.

Amparo, the attractive 22-year-old maid, opened the door when I knocked. Mr. Wannamaker, another American, was the person with whom I'd be sharing the apartment. He was out but Amparo showed me my room and made me feel right at home.

Mr. and Mrs. Shaver had me to their house for dinner. Mrs. Shaver was my friend Linda Ortega's sister. Mickey, her husband, was a pilot. He told me about a plane he was flying that crashed in a jungle area in the far northeast area of the Philippines. Luckily, he wasn't hurt but had to hike through the jungles to safety.

He was lucky, too, because he didn't get killed by a Negrito pygmy with a poison blow dart. "Others venturing in that area had been killed in just such a way," he said.

The Philippines, with its 7,000 islands, 86 dialects and over 50 different tribes, including stone age tribes recently discovered, was a fascinating study. *The perfect place for adventure*, I reflected. *I must check the Negrito tribe area out.*

What were black pygmies with poison blow darts and spears doing in the Philippines? I thought black pygmies were only found in Africa. Research turned up the answers. They are most likely the indigenous people of Southeast Asia—not connected to African pygmies at all. They are among the least known of all living human races and the tribe here was likely part of the original inhabitants of the Philippines.

DNA data from the Negrito peoples have shed light on the origins of modern humankind. The Negrito peoples have one of the purest genetic pools of mitochondrial DNA among any people in humankind. A team of geneticists reported that the genetic drift of this DNA shows that all modern day human beings are descended from one ancestral band of hunter-gatherers who left Africa 65,000 years ago. Fascinating!

I must get to know these Negrito guys, if at all possible, while dodging poison blow darts. Many of them are still living the stone-age lifestyle in the most remote areas of Southeast Asia. The Chinese author, Chao Fuy-Kua, in the

121

beginning of the 13th Century, actually described a tribe of black pygmies dwelling in the Philippine Islands at that time.

On my second full day in this surprising country, I visited with the manager of the Army-Navy Club in the morning. He said, "Clarke, I will help you all I can in your efforts to get a job," since he had no positions open. One contact leads to another.

I had lunch with Mrs. Magsaysay, her daughter Mila, a colonel, and a doctor at her lovely home. She showed me President Magsaysay's museum on the grounds. I thanked her kindly for arranging a free passage on the ship but skipped telling her I thought I was going to die from seasickness.

At 3:00 that afternoon, I met with another contact, Pablo Francisco, at his office in the Hotel Filipinos. He later took me to meet Ramon Fernandez at the famous Manila Hotel about a job. Everyone I met was so kind. No jobs were open there, however.

In Manila, everyone had a driver, it seemed. Lulu and Chit took me to dinner and then we attended a Catholic Church service. I was off to a wonderful start in this country ruled by the Spanish for 400 years.

Lulu Lejano was a Godsend! She and I had become friends on her several visits to the hotel in Hong Kong. Nothing romantic, but we had connected on a spiritual and intellectual level. She truly had a beautiful spirit about her.

On my third day in town, Lulu sent her driver to pick me up at 8:00 a.m. I opened a checking account with the mighty sum of 3,210 pesos. With a free place to stay, I would be able to hold on for several months without a job. That would give me some time to call on the Negritos, headhunters, and the fierce Moros—who delighted in killing Christians—in the south. There were just so many exciting things to do in the Philippines.

At 11:30 one morning, I met Bill Andrews at the Yacht Club. I had gotten to know him in Hong Kong. Bill, Mrs. Andrews, and their movie star-looking daughter, Lorraine, took me to lunch at the Polo Club. This was certainly high living for a country boy from Texas.

Lorraine, her father, and I then went sailing on their yacht in Manila Bay. The sunsets over Manila Bay are famous. So with drinks in hand, we sailed into the sunset. Thank goodness the yacht wasn't rolling crazily. I managed to look somewhat like a sailor.

The next evening Lorraine invited me to a party at a magnificent Spanish-style mansion. The party took place around a gorgeous swimming pool surrounded by statues. It was a look into the rich young set of Manila, polo horses and all. Lorraine and I had a marvelous time dancing the night away. Was this a dream?

What an astonishing introduction into Manila life I had that first week. To top it off, our maid did the laundry, cooked meals, and kept the apartment spic and span. I had never had a maid before. *I could get used to this life*, I thought.

Mrs. Magsaysay personally showed me through the museum dedicated to President Magsaysay. It gave me insight into a dramatic time in the history of this country.

Her son, Jun, soon arrived. Jun and I were both 26 years old and hit it off well. I joined the family for lunch.

Mrs. Magsaysay was so kind. She went so far as to arrange a date for me with her pretty niece, Sylvia, whom I took to a fashion show. This new lifestyle suited me well, but I was anxious to check out the headhunter way of life, too.

Izzy from Hong Kong gave me an introduction to Don Salvador Perez de Tagle. I met this hospitable gentleman in his law office in Escolta. After lunch we drove to his spacious home in Little Baguio. Don Salvador invited me to a party he was throwing the next week. I had been in Manila all of ten days and was already feeling at home.

Colonel White in Hong Kong asked me to look up Colonel Patton at the American Embassy. It never hurt to have a key contact at our embassy. After we had coffee, Colonel Patton invited me to have lunch with him and his wife at the Manila Golf Club. I got an informal briefing on some of the goings on in the Philippines.

I never knew quite what to expect in this extraordinary country. One evening some of the Magsaysay family picked me up and off we went to the Alba Supper Club. It was one of the finest restaurants in Manila with featured entertainers.

Half way through the Maori Hi-Five show, a Filipino Army Officer stomped on stage and grabbed the microphone right out of the singer's hand. The audience was shocked when the officer said, "This is a raid." Soldiers with rifles were standing at the door and across the back of the club. Unbelievable!

This was a posh restaurant where many of the elite of Manila were dining. The disbelief permeated through the people at the tables. Then this dimwit prima donna ordered, "All the men in the restaurant will line up along the left wall and the women along the right wall. Now!" No one moved and he started yelling. There was a shocked silence, then the catcalls began. Hissing, booing, shouts, and some words I can't repeat. It grew louder and louder.

He stalked off stage, motioning the soldiers to follow him into the back room. Here I was with the former first family of the Philippines. Who was this jerk and what did he think he was doing? We later found out that he was a reserve officer, on weekend duty, and a TV personality. Apparently, he had heard there was gambling going on in the backroom of the restaurant. It was his one chance for glory. His career finished, he and his ego rested comfortably in jail after that show.

Nenne, a 20-year-old Filipina beauty, whom I had met in Sydney, invited me for a day of racing at the Philippine Racing Club. It was my first time to bet on the horses. Banks, my roommate, had given me 40 pesos to bet for him. I won 204 pesos with that bet. We split it. I had more than doubled his money and provided myself with a much needed windfall. I went down and kissed the horse.

Just to keep up my intellectual pursuits, I was reading Plato. No matter where I might be, I always tried to have a good book close at hand, mostly classics and history tomes, and still do. In another book, I read Aristotle firmly believed in the existence of pygmies. He was so right. Not only were they in Africa, as he suspected, but they had come to the Philippines 30,000 years ago. It's a fascinating world.

While working at the President Hotel in Hong Kong, I met, only briefly, a beautiful woman around 50 years of age by the name of Mrs. Estrada. It was two and a half weeks after my arrival before I called her to say hello. It turned out to be one of the best calls I'd made in my life.

Almost the first thing she asked me was what I was doing for lunch, in the true hospitable Filipino spirit, of course. She told me later she was on her way to her company office when I called. She dropped everything she had planned to take me to lunch at the Architectural Club. Congenial Mr. Estrada joined us later.

The gracious couple invited me to join them for their Christmas Party that evening for the 150 employees of their cement marketing company. What timing! It was a wonderful party and it helped me to get into the Christmas spirit. I wore my new baron tagalog shirt which is the formal dress for Filipino men.

As often as possible, I went down to Manila Bay to watch the famous sunsets. After one such evening, I caught a cab. The driver, Ramon, and I got

124

into a discussion about life in the Philippines. He told me he would rather talk to me than work. Off we went to a bar.

Ramon and I sat and talked for over two hours about the life of the average Filipino. Up until this time, I had only gotten to know the so-called "upper crust" folks. It brought a new awareness to my mind. As Ramon drove me to my apartment, he invited me to dinner at his home the following week. And so I gained another new friend.

The Estradas had me over for lunch on a Saturday. They had nine kids. The oldest was 17. How Mrs. Estrada managed to look younger than her age, I'll never know. I had a hard enough time just taking care of myself.

My friend, Lulu Lujano, gave a wonderful Christmas Party. I danced with at least 15 girls. I taught everyone how to do the Australian Thredbo Slop. It was a fun dance I learned at the ski lodge.

Peter Nathan invited me to play tennis at the Army-Navy Club. We played for four hours with two other guys. Peter told me about Zamboanga, a city at the southern tip of the country, where he had a branch office. I had to see that city surrounded by the rebellious Moro Moslem tribes.

The Magsaysays invited me to attend the Christmas Eve Mass at the La-Salle College Chapel with them. We got back at their lovely home at 1:30 a.m. where we had a delicious spread of food, including pork adobo, my favorite. We then opened presents. At 3:00 a.m., lovely Sylvia Banzon dropped me off at the Estradas' home, my second family in the Philippines. Mennen and the other kids had stayed up waiting for me. How kind all these wonderful people were! I gave thanks to God for all my blessings on that early Christmas morning.

Bingo and Mennen drove me to the airport to pick up my Australian buddy, Dave Calvert, at 4:25 a.m. Dave had flown in to do an adventure trip with me on his three-week vacation from GM in Melbourne.

As Dave got off the plane, I said, "Welcome to headhunter country, mate." Our goal, if at all possible, was to spend some time with the fierce Bontoc tribe of headhunters in the Mountain Province of the northern Philippines. We got Dave to the Army-Navy Club Hotel so we all could get some much-needed sleep.

One Sunday, Ramon Angeles, the taxi driver I had gotten to know, came to my apartment at 9:30 a.m. From there, we caught a jeepney, a jeep used for transportation, and much cheaper than a taxi. We went to a market where I bought an inflated plastic ball and several bags of candy for his kids.

From the market, we went by bus to the village of Muntinlupa. We visited first with Elino, Ramon's brother. Elino asked me a whole lot of questions. He seemed fascinated about how I was traveling the world and what I had learned. He had not had the opportunity to sit down and visit with an American before.

Ramon and I walked farther down the dirt road to the thatch-roofed house where he lived. It sat on stilts about eight feet off the ground. His wife and two little girls greeted me warmly. Their home consisted of a small bedroom, living area, kitchen area, and porch. It had bamboo walls and wood planking for floors. This was how most rural Filipinos lived.

After lunch, I gave out candy to dozens of kids in the neighborhood. They were about as poor as they come, but friendly, and very polite. Followed by a dozen kids or so, Ramon and I walked down several streets for me to get a better sense of the place. Then we strolled along Laguna de Bay and through rice fields. To top the day off, he introduced me to Mayor Arganna. I boarded the 5:00 p.m. bus for Manila. Now I had an idea of how the great majority of Filipinos lived.

During the week after Christmas, I gave Dave a walking tour of some of the most interesting sights in Manila. I guided him through without getting mugged, stabbed, or shot. Of course, we were just a couple of poor looking guys, who were in good shape.

In reality, there were serious problems with crime. All the nice homes, I had visited, were surrounded by high walls with glass and barbed wire on top. An armed guard always stood at the gates. Even Mrs. Magsaysay's home had been broken into.

Linda, one of the Filipino girls I had met in Hong Kong, had invited me to the New Year's Eve Dance at the elite Baguio Country Club in Baguio, some 40 miles north of Manila. She got Dave a date with her friend, Tessie. Dave and I were ready to celebrate the New Year in style.

We jumped aboard the cheapest bus we could find. Arriving in Baguio, we checked into the small YMCA where we were each assigned a cot. It was like Cinderella going to the Ball. The country club was lavish, the food superb, and the whole night was one to remember. I danced almost straight through to 5:00 in the morning. A cot never felt so good. 1965, here we come!

After several days of getting to know Baguio, we boarded what I would call a "peasant" bus. It had no sides on it, so the pigs, chickens, ducks, and whatever else we carried could get plenty of fresh air. And it was cheap, which was the main consideration. We were off in an enormous cloud of dust for a head-reeling adventure. God be with us!

CHAPTER 25

Headhunters Ahead

We will either find a way, or make one.

— Hannibal

*T*he bus bounced for several hours on treacherous mountain roads full of ruts and rocks from Baguio to Bontoc. If our bus veered two feet to the right, we'd plunge down the side of the mountain into a rocky abyss, just like many buses had done since WWII. I was sure that if the fillings in my teeth didn't fall out during that trip, they never would. I sat next to 23-year-old Dave, a fellow adventurer from Australia. Shaken, in more ways than one, we dragged ourselves off the bus in Bontoc, a logging town that reminded me of old time western frontier towns in the movies.

Dave and I found a place to stay, the so-called Bontoc Hotel, built of logs, just like many of the houses around there. The hotel had two rooms for rent on the second floor and a place to eat on the first floor. I couldn't call it a restaurant or a café. I really don't have the words for it, other than very small, four beaten wooden tables and eight scarred wooden chairs.

Sixteen-year-old Peter, the waiter/dishwasher, came from an Igorat village, home of headhunters, far up in the mountains. Peter had been Christianized by missionaries. Some missionaries, he told me later, had actually lost their heads to headhunters in past years. Dave and I convinced Peter that we wanted to go up and stay awhile, for three or four days if possible, in his remote village. "We want to see how a headhunter tribe lives," I told Peter. The skeptical look on his face said it might not be a good idea, but he finally agreed to take us anyway.

The Igorots inhabit the rugged mountainous terrain of the Cordillera Region of the northern Philippines. There are six ethno-linguistic tribes there, one of them was the Bontoc, Peter's tribe.

Unlike most of the Philippines, which were ruled by Spaniards for about four hundred years, the Cordillera region was generally unfazed by Spanish colonization. And it was no wonder the Spanish stayed out of there.

It's noteworthy that the headhunters' ancestors, namely the Ifugao people, were the creators of the awe-inspiring Banaue Rice Terraces often called the

Headhunter country can be seen in the far distance in the Mountain Province of the Philippines.

"Eighth Wonder of the World." Over a period spanning several thousand years, the Ifugao labored to transform the mountainsides of their homeland into an amazing series of stepped rice terraces. In fact, if the terraces were placed end-to-end, it has been estimated they would stretch half way around the world.

Numbering about 120,000, these Bontoc headhunters were the most war-like of the mountain tribes—absolutely fierce. They were a little less fierce when I arrived, but fierce enough to make the hair on your head stand straight up and reach for the sky.

Wars among the tribes sometimes lasted for years. In addition to being a matter of duty and honor, headhunting was regarded as a sport. I was praying they wouldn't be in a sporting mood on my arrival. I planned to stay ahead of the game, if at all possible.

The next afternoon, Peter, Dave, and I slung our backpacks on and began a four-hour hike over mountain trails. We reached the primitive village of log huts just as the sun was setting. What timing! That evening, as it just so happened, the tribe was going to be celebrating past victories over other tribes in a ritual called the Bontoc War Dance. As I understood it, they used to throw their enemies' heads in the fire and dance around it. Woe is me! Before the ceremony began, the villagers sat on the ground and began to eat together. We sat by Peter's family hut. Peter brought us food in wooden bowls, and we ate with our fingers, and without talking. I didn't ask what we were eating. I was hungry, but most of all I didn't want to know.

During supper, Peter pointed and said, "See that long log hut over there?"

We nodded.

"It is called a U-log. Unmarried girls and guys can go in and sleep there," Peter explained. I envisioned the rest. But it was a cultural habit I had no inclination to adopt. I heard of one foreigner who did and no one has been able to get a heads-up on him since.

In reality, I was in a serious situation and could not be certain of anything. I could have already been selected as the "ritual head" for the evening's main event. The last thing you want to do in such a situation is lose your head. There was a chance my travels could have ended that very night.

After we ate, the men started a huge bonfire in an open area away from the huts. They each wore a strip of red cloth, about six inches wide, in front and back connected by a string. Peter told us that the men never cut their hair. They wore it up in buns.

Seven men soon approached the fire, each carrying a gong in one hand and a stick, with leather at one end, in the other. Then the men circled around the fire, and the colorfully-and-fully-clothed women formed another circle outside of the men. The men began chanting, banging the gongs, and dancing to a rhythmic beat around the fire, three steps forward, two back; the women in a big circle, moving in and out, toward and away from the men, raising their hands as they moved toward the men, chanting all the while.

After about fifteen minutes, one of the headhunters came out from the circle and moved through the surrounding sitting villagers. I was sitting on a huge rock, doing my best to be as inconspicuous as possible, away from the firelight.

He handed out the gong and gong-stick to me. Well, I'd dance for a headhunter any time. There was no way I was going to turn him town. My head could be hanging in the balance. It was like the old-time cowboy shooting at your feet. You better dance.

The women oohed and aahed! I wasn't sure if their sounds were in response to my dancing or if they thought I was about to become the new head of heads. Actually, I had been paying close attention to the steps and picked them up fairly quickly. I had been so shy in high school that I had worked at becoming a good dancer.

I walked back to my rock as that particular dance ended and found Dave looking pale and big-eyed. "I thought you might end up in the fire," he said softly.

Peter said, "They don't burn people at the stake, they just lop their heads off." He half smiled.

"Oh, well, no reason to worry, then," said Dave, his dry sense of humor showing.

"But," Peter added in a hushed voice, "some of the men have been drinking and I can't control what they do. You know, I think we better *head* out now."

That sounded like the best option. I wanted to keep my head about me, or on me, as it were, and we left as inconspicuously as possible. The trek back was not easy, but the moonlit mountain trail felt safe enough. It took us five hours to reach the village of Bontoc—still alive and feeling heady from the experience.

Several days after hanging out with the headhunters, Dave and I went to catch a bus at 7:00 in the morning, but the bus was crammed full. We finally took off at 9:00 on the next bus. In Bontoc, it was clear that no one hurried or paid any attention whatsoever to bus schedules. Because of an accident on the narrow dirt mountain road an hour out of town, everything came to a standstill. Luckily, the bus and car that collided didn't plunge off the sheer cliff, but they came close.

It just so happened we saw a logging camp down from where our bus had stopped. We took off down the steep road to investigate. There we met Allan Harrow. He invited us for lunch and gave us a tour and an introduction to logging.

Our bus had left us, so the real fun began late that afternoon when we departed *on* one of the logging trucks. Dave and I were sitting on the load of logs, half way back, holding on to chains, as the truck careened along the treacherous mountain road. Allan and two of his workers were up front in the cab. I'd heard of riding the rails—but logs?

As we raced around curves to the right, it seemed the logs shifted over the precipice with us looking almost straight down into the abyss. Lovely! This was more adventure than I had bargained for.

Things got even more interesting when night fell. The cold mountain wind whipped through our short-sleeved shirts. We were frozen to the chains and praying for delivery. The great thing about it being dark was that we couldn't see where we were going, and were too cold to care. Bam! All of a sudden we were awakened from our daze. A blowout! Allan was fighting for control as the truck sped toward the precipice, brakes screaming. The front of the truck came to a stop two feet before the truck would have launched off into space.

Our prayers apparently helped bring us through alive. The tire was changed and we sped on through the night as if nothing had happened. Allan could easily have qualified for the Indy 500. By this time, Dave and I were not only frozen, but frozen with fear. This was the third dangerous tire blowout I'd experienced in my travels.

I vowed I would never again ride on a load of logs on a mountain road, holding onto a chain, on worn tires, and in a truck with no inspection sticker. That was it! Finis! I knew I could find more serene ways of reaching heaven.

A harrowing ride it was. Dave and I were shaking when we dragged ourselves off the logs. He was a skydiver, but he had never attempted a dive without a parachute. This would have been his first.

It was 4:00 in the morning by now. Three of us went straight to the Baguio YMCA. No one was up, not even a mouse. When we entered, the long dorm room was dark and cold. There was a lone occupant on one of the twenty beds. His snoring was unbelievable! Allan got us laughing when he said the fellow slept like a mule. Our laughing woke the poor fellow up. He proceeded to give us his life story, in the dark, of why he snored so loud. It put us near to sleep.

We were exhausted, cold, aching, hungry, and dirty. Allan decided to take a shower before hitting the bed with no sheets or blanket. He got undressed and jumped into the shower to wash off all the dust. It was his first shower ever with no water. We all started laughing again. We were on a hilarious downhill slide.

It had been a night of nights. No water, no lights, a blowout, saved by the grace of God, and a guy that snored like a freight train. The beds without sheets felt like heaven.

To make things more interesting, Dave and I were nearing the end of our funds. We boarded a bus for Cresta Ola Beach the next morning, still half asleep. We thanked Allan for the joy ride, and wished him success in finding a shower that had water.

At the beach, we checked into the small, cheap Midway Hotel. Nearby was a small fishing village made up of bamboo huts. We spent the afternoon swimming, walking the beach, and recovering from our night of fright.

I was now down to thirteen pesos, around $8 U.S., to make it back to Manila on. Over rocky, bumpy, dusty roads, the bus took us through Alaminos, Santa Cruz, and into Olongapo that evening. The American naval base was nearby at Subic Bay.

Dave and I toured the fifty or so bars that cater to sailors. It was a wild scene with drinking, fights, and romance to be seen in all directions. It had to be seen to be believed.

At 11:00 that evening, we caught the bus for Manila. At 3:00 the next morning, we arrived on my doorstep after eight days of roughing it. We had a total of eleven centavos between us. What terrific planning! It could only be attributed to our pure financial genius.

The next day I went by to see the girl I was most fascinated with in Manila. Merle was a teen beauty of nineteen. She let me know right away she didn't like the beard I was growing. I just seemed to have a way with women. We sat and talked for two hours about life in the Philippines.

Lulu and her friends took me dancing at the Champagne Room in the Manila Hotel. The Estradas had me over for dinner, and Maggie de la Rivera, one of the Philippines' leading actresses, took me along to watch one of her movies being filmed. There I met Chickie, another actress. All of this happened the first week I was back, plus I kept up my usual daily swims at the Army-Navy Club to keep myself in shape.

Reading a book on Jose Rizal, the national hero of the Philippines, I was inspired by his life. Born in 1861, he attained his BA at the age of 16, became a doctor at 23, traveled extensively, mastered 22 languages, was a genius in many fields of study, and was an expert swordsman and a good shot.

Rizal was the greatest apostle of Filipino nationalism. He published a book exposing the arrogance of the Spanish clergy. Because of his fearless exposures of the injustices committed by Spanish officials, he provoked the animosity of those in power. He was imprisoned in 1892. When the Philippine Revolution started against the Spanish in 1896, he was again put in prison, convicted of

132

rebellion, and shot in a field on December 30, 1896 at the age of 35. He is still adored by the Filipino people.

Dave had headed off for an adventure swing through the southern islands. When he returned to Manila, the Estradas and I saw him off at the airport. We had racked up another adventure together and had kept our heads through it all.

It cost me 133 pesos to have my visa extended for two months. I'd spend that time adventuring rather than trying to work. Hopefully, money would hold out. A free place to stay made all the difference.

Manolo Alvarez, a pilot I got to know, invited me to fly to the south with him. I had no idea what kind of plane he flew, but it would be a new adventure. When I got to Marinduque Mining Company's hangar, I found out that Sipalay, in the south, was weathered in. So, maybe tomorrow!

The next morning Sipalay was still socked in. OK, what now? We took off in an antiquated DC-3 cargo plane and headed for Isabella. My whole life turned around in the opposite direction in a flash, not south but north we flew. The cargo and me were in the back. As we got on board, Manolo pointed to a huge crate that was tied down to the floor of the plane with huge ropes and said, "Sit on top of that crate and hold on to the rope for dear life." "Thanks, Manolo, no sweat," I replied. It brought back memories of riding the logging truck!

As the plane roared off the runway, I realized I'd forgot my rosary beads. Where was the stewardess with the coffee? The plane felt like a cork bobbing in the ocean and I'd finally come to know how it felt to ride a bucking bronco. It was not a good feeling. *Did I hear one of the engines sputtering*? I shuddered.

All of a sudden, the plane started coming down fast in the rain. On the left, all I could see were tall trees in the jungle, on my right the ocean. I trembled and speculated, *Is this a crash landing*? It might as well have been because the plane hit hard. Next time, if there is a next time, I was going to fly only on a plane that serves whiskey. To my immense relief, we had landed on a runway along the edge of the beach.

Dumagot tribesmen, wearing only G-strings, unloaded the plane within half an hour. The Dumagots typify the outstanding Negrito physical traits, have beautifully proportioned bodies and are taller than the Negritos. They live in single-pole, makeshift nipa huts along the riverbanks during the summertime and move to sturdier dwellings on higher grounds during the monsoon rains. Their weapons are bows and arrows.

The flight back was rough and cold, but I had mastered the cargo box and rope. I froze my tail off wearing Bermuda shorts. I thought this was the tropics.

It was good to be on solid ground again. I took Jane, a delightful girl of Caucasian-Filipino descent, to a party at the Pascual Boat Club. Jane and I had met the week before at a concert by two European folk singers. I was impressed by her intelligence and warm personality. She looked like a Filipina Audrey Hepburn.

At the party, I met Ely Chiongbian. She invited me to have lunch with her the next day. Ely and I had lunch at her elegant home. I then drove us, in her Mercedes, to the boat club. We spent a fun-filled afternoon water skiing. My life was quite a contrast, from riding a box in a pitching, old transport plane to riding behind a boat at high speed.

The next day Jane and I sat down in a quiet spot at the Manila Polo Club. We whiled away the pleasant hours discussing philosophy, psychology, history, and goals in life. It was nice having the freedom to go in whatever direction I chose each day, no matter that I had little money.

While Jane went to dinner, I went home to change. She picked me up at 10:30 that evening in the company of two other Filipina beauties. We picked up two more of Jane's good-looking friends on the way to a party for some Shakespearian actors. When we made our entrance, I felt rather conspicuous escorting five lovely women. If they could have seen me back home—all my buddies would have been as awe-struck as I was.

Taking four months off from work to do whatever pleased one's fancy, including dating, danger, sailing, swimming, water skiing, meeting new people, adventuring, learning, studying, reading, a great social life, intellectual discussions, tennis, and parties. I was more than fortunate and gave thanks every day for my health and life.

One afternoon I went to the Manila Hotel for a swim. There I met Cesar, a lifeguard. He invited me to go watch Jai Alai with him that evening. He explained the extremely fast-moving and dangerous game to me. Chalk up another learning experience.

That evening Jane and I went to a coffee shop. We ended up having a long conversation on each other's sexual experience and maturity. I was shocked to learn, that although 23 years old and most attractive, she had only let one boy as much as kiss her. That night she let the second boy kiss her.

CHAPTER 26

The Far Reaches of Zamboanga— Land of the Fierce Moros

Never forget that life can only be nobly
inspired and rightly lived if you take it
bravely and gallantly, as a splendid adventure
in which you are setting out into an unknown
country...

— Annie Besant

*A*fter leaving Jane's house, I got back to the apartment at 5:00 in the morning, packed some things in a small suitcase, and took a cab to the airport.

A new adventure dawned. Early that morning, the Aero Commander lifted off into the blue. It sure beat riding that box in the back of that ancient DC-3. Aboard were Jess Cubaruss and my friend, Manolo Alvarez, the pilots, one Japanese businessman, two Filipinos, and my sleepy self. The destination was Sipalay in the southwestern part of Negros Occidental Province in the southern Philippine Islands.

It was the start of an adventure trip with no idea of where it would take me or where I would end up. My cup of tea! I was lost most of the time anyway. Two hours after takeoff, we landed at Sipalay. We boarded three Jeeps and toured the copper mines from one end to the other. Both gold and copper were mined in the area. I spent the night in the mining company's guesthouse.

Sipalay was used as a garrison for Spanish soldiers in the 1800s. It became a lookout point when the Japanese occupied the country, with the town being used as an outpost by American and Filipino guerrillas.

It was at the age of 26 that I seem to have had an intellectual awakening. There was nothing in the world that I didn't want to learn about. A girl I met told me, "You sound like a reporter." I hardly ever stopped asking questions. The more and faster I could learn, the better.

Off I went again. The next morning I was scheduled to fly to Bacolod City with Tony. The flight was cancelled, so I read all day until I could catch the bus leaving at 8:00 that night. After seven hours of rough roads through the inky night, the bus pulled into Bacolod at 3:00 in the morning. My financial condition stood at 152 pesos, about $100 U.S.

Rene Echauss, a friend of a friend, had reserved a room for me at his Sea Breeze Hotel. He greeted me warmly when I came down to the lobby for breakfast. Not only did Rene insist on buying my breakfast, but moved me into the best room in the hotel at no cost. There is no doubt that the Filipino people are among the most hospitable in the world.

Bacolod is a major seaport and had daily ferry trips to Iloilo City. It was nicknamed the "City of Smiles." Rene gave me a grand tour of the area, and that evening I visited with Dr. Valenzuela and his family. Dr. Valenzuela was the father of my friend Cesar in Manila.

The second day, I toured the Bacolod-Murcia Sugar Plant. Peping Sanchez, the manager, took me to lunch and by Jeep for a tour of a typical sugar plantation. As the sun was setting, we drove 30 kilometers to see where the sugar is loaded on ships.

We had dinner on board the ship *Ma-ao* as Captain Torres' guests. The capacity of the ship was 14,250 long tons. After all this, I had a fair idea of how sugar is made and transported.

However, there was more sugar to come. The next day I got a complete tour of the Victoria Sugar Mill. Izzy in Hong Kong had given me a letter to the manager. Mr. McCann told me, "Clarke, this is the only sugar refinery now operating in the country and produces all the domestic sugar."

I bought a plane ticket for Cebu. It cost me 8 pesos. Cash on hand was 132.50 in pesos. At 8:00 that morning, the PAL flight lifted off. Sitting next to me was an Army captain, whom I visited with. When we landed, the captain introduced me to Major Ba-ad, who was the Philippine Air Force Detachment Commander for the area. Just then, the Task Force Commander of the Philippine Navy for the Visayas walked in and I got to meet him. If I ran into any dangers, I had all the branches of the Philippine Armed Forces behind me.

Commander Asuncion had his Jeep driver deliver me to Philippine Constabulary Headquarters. I had been given an introduction in Manila to meet Captain Alesana. He wasn't in, so I headed for William Shipping to meet Nena Chiongbian. She is the sister of Ellie whom I'd met in Manila.

Nena and her friend, Loretta, took me to lunch and showed me around Cebu in the afternoon. I was still amazed at how one contact leads to another.

My roommate at the local YMCA was Agusto Celis. The room was a bargain at 4.50 in pesos. That evening, three couples of us went dancing at the

Stardust Club. I never dreamed I would be dancing in Cebu. At least it was safer than dancing with headhunters!

The next day, Nena introduced me to her father, William Chiongbian, who owned William Lines Shipping Company. He had once served two terms in the House of Representatives. We had a pleasant lunch at their home. Of course, I had a lot of questions for Mr. Chiongbian about his life and how he built his several business enterprises. It should be noted Cebu City is the oldest city in the Philippines.

That night I boarded the inter-island ship *Elizabeth*. The Chiongbians had graciously arranged a free passage. When I arrived on the island of Cebu several days before, I had no idea exactly how or where I would go next.

My bed was a cot on the top deck. There is nothing like sleeping on the deck of a rolling ship at night. But, lest I forget, it was not costing me one peso. Things could have been worse if a storm had been about. *What was I sailing into,* I pondered. My port-of-call destination was intriguing Zamboanga, "where the monkeys have no tails," as the old song goes.

June 23, 1635 was the day that a permanent foothold was laid on Zamboanga by the Spanish government with the construction of the San Jose Fort. It was the result of continued Moro Pirate attacks on Spanish galleons in the Sulu Sea.

Zamboanga was in the center of Moro Land. In the days of old, Moro-Moslem Pirate vessels infested the coasts ruled by Sultans. The native people of Cebu and other Christianized islands to the north got fed up with the incessant atrocities the Moro Pirates had inflicted upon them for over a century. Along with the Spanish, they were not about to let this opportunity for vengeance fail them. It was time to eliminate the Moro Pirate stronghold.

Even in the 1900s, Moros were still singling out Christians to kill. With the takeover of the Philippines after the Spanish-American War in 1898, it remained for the Americans to carry on the bloody work of the pacification of the Moros. The Moros' favorite weapon for killing was the kris blade. It was a deadly, jagged sword, which made a Moro a man.

No pistol at the time could stop Moros when they attacked. The 45-caliber pistol was developed to do just that.

Back on board ship, Captain Luspo hosted me for breakfast. He was most interested in hearing about my adventures in Tahiti.

When we docked at Tagbilaran, our first port-of-call, Mr. Gulle, branch manager for William Lines, took me on a tour of the town by Jeep. This was on the island of Bohol.

Once the ship had cargo unloaded and loaded, we headed out to sea. It rained off and on all day. I slept almost the whole four hours it took to reach Dumagetti.

Bingo, the oldest child of my friends, the Estradas, attended Sillaman University in that city. I did my best to find him but had no luck. Cash on hand was 117.70 pesos. I was holding my own and spending hardly any money. So far, so good!

When I woke up the next morning, we were sailing along the coast of Zamboanga. I saw no pirates coming to attack us even though it was still a common occurrence in these waters. Thousands of stately coconut trees lined the shore.

As we steamed into port, Moro boys and girls met us in their outriggers. I threw a coin to a pretty girl wearing a bright print dress. After she had retrieved it from the water and climbed back into the outrigger, she yelled up to me in broken English, "I love you very much." Well, I hadn't expected to be greeted with love in Zamboanga but it was a fine start.

Alex Go, a Chinese Filipino who was the manager for Williams Lines, came aboard immediately when we docked at noon. Captain Luspo introduced us. Alex had arranged for me to stay at the local Buddhist Temple, of all places. He felt I would be safer if I became a Buddhist while venturing in Moro country. It took me no time to convert. Pass the joss sticks!

Alex first took me to meet Father Cuna, the Rector of Atenco College. I had been treated to marvelous hospitality since setting foot on Philippine soil. One contact led to another and the unending chain of new friendships continued. How blessed I have been!

Si-Hu, one of the Buddhist priests, and Mr. Ko, a venerable Chinese school teacher, invited me to dinner at the Temple. None of the monks spoke English.

Roy Hammond, another contact, arranged a date for me that first night. I was not sure whether or not Buddhists should be dating. Nevertheless, I went for it and was richly rewarded. My date was a pretty Filipina with a figure to match. Her name was Zenny.

We went dancing at the Aristocrat Club. Zamboanga was not so bad and no one had yet chased me down a street waving a kris.

After breakfast with Alex at his house the next morning, he took me to see a Moslem village. It was an eye-opener. It was built out over the water on bamboo stilts. I managed a few pictures without falling off the bamboo walkways.

Staying in the safety and quiet of the Buddhist
Monastery in Zamboanga.

In the afternoon, Zenny and I went to Ayala beach where I promptly climbed a coconut tree for the fun of it. She caught that high moment on film.

That evening, I took up chopsticks and ate with a Buddhist priest. He spoke not a word of English, so we had some interesting communication attempts. When I went to take a shower, he explained to me in Fukanese how to operate the hot water heater. That had to be one of the coldest showers I had ever taken.

Zenny and I spent a romantic evening listening to music on a jukebox, dancing, and talking. I invited her to come back to the temple with me at the risk of being drummed out of Buddhist ranks. We quietly tiptoed past the Buddhas and burning incense at the midnight hour. My room happened to be in the Chinese tower accessible only by a narrow, steep, squeaky staircase. I thought I'd wake up the monks with every delicate step and that would cause gongs to go off.

The room had no glass or screens on the window openings. The mosquitoes were big enough to carry one off, so a mosquito net covered the bed. I always went first class. Nonetheless, it was quite romantic in that tower overlooking tranquil Buddhist gardens filled with fragrant flowers and imposing fountains bathed by the light of a full moon.

Before we knew it, it was 4:00 in the morning. The huge bronze doors that were twelve feet high at the entrance of the monastery were opened at sunrise and closed at sunset. The doors had to be well over a hundred years old. I had been given a skeleton key to open the 2' by 4' door in one of the giant bronze doors anytime I got back after sunset.

Zenny and I tiptoed back through the temple and across the gardens to the giant bronze entrance gate. I gingerly opened the small bronze escape door. It sounded like the creaking of a door in a haunted house. I held my breath as it squeaked open.

As I slowly pulled the door toward me, it wouldn't close all the way. There was only one way to shut it. I pushed it open half way and then pulled it forward with all my might. There was an ear-splitting gong that must have woken up half of Zamboanga. I looked at Zenny and said, "Run!" Off we went down the street setting a new hundred yard-dash record for the Philippines.

After walking Zenny home, I sat on the wharf and watched a full moon sink into the Sulu Sea. It was 5:00 in the morning.

Back at the temple, I had Chinese porridge and bean sprouts for breakfast. None of the monks mentioned the gong that was heard around the world. I lit an incense stick to give thanks.

In the afternoon, I went swimming at Pasonanca Beach. There I met the Jove Jagers, a group of college kids. Apparently, they had just made up that name for themselves. Before I knew it, I was adopted as a Jove Jager. I was honored.

CHAPTER 27

Jolo Lot of Danger

Success is not final, failure is not fatal. It is the courage to continue that counts.

— Winston Churchill

$\mathcal{T}$he next morning I was up at 4:30. When I got to the airport, I found the plane to Jolo was full. I went back to the temple and then had a talk with some Peace Corps workers. Never was I one to let grass grow under my feet. There was always someone to meet and something to learn.

Why on Earth would I want to go to Jolo where the Moro guerrillas had recently attacked the courthouse with machine guns, bazookas, and grenades? It sounded like an adventurous place to check out. I understood the Mayor was considering changing jobs. I would've.

I was able to get on board the 2:00 p.m. flight. It was a Philippine Airlines' DC-3 with real seats. I'd had it riding on cargo boxes.

The history of the Moro capital of Jolo read like the plot of a war novel. The town was officially captured by the Spanish on five occasions. Eleven unsuccessful assaults were made by Spain between 1598 and 1899. Jolo was, to put it mildly, a bone of contention for 321 years. In all that long struggle, Spain held it but 31 years. The Moros for 290 years. The score, Moros - 290, Spain - 31. In 1899, Spain relinquished the post to the United States. Lucky America.

The Moros fought with their deadly kris swords against the rifles of the Spaniards. The Moros adopted a system of guerrilla warfare and were known as Juramentados. These fierce fanatics penetrated the walls of the Spanish fort every day, inflicting heavy losses. Not much had changed.

When the Spanish finally quit Jolo altogether in 1909, they left the Moro province in much the same state as Magellan found it. Then came the Americans. They carried on the bloody work of pacification of the Moros. When Captain Vernon Whitney became Governor of Jolo, he undertook the leadership of a jungle province that was one of the oldest battlegrounds in the world.

The patrols that were sent out reported that often the mere sight of their bayonets was sufficient to start "amucks" on their course of death. The Moro warriors were not about to turn in their kris swords to the Americans. They preferred death and took anyone they could with them.

I'd been warned that every once in a while a Moro would go berserk, dress in white and kill everyone in their path until he was killed. This was enough to keep me on my toes.

In fact, as I strolled the cowboy-town-like-streets of Jolo by myself, I would stop at each alleyway, peek around the corner, and make sure the coast was clear. I only came across four alleys where guys dressed in white were coming full speed ahead, yelling for all they were worth. I would take off in the opposite direction yelling for all I was worth. It was a terrific game of "run and hide."

Herman, from the Office of the City Court, showed me around Jolo on foot. He was dressed in black, so I knew I was safe.

Ben Villa Senor, with the Philippine Airlines, and I spent an hour at the Constabulary Headquarters. There I got a briefing on the outlaws and crazies on this charming island.

I spent a fitful night at the Victory Hotel. Victory over whom? Hopefully, the amucks would not find out another Christian had arrived in their paradise.

It was back to sedate Zamboanga by plane the next morning. Maybe in another 300 years, the Moros will settle down, but one can't count on it. And up until this very day, they have not, in fact, it may be worse than ever.

It was good to be back among my new friends, the Jove Jagers. That evening, it was dancing at a popular nightspot. I kind of fell for Vicki, but the duty of adventure called. The Jove Jagers came to see me off on the ship *Davao*. They presented me with an exquisite shell-inlaid swagger stick, or maybe it was a pointer.

It was smooth sailing all day. It was so smooth I didn't get seasick. A first! I wasn't a sailor but I put on a great act.

When I woke up at 4:00 in the morning, I headed up to ship's flying bridge. We were steaming around the point of Davao Gulf under a full moon. After drinking in the surrounding beauty, I went back to my deck cot to sleep until sunrise.

Later that morning, I finished reading *Japan: Past and Present*. Japan was my next planned destination. The ship docked at 1:00 in the afternoon at Davao.

I headed straight for the Apo Hotel to meet the owner, Mrs. Pamintuan to whom I had an introduction. She kindly gave me a "comp" room.

At the swimming pool, I met an attractive Filipina girl. Delia was a physical education instructor at Ateneo University and she had the body to prove it. She gave me a grand tour of the university that afternoon.

Somehow my contacts always seemed to come through in style. That evening I went to a fun party with Bobby Sorianno and some friends.

After attending Mass at Santa Anna Church, Delia took me to see her family's fruit and coconut farm near Mt. Apo, a dormant volcano. Mt. Apo, at 10,000 feet high, is the highest mountain in the Philippines. Ancestral tribes live in its valley, like the Bajobo, Manobo, Mandaya, and Bilaan.

Delia kindly saw me off at the airport at 2:00 that afternoon for my flight to Cebu Island. The Filipinos I'd met everywhere had been so gracious.

What would happen in Cebu I had not an inkling, but at least I had some contacts there. Always hope for the best was my motto.

A quote I came across in a newspaper in Calcutta came to mind: "I am a wayfarer and the path is my companion."

CHAPTER 28

Sitting on the Dock of the Bay

"You have plenty of courage, I am sure,"
answered Oz. "All you need is confidence in
yourself."
— L. Frank Baum (*Wizard of Oz*)

*I*n Cebu, Mr. Ramon Binamira put me up at his Life Hotel in the heart of this oldest city in the Philippines. After a delicious dinner with him and his wife at their palatial home, I went back to the hotel to crash.

When I got up the next morning, I had no idea where I was going or how I would get there. I had only 25 pesos left in my pocket, about $15 U.S. And I was hundreds of miles and islands away from Manila. What to do? Something would turn up, I was sure, so, as always, I took each day as it came and kept listening and learning.

Maybe I could find a free private plane flight or ship sailing north. In the meantime that early morning, I wandered through the Spanish triangular stone fort built in 1739.

When I told Victor at William Lines, I would like to try to find a private flight or ship to Manila, he said, "You're in luck. My parents are flying there this afternoon." A miracle! There were six of us in an Aero Commander. We landed smoothly at 3:00 p.m. Praise God for watching over me on this eye-opening, day-to-day exciting adventure trip. I was in his hands.

I had seventeen letters awaiting me from all parts of the globe. One was from my parents. I tried to let them know I was still alive at least once a month, if that was the case.

The first task on returning to Manila was to write thank you notes to all those who helped me on my trip to and through the southern islands. I had arrived back at the capital with pesos worth about $6 U.S. out of the $110 I started with. I had been on the "Road to Jolo" and back for 17 days, and was able to keep my head in the bargain. It reminded me of one of the road series of movies made by Bing Crosby and Bob Hope. *The Road to Mandalay* is but one example of those funny adventure films I had watched as a kid.

It was nice to be back to a so-called life of luxury. The next several days found me playing tennis, swimming, watching Manila Bay sunsets, and sipping the occasional rum Collins at the Army-Navy Club. One evening, Gony, the lifeguard, and I had dinner at Taso de Oro Mexican Restaurant. We had become friends over a number of weeks in my swims at the club.

Jane, who I had dated earlier, invited me to the most elegant ball of the year, the Kahirup Ball, at the Manila Hotel. She wore a stunning red silk ball gown. I wore Bermuda shorts. Actually, I broke down and rented a tux. I made quite a dashing figure for a broke guy, but I felt rich indeed in such esteemed company. It was a far cry from experiencing life as a Buddhist monk.

Another adventure jumped out at me. I got an invitation from the Magsaysay family to fly to Legaspi. This was an opportunity to visit Mrs. Magsaysay's daughter, Terisita, and her son-in-law, Frankie. Frankie's father was Commander of SEATO, the NATO of Asia.

The first thing they did was drive me around the Mayon Volcano in their Jeep. Its base was 80 miles in circumference. This active volcano has the world's most perfect cone. It was considered by many people to be more beautiful than Mt. Fuji in Japan.

Mayon's eruption of February 24, 2000 was its 47th since its first recorded upheaval in 1616. Its deadliest eruption was on February 1, 1814, when it buried the entire town of Cagsawa under ash and killed more than 1,300 people. Mayon seemed to be sleeping as we drove around it. That was fine with me.

Legaspi City, a port on Albay Gulf, was in the southeastern part of Luzon Island. In December 1941, during World War II, it was the debarkation point for Japanese troops invading Luzon. Founded in 1639, it was named for Miguel Lopez de Legazpi, conquistador and first Spanish governor general of the Philippines.

Terisita liked my new mustache. She said, "I think it makes you look like actor Peter O'Toole." In those days, as a matter of fact, I was always being taken for many nationalities. On the flight down, the lady sitting next to me thought I was Swiss. My Texas accent had long disappeared.

The next morning I walked all around the city, as was always my way when I was in a new place, to get a feel for the area and its people. I then walked out to the end of the ship pier. Hanging my legs off the end of the dock, I took in the sun, the cool sea breeze, and the exhilarating view of Mt. Mayon across the water.

When I think of that perfect day, the song "Sittin' on the Dock of the Bay" comes to mind. There I sat for two hours in that beautiful spot thinking about many things and contemplating life and its purpose. I gave thanks for being alive and the opportunity to explore the world. I was content.

Terisita and Frankie made me feel right at home. After several days of visiting and sightseeing, I headed back to Manila.

It was time to somehow get my act together and find a job in Japan. Money was starting to run low and I had no backup of any kind.

A letter had arrived from Emoto-san in Hong Kong. It upset me at first and then galvanized me into action. He wrote, "The job I thought I had lined up for you fell through."

For nearly four hours, I thought, figured, contemplated, made calls, and worked on the problem. In the end, I made a decision on the course of action I would take. *I resolved not to worry, but head for Japan and work it out there, as I had done everywhere else.* It was once again time to cross the Rubicon.

I went to the Finance Building to start the procedure for tax clearance to leave the Philippines. This was easy, since I hadn't earned one centavo, unfortunately. The rich experiences and new friends were my compensation.

The next morning I went to the Immigration office to complete my alien registration. It was the first time I discovered I was an alien. That was required for anyone who stayed in the country over 59 days. As always, when they asked me where I was from, I replied, "Texas." It always brought a positive response.

Jane and I attended the French Ballet with some friends. *Amazingly*, I thought, *I have been getting really cultured in the Philippines, thanks to Jane.* There was hope for me yet. The next night, we went to three parties. Never had I seen a place with so many parties as Manila.

My wonderful, exciting, challenging, adventurous days in the Philippine Islands were coming to a close. For a broke guy, I had lived them to the hilt.

Mr. Lutey at American President Lines gave me a $173 first class cabin for $41, which was the lowest economy fare to Hong Kong. If I was going to be seasick, I might as well go first class.

The *President Wilson* was scheduled to sail in two days. Butch Rous of the *Manila Times* interviewed me for a story about my travel adventures.

I got my Visa at the British Embassy. At the bank I bought $380 in travelers' checks and closed my account. *How far this $380 would take me* *was anybody's guess,* I thought. My three-and-a-half-month stay had been an education and a joy.

I made the rounds to thank all the people who had been so gracious and kind to me, especially the Magsaysays, the Estradas, Lulu, Jane, and Mr. Scheff. I took Celi to the Orchid Restaurant in appreciation of her help. She was the private secretary to the Secretary of Finance of the Philippines and had introduced me to a number of Congressmen and Senators during my sojourn in the Land of Mabuhay, including Ferdinand Marcos, later to become President of the Philippines.

On Wednesday, October 10th, I packed from 4:00 to 6:00 in the afternoon. I said goodbye to our wonderful maid, Amparo. Jane and I had dinner at the New Europe Restaurant before she drove me to the docks.

Twenty-six friends waved me off as the liner *President Wilson* pulled away from the dock at 10:00 that night. I had tears in my eyes as I waved back. The warmth of the Filipino people and those friends would remain in my heart forever. God bless them all.

One of my favorite sports—climbing a coconut tree in Zamboanga.

CHAPTER 29

Japan or Bust

Optimism is the faith that leads to achievement.
Nothing can be done without hope and
confidence.

— Helen Keller

What is it about me and the sea? I wondered. The next morning I got seasick even after taking four bottles of seasick pills. I stayed in bed most of the day. At least I was doing it in first class, which was some consolation.

By dinnertime, I was starving. Again, after the first day of sailing, everything always righted itself. That night I could hardly sleep I was so excited about seeing my friends in Hong Kong.

At 6:00 the next morning we sailed into the misty harbor. When I got to Chim's flat, she was still asleep. She woke up fast when her roommate told her I was there. It was a happy reunion with the pretty Thai princess-stewardess.

After a hearty breakfast at a favorite restaurant around the corner, we went to see my Mexican hotel manager friend from the President Hotel. The timing was right because he was heading back to Mexico that very afternoon. He had been fired but was taking away a substantial compensation package. "It pays to have a contract," he told me.

Chim was off on one of her flights to Singapore at 7:00 that night, so Emoto-san and I got together to talk about the job situation in Japan. He asked me to do a favor for his rich friend from Okayama. I told him, "I'll help in any way I can."

The Cablao family welcomed me with open arms and warm affection. They fed me, we talked together of their native Philippines, and then they gave me a bed to sleep in. Life would be empty without friends.

That day showed how international my life had become. I spent time with a Thai stewardess, visited my many Chinese friends at the President Hotel, said goodbye to my Mexican friend, had a drink with a Japanese friend, and dinner with Filipino friends—not one American did I see.

Now, all I needed to do was get to Japan and find a job. That didn't appear that it was going to be an easy task. Nothing was even remotely on the horizon.

The day after I got back to the British Crown Colony, I met with my friend Fred Aw at the Bayside Coffee Shop. He invited me to stay at his Tiger Balm Mansion until I shipped out for the Land of the Rising Sun. I was saved once again from a headlong rush into poverty.

At noon, a truck arrived to take my bags to Fred's mansion located in the Tiger Balm Gardens on a mountainside, one of the famous tourist sights in the Far East. There was no doubt about it, it was uptown living at its finest.

While having breakfast at one of my favorite spots—the roof garden cafe at the YMCA overlooking the entire bustling harbor—I marked all of the ships sailing for Japan listed in the shipping section of the *Hong Kong Tiger Standard* newspaper.

Next, I met with Mr. Gaffey of American President Lines to see if I could work my way on one of their ships. All he could offer was the minimum fare.

Two days later it *happened*. Serendipity picked me up by the collar and shouted, *I'm back*! I was overjoyed to see my old friend "serendipity" once again.

My one Japanese friend in Hong Kong, Emoto-san, arranged an evening meeting for us with Akazawa-san, who had just arrived from Tokyo. Several days before, Emoto-san had asked me if I could get an article in the *Tiger Standard* about Akazawa-san coming to Hong Kong and his business interests. Well, I checked with my friend Fred, who was one of the owners of this major newspaper, to see if he could assist. Fred gladly agreed.

There it was—a great article on Akazawa-san in the newspaper on the day of his arrival. He expressed his gratitude in Japanese, as we sat down in his suite in the President Hotel. Emoto-san was sitting between us to act as interpreter.

Emoto-san had previously informed me that Akazawa-san, at 33, had recently inherited his late father's fortune and was somewhat of a modern day shogun. He was a handsome man with almost movie star looks, and he was tall for a Japanese man. Added to that, he had an infectious smile and warm personality.

After introductions, Akazawa asked Emoto what I had done and what my plans were. Emoto told him, among other things, "Clarke is traveling the world studying and learning about the history and cultures of as many countries as he possibly can."

At that point, Akazawa said, "Tell Clarke that he is welcome to come live as part of my family for as long as he likes, with no expenses." Emoto translated and all I could say was, "That is wonderful. Thank you so much for your kindness and generosity. I am deeply honored by your invitation and I accept with a grateful heart."

My Japan dilemma had just been turned into a miracle. *Who would have ever dreamed of such a thing happening?* I thought. Certainly not me! Yippie-yi-ti-yea!

I had always been fascinated with Japan, especially after having seen the movies *Tea House of the August Moon* and *Sayonara.* Now I was going to have the opportunity to create my own Japanese story, and it was going to be a fascinating one.

I spent the next morning going from one shipping company to another. I had no luck whatsoever on finding a ship I could work my way to Japan on. On March 27, I finally booked a passage on the cargo ship *Oregon Bear* of the Pacific Far East Line sailing April 2. The ticket cost me $85. That left me with a grand total of $295 to my name. I was now rich, when I thought back to the time I had only $3 when I started work in Hong Kong.

My true friend Flora Ho and I got together for dinner and a movie several days before I sailed. Her English had improved considerably since we last met. She was still doing bit parts in Chinese movies hoping for the big break. She truly was one of the sweetest people I had ever known.

At 2:30 in the afternoon on April 2, I took a Wala-Wala from the dock to the ship anchored in the harbor. The Wala-Wala is a wooden boat not much bigger than a rowboat.

In the evening, my close friend, Fred Aw, and I went to the Neptune Bar, similar to the bar in the movie, *The World of Suzy Wong,* in the Wanchai area. We vowed to keep in touch.

So it was goodbye to Hong Kong for the second time. At 6:00 the next morning the *Oregon Bear* cargo ship sailed for Pusan, Korea. My cabin mate was K.J. Ahn, a Korean born in Japan who had graduated from the Foreign Language College of Korea. He had been living in Taipei for the past five years while studying in the School of Diplomacy of Chengchi National University.

K.J. was on his way to an arranged marriage with a Korean girl. After his marriage, he would go to Tokyo to work on a doctorate at Miji University. He most likely became an Ambassador with all that education. One just never knows whom they are going to bump into on the *Oregon Bear,* or anywhere else for that matter. That's what makes traveling fun, exciting and, at times, enlightening.

After dinner one night, K.J. and I were discussing the problems in Asia, from war to the price of bananas. Rossi, our tall, black ship steward, politely interrupted us to give his views. We invited him to join in. For the next two hours, an oriental, a black, and a caucasian sat and discussed some heavy world issues as the ship plowed through the South China Sea.

As we entered the harbor of Pusan, I saw that the mountains were totally treeless. It was a drab looking city. I ended up going ashore with Rossi and spent most of the day walking around the city observing people and the sights.

We sailed for the Port of Inchon that evening, I recalled General MacArthur's brilliant attack landing plan for Inchon during the Korean War. Now I was getting ready to land there myself.

The Inchon Invasion on September 15, 1950 was more than hazardous. No one except MacArthur thought it was possible. There was a narrow channel and extreme tide changes. The tide actually falls more than 30 feet twice a day. Most thought Inchon was the "worst possible place" and September the "worst possible time" for a landing.

During the amphibious operation, U.S. Marines under the command of MacArthur secured Inchon and broke North Korean control of the Seoul region. It was a stunning plan and victory.

I had high hopes Captain Cotter would ride a high tide through the narrow channel and keep us from getting grounded on the mud flats. He did it! That next morning six passengers, the Captain, and myself took a small launch into port. Large ships were not able to go into the harbor because of the tides.

We boarded a bus and headed into Seoul, thirty miles away. The first thing I did was to go to the U.S. Embassy. Once there, I talked to a political officer about current and long-time problems in Korea. Of course, war could have broken out with North Korea at any time.

Next I toured the ancient palace. From there I took a bus to Seoul University. As I was wandering the campus, I met three students when I asked them a question. They immediately offered to show me around the university. This is what makes traveling alone so special because there is much more opportunity to get to know the local people firsthand.

They then said, "Come, we will show you the city." One of them, Kim, was even so kind as to ride the train with me back to Inchon that evening. People are wonderful.

The *Oregon Bear* set sail for Japan. At long last, I was going to become a samurai and learn the ways of the ninjas, or at least learn how to bow and make tea.

The day of sailing was uneventful and fairly smooth. After doing a great deal of reading about Japan, I went to bed late that night. Our ship docked at noon at the port of Moji-Ko, City of Kitakyushu, on the northern tip of Kyushu Island in southern Japan. There I was in the Land of Cherry Blossoms at the beginning of cherry blossom season. It was a glorious spring day.

What is my life going to be like in Japan? I wondered.

A Japanese welcome at a tea house.

CHAPTER 30

The Land of the Rising Sun

*It is only when we truly know and under-
stand that we only have a limited time on
earth and that we have no way of knowing
when our time is up that we will begin to live
each day to the fullest...*
— Elizabeth Kubler-Ross

After going through Immigration, I took off to walk the streets of the city. The only people I found who could speak English were a schoolgirl, one clerk at the Japan Travel Bureau Office, and a little old lady who wanted to arrange a girl for me.

Kitakyushu retained the sense of being a country area full of natural beauty, despite its reputation as a steel town. It had been the target of the second nuclear bomb to be dropped in World War II. However, it had been cloudy the day of the attack and the plane had diverted to Nagasaki instead. My uncle was a prisoner of war not far from Kitakyushu at the time, so he survived.

To save money, I spent the night aboard ship. When I returned to the ship after six hours of walking and exploring, I met one of the night watch-men aboard. Hirokazu Yazaki, 21, was a university student and spoke English fairly fluently. We hit it off immediately over a cup of tea.

Yazaki-san knocked on my door at 4:20 the next morning. I had to rush to make it off the ship by 5:00 when it was time to sail. My new friend had saved the day. He took me to his small but neat home for breakfast, where I met his family. Never had I experienced greater politeness or graciousness.

Yazaki-san accompanied me to the train station at Shimonosaki. My train arrived at 4:48, precisely on time, that afternoon in Okayama—my new city of residence. It was not far from the Inland Sea of Japan and is located be-tween Kobe and Hiroshima.

Mention the name Okayama, which means big mountain, to any Japanese and he or she will immediately conjure up visions of an ancient castle town ruled by the Ikeda clan and Korakuen. Okayama is among the earliest civilized regions of Japan.

Korakuen Garden is one of the three most beautiful gardens in Japan. After 14 years, it was completed in 1700 by Ikeda Tsunamasa, the Lord of Okayama. It contains streams, waterfalls, and ponds with distant views outside the garden to enhance its beauty.

The history of Okayama goes back to 1573 when a local warlord built his fortress here. The city prospered as the castle town of the Ikeda clan for more than 200 years.

Going way back, the history of Japan probably started around 10,000 B.C. The rise of the military class took place in the 11th century.

The samurai, or bushi, were the members of the military class. Samurai were supposed to lead their lives according to the ethic code of bushido, "the way of the warrior." It stressed loyalty to one's master, self-discipline, and respectful, ethical behavior. For anyone who saw the movie *The Last Samurai*, it gave a fairly accurate picture of the life of a samurai.

As I stepped off the train at Okayama Station, there was Akazawa-san and Sato-san to welcome me. Neither, of course, spoke English, but their greeting was warm. We crossed the street in front of the station to the New Okayama Hotel owned by my benefactor, Akazawa-san. Ogawa-san, the front desk manager, became our interpreter.

This was going to be fun. Guess who had to learn Japanese? And fast!

I was given a nice room in the hotel for the night. As I wrote in my diary that evening, I mentioned, "I can hardly believe I'm in Japan. I not only did not go bust but have ended up staying with what I would call a modern day shogun's family with no expenses." It was almost beyond my imagination.

The next morning, I was introduced to Ok-san, 28, the lady of the house and very pregnant, her two young boys, Hideki-chan and Yoshiki-chan, five and four years old, respectively, and two servant girls (a combination of maid, nanny, or whatever needed doing who were considered almost a part of the family). Ok-san spoke English fairly well but no one else in the household could even understand it.

Ok-san proceeded to give me a tour of my new place of residence—the extensive acre of gardens surrounded by a 12-foot masonry wall, the teahouse, and the main house, which was over 100 years old. This was the real Japan of old.

She then introduced me to Azuma in his cage. It was one of the biggest

154

dogs I had ever seen. He seemed friendly enough, but I wasn't about to put my hand out.

Ok-san told me he was an Akita dog. Azuma was let out of his cage each night at 10:00 to guard the grounds. He and I would have some interesting times together, as it turned out.

The Akita is more than special and had been named a national treasure in Japan. The breed dates back some 300 years. There is a spiritual significance attached to this large powerfully built dog. In Japan, Akitas are affectionately regarded as loyal companions, pets, protectors of the home and children, and a symbol of good health. They are alert, responsive, have an attitude of nobility, an appearance of strength and power, courageous, and friendly towards people, unless it's a ninja coming over the wall. Then watch out!

When people first see an Akita, they may say, like I did, "Excuse me, but what kind of dog is that? He looks like a big bear!" No kidding! A mature male is imposing because he weighs over 100 pounds and, what's more, the Akitas have captivating personalities. In the old days, they were owned only by shoguns.

On Helen Keller's arrival in Japan in 1937, she expressed a keen interest in the breed. She was presented with the first two Akitas to enter the U.S. One of them became her constant companion. She wrote, "If ever there was an angel in fur, it was my puppy Kamikaze."

This was all so fascinating. Just why is the Akita dog so revered in Japan? It is an awe-inspiring story. Hachi-Ko is one of the most revered Japanese Akitas of all time. He was born in 1923 and was owned by Professor Ueno of Tokyo. The professor lived near the Shibuya Train Station in a suburb of the city, and he commuted to work every day. Hachi-Ko accompanied his master to and from the station each day.

On May 25, 1925, when the dog was 18 months old, he waited for his master's arrival on the four o'clock afternoon train. But he waited in vain. Professor Ueno had suffered a fatal stroke at work. Hatchi-Ko continued to wait for his master's return. He traveled to and from the station each day for the next nine years.

Hachi-Ko allowed the professor's relatives to care for him, but he never gave up the vigil at the station for his master. His vigil became world renowned, and shortly after his death, a bronze statue was erected at the train station in his honor. Each April, tens of thousands of people visit the statue and leave offerings in the hope that the spirit of Hachi-Ko will visit the hearts and souls of all humans. This was truly a story for the ages.

I digressed, but the Akita is truly in the heart and soul of the Japanese people.

I believe one of the reasons Akazawa-san invited me to be a part of his family was in hopes his two young sons would get to know something about the language and ways of a *gaijin*, the word for "foreigner" in Japanese. English had become the language of business around the world, and Akazawa-san was a businessman.

After a Japanese dinner served by the servants, Akazawa-san and I studied Japanese and English together. I was now a part of the real Japan, not the part most tourists experience.

That night I took my first *ofuro*. It was a bath in a huge, round, wooden tub. I found out how lobsters must feel. With a chill in the air and no heat in my room, I stayed warm the next several hours with a light cotton kimono that Akazawa had given me.

My room was in a wing off the main house. It was the closest room to the wooden front gate. To use the toilet and sink, I would have to slide open the shoji doors, take one wooden step down to the ground, and then walk on the stepping stones to a door next to my room. The room on the other side of the toilet was occupied by Akazawa's bodyguard, Mizuuchi-san. Going to the bathroom after 10:00 at night always proved quite an ordeal with Azuma roaming the grounds, but more about that later.

The room had no chair on the tatami mat. I would sit cross-legged on a cushion if I wanted to sit. My futon bedroll was kept in a closet behind sliding doors.

I would venture to say that there were not many homes in Japan with a more beautiful garden or a more traditional house than my new home. It was as if I had arrived in a Japanese fairyland! Almost overnight, my life changed from the Western way of living to an almost pure Japanese way of living.

On my third night in Okayama, Akazawa had his geisha come to the house to meet me. She spoke not a word of English. I was rather amazed that he would bring that beautiful young woman home with his wife there. It was the beginning of my Japanese education. Kyoko-san, 21, was the number one geisha in Okayama and was interested in me teaching her English.

A true geisha, she was well-educated, and highly skilled in singing, music, dance, and entertaining Akazawa's business contacts. It had nothing to do with sex in any way.

In Japan it was proper, as I understood it, for a successful businessman to have a Geisha or Geishas in his employ. Ok-san (pronounced "oak-san") treated Kyoko as a friend. This experience took me right back to the memory of the movie *Sayonara* starring Marlon Brando.

My welcome to Japan was a grand one. Now I had to learn the language and absorb myself into the culture.

The Akazawas gave me an old bicycle to ride. This was how students and most people got around this medium-sized city.

While I looked for an English-Japanese dictionary in the Maruzen Bookstore, three English-speaking college students offered to help me. Timing is sometimes everything. My new friends told me about Paul Griesy who was their American English teacher at Okayama University. As it happened, Paul lived in a small house on the narrow street directly across from the entrance

Me in a kimono and wooden geta, the usual attire
around home and for walking in the exquisite garden.

gate to my place. He was happy to learn that I was his neighbor.

We all peddled to the university several miles north from downtown. After lunch, my three new friends took me to meet some more members of their English Speaking Society (E.S.S.). Sixteen of us then headed for Korakuen Park.

At this breathtaking park, we sat under Cherry trees in full-blossom, sang songs, and conversed in English. I began my study of Japanese that evening using the two books I had bought at the bookstore, *Essential Japanese and Japanese Conversation—Grammar* (a thick book) by Vaccari. My goal was to study the language at least four hours a day.

Several days later, Hashimoto-san and Tateishi-san showed me the sports facilities at the University, and we then bicycled into town to have dinner. Afterwards they pointed out all the theaters, nightspots, and coffee houses in the downtown area.

On Sunday, Paul took me to a Japanese Protestant Church where he sometimes preached. Actually, he considered himself a full-time missionary. To me, he had a touch of saint in him. Paul, 35, was tall, blond, and of Scandinavian-descent from Minnesota.

I wrote down my tentative plan for Japan in my diary. Stay in Okayama from April through December; learn Japanese, and teach English to make money; live in Tokyo from January through March to learn all I could about the capital and the government; and travel to every corner of Japan in April and May. My daily schedule plan went as follows: study Japanese from 8:00 a.m. until noon; teach English from 1:00 to 4:00 p.m.; get involved in Judo, Kendo (sword fighting), Karate, and exercise from 4:00 to 6:00 p.m.; and teach English on week day evenings as much as possible.

One evening, Paul gave me a thorough briefing on the culture and ways of Japan. It was surprising and enlightening.

Combined with Paul's knowledge and my reading on the Japanese culture, these are some of the things I learned: Number one, there are many reactions and attitudes the Japanese give off, many of which the typical westerner would ordinarily not pick up. I was still a babe in the woods.

From my understanding, multitudes of westerners had found Japan captivating, bewildering, enchanting, humorous, frustrating, loose, uptight, and accommodating, sometimes all at the same time. I was half-way through this list.

The Japanese have been raised to think of themselves as part of a group (us and them). Internationally it is, "We Japanese vs. everyone else." Dealing with them on a one-to-one basis usually comes very easy to non-Japanese, but dealing with them as a group is a whole different ball game. One will always be treated as an outsider. In fact, the literal meaning of *gaijin* is outsider or alien, but in most all cases "white person."

The Japanese, it seemed to me, didn't think in a logical, rational fashion, at least in western terms. It is no exaggeration to say that they see things through race-colored glasses, but in almost all cases, it is never hostile towards others.

The Japanese try to establish rapport with a westerner by saying things they think he would like to hear. Many view westerners on two levels—if you are taken as a temporary visitor, they nearly always treat one warmly and helpfully. But if you are someone trying to become a member of their society, there can be quite a different attitude involved.

Then there is the reality and the facade—the real reason and the pretext. Since avoiding conflict and trouble is extremely important, they use diplomatic language often rather than the direct approach as Americans are inclined to do. The Japanese may stress harmony but the reality is they push the image of harmony. What lies beneath may be completely different. Boy, was I learning fast.

If a Japanese person said, "Come over to my place sometime," it really may mean, "I hope we get along well together." What is not said may be more important than what is said.

There is overwhelming social pressure to conform. The Japanese have a saying that goes, "The nail that sticks up gets hammered down." Forget about being a star, getting a group consensus is the only way.

Tate-Shakai means a vertically structured society, like the military or caste system. From 1600 until 1868, Japan was an officially segregated society with five classes of people. At the top were the samurai. Even today, a shadow of this system is still around. Japan could still be considered to have a plutocratic government "of the rich, by the rich, and for the rich," or so some might say.

From the day they are born, in most cases, the Japanese were taught to conform and follow orders without question. A philosophy that basically dictates that the strong control the weak and the weak exist to serve the strong—be it the Almighty Company, or the Establishment.

For a foreigner like myself and other foreigners, one's attitude usually goes through three predictable phases of varying links: (1) The Honeymoon Phase, (2) The Critical Phase, and (3) The Integrating Phase. I was certainly in the first phase.

The foregoing is but a brief look at what may be termed the mysteries of Japan. Now it was time to sort out the mysteries for myself.

CHAPTER 31

An Intriguing Life

Who reads much and travels much, sees a lot
and knows a lot.

— Cervantes

Eleven days after I arrived in Japan, Ok-san gave birth to a baby girl. My would-be baby sister was given the name of Tomoko. No doubt she was going to get plenty of attention with two young brothers watching over her.

My first trip inside Japan was to Kyoto to see my English friend Mike, whom I'd met in Hong Kong. Three young people took me in tow at the train station and escorted me all the way to Mike's house. Everywhere I went in Japan, eager young people always welcomed an opportunity to practice their English.

The next day, Mike and I had tea at the Ura Senke Tea House. It was the largest, most respected, highest and oldest tea sect in all of Japan. Mike's Japanese is nearly fluent, so our tea party went without a hitch. "Every woman in Japan would give almost anything to have tea at this most famous of all teahouses," Mike told me.

That afternoon, I watched Mike teach English to a class made up of Japanese businessmen. This was fortunate, since I planned to do the same to earn money. I now had a guideline to follow.

Kyoto was not only a beautiful city, it was the ancient capital of Japan for 1,000 years until 1867. It can be said Kyoto touches the heart of the Japanese people like no other place.

Almost all of the National Treasures of culture are located in Kyoto and in nearby Nara. If one goes to only one place in all of Japan, Kyoto is a wise choice.

In Nara, another former capital even more ancient than Kyoto, is Japan's largest bronze Buddha. Planned on a grand scale, the walled city measured 2.7 miles from east to west and 3.1 miles from north to south. It was modeled after the Chinese capital of the time.

At this point, I must relate the unbelievable Nara Park episode that occurred during my stay with Mike. I would speculate that never has such a thing happened before or since in Nara. I never thought I would be among those who were the object of a search by the police in that ancient capital.

Mike and I had gone to Nara for a day to visit some of his friends. One of them was Patrick, a 6'8" giant from Virginia. Another was Iwata-san, 5'8", who worked for a Japanese movie company in Nara. Mike's height fell in between the two men, at 6'2". They were an interesting trio when they dressed up in authentic samurai costumes, wigs, swords, and put on hideous Japanese masks that would have scared the devil himself.

What were they up to? At dusk, they paraded through the entrance of Nara Park strutting like the Three Musketeers. Mrs. Iwata and I followed twenty yards behind.

Hardly anyone was visible in the park as night fell. All of a sudden, the three samurai spotted a young couple on a park bench about forty yards to the right, kissing for all they were worth. The couple had no sense of the Samurai warriors that had halted ten feet in front of them. With a deep samurai voice that would strike terror into any enemy, Patrick roared out in Japanese, "What on earth are you doing with my daughter?" swords poised overhead ready to do them in. The young man lit out running to his left with no thought of his girlfriend. Thirty yards away, we saw him disappear into a culvert and then scramble up the other side and into the trees to save his life.

The poor young woman was frozen in place for a moment and white as a sheet. She then dashed off in the opposite direction. Her boyfriend had deserted her with abandon. I believe I would have done the same in his case. These Samurai indeed looked formidable and fierce, especially in the dark.

The "samurai scourge" advanced deeper into the park. It was inky black. No one else was in sight. That's when we heard a band playing in the distance. As the samurai snuck through the huge trees, we could see there were about twenty members of a high school boy's band practicing under one of the park lights. They were lined up in three rows facing the path, the band director's back to the path.

To make things interesting, Samurai #1 walked from behind a tree to another tree 20 steps away, being about 20 yards away from the band. On cue, Samurai #2 walked across the same space. The area was dimly lit and they must have appeared almost as apparitions to the members of the band who noticed them.

The band was blaring out a tune with the bandleader in full swing with his baton. Samurai #3 appeared and then disappeared. As #2 had made his way across, the music had slowed considerably and the eyes of the band members grew big.

As Samurai #3 appeared, the music trailed off and the band director had no idea what was going on. Puzzled, he turned around to see what everyone was gaping at, but saw nothing. The Samurai had melted into the darkness. The band finally began playing again, after some discussion with all the musicians keeping one eye on their music sheets and the other eye on the trees.

As we all sat at a small bar in town, drinking sake, the police arrived on the scene. They wanted to know if the three samurai were carrying real swords. Fortunately, the swords were dull movie versions of the real thing, or the whole lot of us would have ended up in jail.

No telling what shenanigans Mike and his friends would come up with in the future. They certainly would be unique, of course, with Mike as the ringleader.

A Dr. Kawada became my first student. I would be charging $25 an hour for private lessons. This was the going rate and would be a boon to my lowly finances. At Oka-yama University, Professor Yano introduced me to a company manager who wanted me to teach English to his employees. Yes! I opened an account at Mitsubishi Bank to be used only for the money I made teaching English.

As I sat down on my Tatami mat late one evening to write in my diary, this thought struck me, *How many different kinds of life I had led over the past three and a half years—Hawaiian, Tahitian, Australian, Chinese, Filipino, and now Japanese.* At this point, I had learned to adapt to almost anything and to take things as they came—and make the best of any situation. Liking, respecting, and getting along with people was certainly one of the keys to any successes I had had to that point.

I was soon initiated into the Art of Judo at the University Judo Club. The members select the three best fighters to lead the class, co-captains, so to speak. To initiate a new recruit properly, the novice is paired up with a black belt. As the black belt slammed me to the floor over and over he would look down and say, *Diajobu-deska?* which means "Are you ok?" in Japanese. *Hai!* meaning yes. I would slowly pick myself up only to be slammed down once again. *This is ridiculous*, I thought. Enough is enough. I started learning fast. Easing into it was out of the question.

The modern form of Judo was developed at the end of the 19th century from the ancient martial art of Jujitsu. In Judo, the aim is not only winning fights but also training the body and spirit. It is "the gentle way" where

Clarke holding up his little Japanese brothers
before Judo practice.

techniques are more important than stamina. After that first lesson, there was nothing gentle about it as far as I was concerned. I couldn't wait to get hold of that guy tomorrow.

In Okayama, young people didn't seem to date but went out in groups. It was a challenging situation, since I was used to asking out a girl I was attracted to. Of course, most could not understand a word I said. This was great incentive to go all out in learning Japanese.

I landed two more teaching jobs at Japanese companies. One was at Tenmaya, the largest department store in town. There I had 15 men and women students. Second was Exlan Chemical Company with a class of 30 men. The latter company was located in the country about five miles out of town. It was a great bicycle ride.

One gorgeous afternoon, I mounted my trusty bicycle and peddled carefree all the way around the outskirts of the city. The thing that most impressed me was that every square inch of ground right up to the mountains was being used to grow crops. Because of the mountains, only about one sixth of Japan is plantable.

At Club Sanyo, a private club at the New Okayama Hotel, I became totally smitten with Satomi-san. She looked like Ava Gardner in her prime, in looks and figure. And Ava had been the most beautiful woman in the world, in my mind, as I was growing up. I struck out completely with Satomi because of the language barrier. I tripled my efforts to learn Japanese.

Murai-san, a university student, was becoming a good friend. He was kind, soft spoken, had a most pleasant manner about him, and was always there to help me in any way he could. One weekend, he took me to his home in the far reaches of the mountains that few foreigners ever penetrate. After taking a train and three buses, we reached the mountain village of Bicho-Cho.

It was as if I was stepping back 100 years into old Japan. His home was located on a hillside and was made of wood with a thatch roof, and was very dark inside. His parents and young brother welcomed me warmly. I learned they grew rice for a living. I had been transported from a rich home to a poor home and from modern day Japan to ancient Japan in a matter of 50 miles.

It was now time to give Karate a try. In this martial art you defend yourself with fists, elbows, and feet. It is related to Chinese Kung-fu. Karate-do means "the way of the empty hand," since usually no weapons are used.

From my brief experience, it was "the way of the uncovered foot." On my first day of training, the class decided it would be fun to run over a rocky mountain trail barefooted. I could hardly walk the week after and decided to take up something less grueling, like Kendo, now that my feet were damaged for life.

Kendo is Japanese fencing, football style. It means "the way of the sword." By this time, I was losing my way in this complicated society, so it promised a new chance to look at the world of Japan.

Swords were the main weapons in Japanese warfare for centuries. They continued to be the symbol of the samurai into the 19th century.

The participants in modern Kendo are well protected, or so I was told. You wear pads everywhere and a big mesh mask with plenty of padding on its top and sides. I was ready for anything, "Bring those samurai on." Within a week, my head was ringing and I was black and blue on almost every part of my body, what there was left of it. What great and bruising fun!

I must admit that my Kendo training did serve a useful purpose. Any time I had to leave my room after 10:00 p.m. to walk the rock path to the bathroom, I would take my bamboo sword in hand and fight off "Azuma the Great," our Japanese guard dog, all the way there and back. This bear of a dog always thought I was coming out to play, as he stayed in his cage all day. After being knocked down several times by this "friendly" canine—he was 6 feet tall when standing on his back paws—drastic action was called for. That's when I brought out my bamboo sword as a matter of survival. Azuma enjoyed every single minute of it. Of course, I was his favorite playmate.

My Japanese tourist Visa was about to expire. My philosophy was "go to the top," if nothing else worked, so I wrote to the Prime Minister for his help on an extension. I was carried away in chains a week later.

Actually, after writing to the Prime Minister, my friend Sato-san, along with Noma-san as an interpreter, drove us to Tamano-shi where I put in an application for the extension of my Visa. If it didn't come through, I would be required to go to another country to get a new tourist Visa. That was something I couldn't afford.

I was invited to a party for Japanese teachers. The next day, Hashimoto-san called me. I had met him at the party. He invited me to visit and talk to some of his classes at a junior high school. The students were so eager to learn.

I was invited to another teacher's party a few days later. At that party, I met a classic Japanese beauty by the name of Yamada-san. She was 24 and pretty enough to be a movie star. Even though she spoke no English, the language of the eyes said it all between us. Hashimoto played the role of matchmaker.

Kawamoto-san had become my main Japanese teacher. She was a student at Seishin University, an all-girl Catholic College near where I lived. My language ability was picking up steam, thanks to her and many other students.

My finances had reached a desperate low. I was down to 20,000 yen or $60 U.S. It was time to beat the bushes hard for teaching jobs. Just in the nick of time, I signed up Shiseido Cosmetics and Diamond Rose Department Store.

Hashimoto-san had a sukiyaki party at his home. Yamada-san just so happened to be his next-door neighbor and was there in all her beauty. He invited me to spend the night and talk longer with everyone. I didn't hesitate for a second! Yamada-san walked me to the bus stop in the rain the next morning. She presented me with an ornate fan, which had the wonderful smell of her perfume on it.

Judo was progressing nicely. I had a badly twisted right arm, bruises and mat burns, two skinned knees, stubbed toes, a pulled right calf, and a sore back. Other than that, I was in great shape. All this damage was just from Judo. I wouldn't tell what Kendo had done to me.

165

With the Prime Minister's help, I had managed to get my Visa extended. I worried if I could get it done a second time. The time was fast approaching and I was shooting to get a one-year Visa this go round. *Maybe the Emperor can help*, I thought.

My first class at Shiseido Cosmetics was an eye-popper. Twelve beautiful models showed up. Miyoko stood out above all the rest with her silky black hair falling to her waist. Had I died and gone to heaven or was this just a stop along the way?

My first lesson in tea ceremony was at a Zen Buddhist Temple in the city of Tsuyama. The ceremony was a traditional ritual influenced by Zen Buddhism in which powdered green tea, matcha, is ceremonially prepared by a skilled practitioner and served to a small group of guests in a tranquil setting. Given all that, I wasn't fond of the tea's taste, but that wasn't the point of this exquisite ceremony.

Though not native to Japan, the drinking of tea was introduced to the country in the 9th century by a Buddhist monk from China. By the 13th century, samurai warriors had begun preparing and drinking matcha. The tea ceremony, even today, is characterized by humility, restraint, simplicity, naturalism, and imperfection. It celebrates the mellow beauty that time and care impart to materials. The principles set forth are harmony, respect, purity and tranquility. I needed all of this I could get.

I was in the process of soaking up every bit of Japanese culture I could in the way of, and including, the martial and fine arts. Of course, I had trouble raising my teacup with my "martial arts" right arm.

To round things out, I launched into the fine art of flower arrangement, known as *Ikebana*. Saito-sensei, 73, my esteemed teacher, *sensei* means teacher, was 4'10" and weighed less than a hundred pounds. But her heart was big. She always welcomed this *gaijin* with a smile and warmth, even though she spoke not a word of English.

When I would arrive at her small house, I would take off my *geta*, or wooden sandals, on the front porch and line them up neatly with the ten or so pairs of *geta* of the women students. Mine looked like gunboats compared to their tiny *geta*.

I would slide the wooden door open, go to my knees on the tatami mat, bow my head all the way to the floor and say, *mina-san, konichi-wa*, which meant, "All, good afternoon." Then Saito-sensei would show me my place at the long table, two feet off the floor, in the middle of the room.

Slowly I began to learn this cherished art, and there was nothing easy about it. Especially sitting on one's legs for long periods of time.

The origin of Ikebana stretches back over 500 years. The oldest manuscript dates from 1486. In Japan, "the way" of arranging flowers and plants has been carefully systematized and is called *Kado*.

When Buddhism was introduced to Japan in 538 A.D., exactly 1400 years before I was born, monks started to arrange flowers to decorate the alters and temples. In Japan today, there are over 3,000 different schools of Ikebana.

One evening, when Akazawa arrived home, I was in the breezeway working on a flower arrangement. All he could do was laugh, seeing this *gaijin* trying to stick flowers in a vase. It had to be quite a sight, me black and blue from Judo and Kendo, fiddling around with this delicate art. Practice makes perfect in all disciplines.

My English class at Shiseido, all 16 men and women, took me to Kamashima Island for a day of fun. It is one of the most beautiful areas of Japan's Inland Sea. It was here I got to know model Miyoko for the first time. She looked stunning in a bathing suit. I had been attracted to her from the day I started teaching the class. We all swam, ate, sunned, and played games. The language barrier was lifted in the face of a day of fun!

About this time, I had written in my diary, "Even though I'm dedicated to my studies, it sure would be nice to date and have a girlfriend. Language and customs have been real barriers in this pursuit. I have been four months in Okayama with not even one date."

One week later, I met Miyoko at the Tenmaya Bus Station. We took a bus to Paul's house. He was out of town and told me I could use his house whenever I liked. Miyoko and I listened to records, danced, and did our best to communicate with a little English and a little Japanese. As we were getting ready to leave Paul's house, she threw her arms around my neck and kissed me as hard as I'd ever been kissed. Life is full of surprises.

I visited Shizutani with some friends. It was supposedly the oldest continuous school in the world. It opened its doors to the common people and ruling classes, on an equal basis, in 1701. There was still so much to learn in and about Japan.

CHAPTER 32

Life's Oriental Ups and Downs

Each individual reflects the many different combinations of people to whom he has been exposed.

— Disraeli

Soga-sensei gave me my first lesson in brush writing—also known as calligraphy. Shodo, "the way of writing," is the art of writing beautifully.

This art form has been studied for over 3,000 years. A knowledge of calligraphy is an important step in the understanding of Japanese culture. It was my 894th step into the culture.

Sho is the attempt to bring words to life and endow them with character. The characters must be written only once. There is no altering, touching up, or adding to them afterwards. I was in deep trouble right off the bat.

Calligraphy began to filter into Japan during the seventh century A.D. Buddhism from India had traveled via China and Korea and was making converts in Japan, including the Emperor. At the time, the Japanese had no writing system of their own. In the hands of Japanese noblewomen, hiragana developed into a beautiful script, which is the unique calligraphic style of Japan.

I was off to a fine start in brush writing for someone who had no idea what they were doing. I will say this for Soga-sensei, "He had the patience of an elephant." Slowly but surely I started to come around in the improvement of my brush strokes.

How fortunate I was to be completely free every day to pursue the two things I liked most, being a scholar and a sportsman. Never had I had so much financial security in my travels. The only expenses I had were for personal items. All else was furnished through the great kindness of the Akazawas.

My friend Emoto-san from Hong Kong called me out of the blue from Tokyo. He asked me to join him there ASAP. The very next day I took a train to Osaka and a flight from there to Tokyo. Emoto said he would reimburse me for any expenses.

This was my first time to be in what was purported to be the largest city in the world. Tokyo, at that time, had a population of 15 million in the metro area.

Emoto was in the process of doing a guidebook for Hong Kong in Japanese and English. He needed me to proof read the English section of his guide and I spent a full day reading and proofing. He said he would reimburse me in Tokyo but did not. This put me in a bit of a financial bind. I wasn't happy.

That evening, I had an unbelievable surprise! After visiting the famous Ginza area with Afifa Raham (her dad was of Iranian, Indian, and English descent and her mother was Japanese, which resulted in a beautiful creation), I was walking across the Palace Hotel lobby. Someone tapped me on the shoulder and said, "Do you have a match?" I turned around to see my college roommate, Roger Moran. We had not seen each other since graduation five years before and had totally lost touch.

All I could say at first was, "Unbelievable! This is just too good to be true." Think of it. He had no idea where in the world I was and visa versa. It just so happened that we were in the same hotel lobby at the same time in a city of millions of people with hundreds of hotels.

Roger had arrived two days before to start a new job. We went to the bar and spent four hours catching up on our lives since graduation. Roger was one of the most "full of life" guys I had ever known. We were an unlikely pair to be the close friends we had been in college. He was a damn Yankee from New York and I a rebel southerner from Texas.

Back in Okayama, I went to a dance put on by University students. I was dancing with a girl named Sugako. I thought I was making a fairly good impression when she bluntly told me, "It is rude to have part of your t-shirt showing at the neck. I thought you were a sailor." Of course, in America this was a totally normal thing.

Her sentiment came as a bit of a shock. I started to reply, "Actually, I'm an assistant cook on an old garbage ship," but thought better of it. On hot summer days, I had seen a university student walking down the street in his jockey underwear to mail a letter and men board trains, strip down to their underwear, sit down, and leisurely read their newspaper. Perceptions can certainly color peoples' thinking. If I had taken off my shirt and pants, she probably would have felt right at home.

I sampled a little of everything in Japan. My friend Paul loaned me his Yamaha motorcycle to go to the city of Kojima. A trusting soul! It was the first time in my life to ride a motorcycle. This called for sheer bravery in kamakazi traffic, especially when I was doing good just to keep the precision machine upright. Now that was a "real" adventure, literally taking my life in my hands on the seat of my pants.

I followed Sato-san and Momoda-san, who were riding double on a Honda. They kept looking back to see if I had become part of the dearly departed. It took us an hour and a half to reach our destination, riding over every kind of road imaginable. Nonetheless, it was exhilarating to be sitting on so much power.

We went sailing on the Inland Sea and had lunch on Tateba Island. By a miracle, I made it back to Paul's house in one piece and joined the motorcycle elite for bravery beyond comprehension or good sense.

A new adventure was just around the corner. I had heard of people losing their shirt, but this one would be totally ridiculous. Be careful where you take off your shoes.

Preparing for my trip to the island of Kyushu to visit Yazaki-san, the student I had met when I arrived in Japan by ship, I bought an advance ticket at the train station. When I got home, I discovered I had been charged 1,000 yen too much.

The next day Ogawa-san accompanied me to the station as my interpreter. Upon entering the ticket manager's office, we had to take off our Japanese sandals in the foyer. After half an hour of discussing the ticket overcharge in excruciating detail, the manager refunded my money and apologized profusely. All was well. He walked us to the door still apologizing. As I went to put on my shoes, they weren't there! The poor manager was embarrassed beyond the bounds of sanity. He had worked so hard to put things right.

For a while, it looked like I was going to have to walk out of the station barefoot but the manager finally came back red and panting. In his arms in a jumble, he was carrying five pairs of shoes. If one pair of them was mine, there were four other people missing their shoes. This was getting serious. There was no telling where he collected all of them. Luckily one of the pairs really was mine. Four others were now searching for their shoes. Ogawa-san and I walked out of the station bursting with laughter. Those sandals had cost me $2.99.

On the way back from visiting Yazaki-san, I got off the train at Iwakuni Marine Air Base. While I was there, I talked with Captain Cunningham about getting on a Marine flight to Hong Kong to renew my Japanese Visa. Even though I was a Marine, "Once a Marine, always a Marine," I had no luck. I was willing to try anything to save money I didn't have.

On September 3rd, I filled out a form for the renewal of my passport, which was due to expire on the 13th. That was all I needed—no passport and no Visa. It looked as if I would have to leave Japan to renew my Visa. I had pushed my renewals to the limit but had achieved the all-time record for extending a tourist Visa. Such is life, win some, lose some.

In Japan, the most beautiful moon is the September full moon. It is called *Meigetsu*. The Japanese have paid special deference to this moon for centuries. Poets have praised it and lovers have been moved by its romantic tidings. Miyoko and I decided to take full advantage of the situation. She was a lovely vision in and out of her kimono on such a lovely moonlit night.

The next day, the fifth typhoon (hurricane) to hit Japan directly was approaching, and it rained all day. The 24th and 25th typhoons of the season passed Japan soon after, one off each coast. Now all that we needed was a giant earthquake like the one that hit Tokyo on September 1, 1923.

That earthquake destroyed Tokyo and Yokohama. One hundred forty thousand people died. Most of the fatalities were caused by 88 fires, which broke out separately and spread due to high winds from a typhoon. In 1960, September 1st was designated as Disaster Prevention Day to commemorate that great earthquake, and remind people that September and October are the middle of the typhoon season.

Six months in Japan brought some interesting changes to my life. I was beginning to look at things through Japanese eyes rather than American eyes. Also, I was entering the phase of disillusionment. Things were not as I first hoped, all bright and wonderful. Until then, I thought there were certain solutions that would work for all the people the world over.

Life was smoking. I signed up a tobacco company for an English class. I was convinced almost every man over 30 years old in Japan smoked like a chimney. The only thing I had ever smoked was cedar bark as a kid and it always managed to turn me as green as the tree.

I had a rather unpleasant experience when I went to teach an English class at one of the companies I worked for. When I got there at 7:00 in the evening ready to teach the class, one of the employees informed me, "We have something else we need to do."

"*Ah, so desu-ka*," I replied, which means "I see" in Japanese.

No one had called to inform me ahead of time. It was a subtle way, I was finding out, to say we don't need your services anymore. I had noticed less and less people were attending class each time. It was a shock and disappointment.

No matter, the company was sure to go down the tubes in the near future without my expert instruction.

On the other side of the coin, the other English classes had virtually adopted me as a member of their companies. One company even had a mock Olympic game every year and they had me involved in three events. One was a three-legged race, where the guys had their inside legs tied together and an arm over each other's shoulders.

In the fifty-yard race, we managed to knock another team down, fall twice ourselves, and come in third from last. If we could just have knocked four other teams down, we would have won. As almost everyone in the world knows, the Japanese are extremely competitive. Try running with your leg tied to someone else's leg sometime. "It ain't easy," as we would say in Texas. So there were plenty of ups and downs as I edged my way into Japanese society. There were still many lessons to learn, but each day revealed new insights into the Japanese way of life.

Participating in a mini Japanese Olympics.

CHAPTER 33
Walk Softly and Carry a Big Zen Stick

Whatever accords with your own experience—
and after thorough investigation agrees with
your reason, and is conducive to your own
welfare and that of all other living things,
that accept as truth and live accordingly.

— Buddha

*T*he Japanese seem to prefer autumn over the other seasons. Because a harmonious connection with nature has always been particularly important, observing the distinct seasons of the year is a valued part of the culture. The customs and traditions used to observe the arrival of each season conveyed the spirit and beauty of Japan. I was enchanted by autumn in Okayama.

Autumn was considered by many to be the most beautiful season in Japan. It was marked by an invigorating crispness in the air, clear skies, and rich harvests. Festivals of thanksgiving prevail. I jumped in and participated in a number of these. *Momiji-gari*, the viewing of autumn leaves, is a treasured pastime in the scenic regions of the country.

Autumn was a wonderful time to do my studying in the Japanese garden surrounding the house. After six months of concentrated study, I completed the 774 pages of the *Complete Course of Japanese Conversation-Grammar*. The pages were in Japanese and English in very small type. It was a chore, but well worth it in the improvement of my conversational abilities. I also finished reading *Meeting With Japan* by Maraini. Paul then loaned me another one of his books, *Japanese Sentence Patterns*. It was about the most exciting thing I had ever read.

Kameoka-san, a student friend from the University, took me by train to Konko. A famous religion in Japan, known as Konkoyo, originated there. This center is located in Okayama Prefecture.

The founder, Kawate Bunjiro, born a peasant farmer, lived a life (1814-1883) that spanned many significant time periods in Japan's history. These periods created instability within society and inclined people to look toward Kami, or God.

Bunjiro was nicknamed "The Pious One." His adult life was full of hardships. At 42, he became fatally ill but was believed to have been saved by a "spirit." He recovered fully. Bunjiro reflected on the experience and received assurance of divine favor from the god Konjin. This religion was born as a Shinto sect.

In 1858, Bunjiro began full-time service to this deity. He abandoned his life as a farmer and for the next 24 years, he served as a "mediator between man and God." The leaders that followed were of direct lineage of the founder and I was about to meet the leader.

In Konko, we went to the main temple where the Patriarch was officiating. He was the spiritual leader of 600,000 people. At least 100 people were on their knees bowing to the Patriarch. I was led to the front of the huge tatami-matted hall to meet him. Kameoka did most of the talking and translating. I was most honored to be introduced to a man of such eminence. He took kindly to a poor sinner such as myself. It was another insightful experience into the mystery of Japan.

Kendo was taking its toll on me. With two rugged hours of training in the morning, I had a terrible headache after being hit hard on the head, and everywhere else, so many times. *I'll get those guys back good tomorrow*, I always said to myself. *Just wait till I learn what I'm doing*. It never happened. Some mornings I woke up so stiff and sore I could hardly move.

But why would I want to get up anyway in my freezing room that had no heat? I had to sleep with two pairs of socks on just to keep my feet warm.

I started missing my own culture after four years of adventure on the road. I longed for the warmth of my family and friends back home, Mexican food, and football games. Japan was starting to grate on me a bit, while at the same time, it was fascinating. One can't have it all.

One evening Akazawa-san and I were joking around. He was surprised to find out Texas is bigger than Japan. He knew Texas was big, but not that big. I owed so much to him and Ok-san for their great kindness toward me.

I had gained two close friends that I trusted implicitly: Murai (family name) Mitsumasa (first name) and Kazahaya Yoshiko. Mitsumasa was a student at the University and a gentle soul if ever there was one. Yoshiko and I had met when I had first arrived in Okayama. She was an English teacher and good to the core. Both of them became like family to me. With Yoshiko, there was no romance, just friendship.

The Japanese have a saying, "This is a fleeting, temporary world." One never quite knew what people were thinking and what was going on in Japan.

174

My pendulum of feeling for Japan and the Japanese was constantly swinging from optimism to pessimism and back again. It was only through the deep kindness of Mitsumasa and Yoshiko that I was provided with an important balance and anchor.

Lafcadio Hearn, a true scholar of Japan, wrote about this duality of feelings back in 1892. He noted this happened once a person became more than a tourist. And I was light years beyond being a tourist.

Yoshiko asked me to her home for dinner on numerous occasions. She was my best teacher in everything Japanese. On one occasion, she arranged a trip for me to Kyoto, and three families for me to stay with.

It took me half an hour by train to get to Kyoto. I was met by Oyabu-san of the 3F (Friendship-Freedom-Forward Action) Club. He was the club president and one of my hosts for my visit. Everyone treated me royally. Long live the Kyoto 3F Club.

With the weather getting colder and colder, I stayed close to the oil stove in the main house in the evenings, took a hot, hot bath in the wooden tub (I always bathed last as a guest of the family), and then retired to my small tatami-mat room with sliding doors. With a pair of long underwear and two pairs of socks on, I would crawl into my futon on the floor and sleep soundly. If it got any colder here, I might decide to move on to the North Pole.

Yoshiko accompanied me to the Uno Immigration Office for my fourth bid to renew my tourist Visa. I was pushing the envelope at that juncture. The next day I had my Alien Registration Book stamped at City Hall. Again, I was an alien.

I was in the middle of laying any groundwork possible to be able to work and live in Tokyo. A Japanese gentleman who had offered me a place to stay and a job teaching him English, sent me a letter that contained conditions and pay far from acceptable. Another disappointment. As always, I went right to work to make good things happen.

Life, what is it? I pondered this weighty question at times. Whatever it is, I love it. What puzzled me was there are so many ways of living life— considering all the philosophies and ideologies that exist. I had found there are certain truths that are similar in all societies. For me personally, my guide was the simple Golden Rule. There's no better way to live than that, in my mind. I prayed to God that I could help build bridges of peace and understanding as I traveled the world. In many ways and places, I had done just that.

It was November 30 already. How the days march so quickly into history. It was exactly one year ago that I sailed from Hong Kong to the Philippines.

To toughen up for my coming three-day stay at a Zen Temple, I decided to sleep without my long underwear. The temple on the mountaintop had no heat at all. Temple life is austere from what I'd heard. I could hardly wait to experience it!

My room in Okayama was like an icebox. I seemed to be frozen to the floor as I wrote in my diary. This was perfect training to be a Zen monk, or an Eskimo.

Well, there I was finally sitting in my eight mat room at the Zen Buddhist Temple at Hofukuji. I had just finished eating my dinner, which was a bowl of rice, a small plate of vegetables, two small pickles, some cold greens, and a bowl of piping hot clear soup.

Dinner had been served to me on a small tray by a young boy named Genkai. He was 13 and in training to be a Buddhist priest. Sitting on the floor at a small two-foot high table, I ate alone. The temperature in my room was 38° F. Fortunately, there was a small hibachi in my room. It was full of hot coals and, at least, helped keep my hands from freezing.

Looking back on that day, I recalled Yoshiko rode the train with me to Soja. We then walked 30 minutes across rice fields and up a mountain trail to reach the temple. Genshin-san, a 24-year-old apprentice priest welcomed us. He served us green tea and small cakes soon after we arrived. The temple and its environment were in a world of their own, completely isolated from society. It was truly a place of peace and tranquility.

After Yoshiko left, I took a long walk through the surrounding mountains that afternoon, with only birds keeping me company. Japan is so crowded that this was a quiet paradise in a land of almost frenetic activity. It was soothing to the soul, solitude provided its own healing balm.

My first session of Za Zen the next night was a chilling experience. For a while, I wasn't sure if my bare feet were frozen from the biting cold in the open air hall, or if they had just gone to sleep from sitting in a rigid lotus position. I do believe it was a combination of both.

The first session lasted an hour. The first half-hour, I concentrated on what it would be like to achieve world peace, as it is a rule to concentrate only on one subject. By the second half-hour, all I could think about was the pain and numbness in my legs and feet. World peace was out the window, or would it be better to say escaping into the frigid night air? This Zen stuff was going to take some serious practice, if I didn't freeze to death first.

The sixteen of us attending the three-day contemplation session arose at six the next morning. For an hour we chanted prayers, accompanied by the ringing of a small bell and the beating of a wooden drum. For breakfast, we each had a bowl of rice and soup.

Through the morning, I assisted Hojo-san, the head priest, as he made a sign using white paper and black paint. On it, he brush stroked large Chinese characters. I think it must have said, "Get prepared for tonight's session with the big stick." If I only had known what was coming.

That afternoon, with an old Japanese umbrella made out of bamboo and paper, I walked in a light drizzle over the hills and through the farm fields. It was as if I had gone back in time. Things could not have changed much in the last 100 years in the places I strolled past.

That evening, as we sat in the dark in the long narrow hall with no walls. It was approximately six yards wide and twenty yards long. The Zen priest slowly walked from one end to the other and back. In his hands he held one of the stoutest sticks I had ever seen. It was about five feet long and had a circumference of six inches round.

We had been told that we were to concentrate on one subject so completely while in the lotus position that literally we would be out of body and nothing in the world could faze us. The trick was not to flinch when the priest all of a sudden whirled on you and came down on one of your shoulders with the stick in a convincing manner.

Well, this was carrying it a bit far, I thought. All I could think about the whole time was, *I sure hope in hell he doesn't turn on me*! If he had, I would have done a back roll off the raised platform and headed for the hills. So much for my Zen training! My shoulders started hurting just thinking about it.

Zen has many wonderful benefits. *Getting the stick* was not one of them, as far as I was concerned. The next day I headed back to my Japanese home, wiser and with shoulders intact.

CHAPTER 34

The Lure of Tokyo

A good traveler has no fixed plans and is not intent on arriving.

— Lao Tzu

Unfortunately, Okusan hadn't been successful in arranging a place for me to stay in Tokyo, so it was back to square one.

My goal was to stay in the capital city for two or three months to learn all I could there, while earning my way teaching English. I vowed to myself, "I shall persevere."

Okusan, feeling sorry for me, had arranged for a small kerosene stove to be put in my tatami-mat room. It was the dead of winter and even with the stove going full steam, I would sit studying in my room at night wearing a pair of long underwear, two kimonos and two pairs of socks. It was an inadequate attempt to keep warm, but I was about as alert as one could be.

Each week at my Exlan Chemical Company class, I'd ask each student, all managers, what he would like to talk about in English. For example, it could be the Vietnam War, the purpose of life, perceptions of America, the future of science, and so on. After a student gave his view, he would always want to know mine. It was a great learning process for all of us.

My Japanese was getting better after eight months of mumbling and bumbling. I had gone completely through the 774 pages of the book *Japanese Conversation-Grammar* twice, and had finished studying the book *Essential Japanese*.

After everyone had had their bath one evening, the Akazawas presented me with an exquisite formal, dark blue silk kimono that had been especially made for me. Needless to say, I was touched and thanked them profusely. Never had I, or would I, receive greater kindness than this family showed me. They wanted me to have the kimono as a remembrance of my stay in Japan.

My calligraphy class gave me a *sukiyaki* dinner going away party at a fancy restaurant. They were fascinated about my having assisted a head Buddhist priest with his calligraphy. It was just another step in the commitment I had made to myself to *learn the way of Japan.*

178

Still no good news from Tokyo. There was nothing like a good challenge! I had no idea where I would stay or what I would do there. I was counting on serendipity to once again provide the means. Serendipity hadn't let me down yet.

In the meantime, my class from Tenmaya Department Store gave me a farewell party. Each member made a speech in English and then I was given an expensive sweater. I was somewhat of a celebrity at Tenmaya, after I participated in their annual company Olympic games. It had been the first time a *gaijin* (foreigner) had ever taken part in that annual event. Needless to say, I was honored.

Soon after, I was asked to give a speech on the Japan—Republic of Korea Normalization Treaty to English clubs from ten Japanese universities, all located in the Chugoku District. It was part of a yearly three-day camp at Shizutani.

After spending several weeks preparing, I spoke for 30 minutes and answered questions for an hour and a half. Most of the questions came from a student who was steeped in Communist ideology. However, I believe I won the day with the great majority of students in the audience.

In 1960, President Eisenhower's visit to Japan had to be cancelled because of protests by "snake dancing" radical Zengakuren students, most of whom were communists. Apparently, some of those leanings still existed among small factions of University students.

Besides studying Japanese, the Japanese martial and fine arts, and the country's history, I continued reading books on many subjects. I finished reading *The Taming of the Nations*, which I found to be enlightening. Northrop's insight into global cultural assumptions is joined to the difficulties of world peace. It has been said that his observations were accurate to the degree that the book was prophetic, as he predicted the inevitable rise of Islam.

It was time to take off for Tokyo, with no job or place to stay in sight. Okusan, the three maids, and baby Tomoko-chan waved goodbye as I left the Akazawas' home by taxi at 9:00 in the morning.

At the train station waiting to see me off, were five managers and a secretary from my English class at the tobacco company, one of my high school students, beautiful Miyoko, Matsumoto-san and daughter, Suto, Momoda, Mizuuchi, and Yamada-san. It was a gratifying send-off. My dear friend Yoshiko rode on the train with me as far as Osaka.

I had only one solid contact in Tokyo. Shunsaku Nakajima met me at the train station. After a pleasant dinner at his home, Shunsaku, his brother, and I discussed politics for three hours.

The next day, I checked into my old standby, the YMCA. My room cost 1,000 yen a day, about $3 U.S. I hit the ground running, making contact by phone with people who had offered to help me find jobs teaching English and a family to live with. At the U.S. Embassy, I talked with Mr. Christensen, an economic counselor, who promised to help me in my purpose to study and observe the Japanese Diet (Congress) in action.

On day three, I went to a department store to see about a teaching job. No luck, even though I had taught at such a store in Okayama. I walked the cold, windy streets to eight other companies with the same results.

Shunsaku and I went for a bowl of noodles at suppertime. We then headed off to a party given by some of his friends. There I saw a vision in a tight, yellow knit dress. I was soon conversing with Kazuko-san in my faltering Japanese. Despite my stumbling efforts, there seemed a romantic spark between us.

The next evening Kazuko and I spent several hours talking at a coffee shop. This was only day four in Tokyo and I was infatuated by her looks, figure, manner, allure, and femininity. Wow! During the day, I had spent the time making cold calls to find a teaching job with no success. Her presence provided a soothing balm for my flagging spirit. It was December 30.

There I was, in the world's largest city, on New Year's Eve. Kazuko and I paid a visit to the seven best hotels in our rounds to eat, drink, and be merry, and observe the varied festivities to bring in the New Year. This was our third night in a row together. My Japanese was improving at breakneck speed. Fireworks went off all night long.

Then, it was the first day of the New Year. With it came some doubts and fears. I still had no permanent Visa, no job, and no place to live lined up. What a challenge laid ahead! Poverty was closing in.

The YMCA would have to do until I got a break. That morning while I was shaving, I met two French brothers, Jacques, a French West Point graduate, and Bernard Gourcuechon. They invited me to join the Foreign Legion, and I was greatly tempted. Actually, they asked me to look them up when I got to Paris. They worked for the French TV Network and were on a filming mission in Japan.

Not having anything else to do on January 2, I walked through the Emperor's Imperial Palace grounds. They are open to the public only two days a year. The Palace sits in the center of the city on the site of the original Edo Castle. It was where the Shogun was located in the Edo period from 1603-1868. The Castle was the largest in Japan and surrounded by double moats.

As I walked the impressive grounds, I thought to myself, *It was just twenty short years ago that World War II ended and my Uncle Millet was released from a Japanese prison camp.* What a difference twenty years makes. And there I was immersed in the Japanese culture where my uncle had been beaten and suffered every degradation imaginable over a three-year period.

With money running low, it was an all out push to find a job. On January 5, I met the following people in their offices: Okutsu at Pan American Airlines, Mr. Weeks at Quantas Airlines, and Mr. Takeda at Air France, among others. It was airline day. Nothing took off. After all this hustle, I got completely lost looking for the Diamond Hotel and ended up right back where I had started walking an hour before. I had gone in a big circle and was made painfully aware of the saying, "Going around in circles." Things just had to get better.

The next day I was back on the streets determined to get less lost than I was the day before. I knocked on the doors of Shiseido, Fujita Travel, and Ga-mo-san, the General Manager of the world famous Okura Hotel. The Okura was considered the best hotel in Japan and one of the top ten hotels in the world. My philosophy was to always go for the best.

That evening, being a Toastmaster, I attended the Toastmasters meeting at the American Club. I was determined to leave no stone unturned. One never knew where one might stumble on a job. It was Thursday.

CHAPTER 35
Serendipity Ichiban

Hour by hour, resolve firmly, like a man,
to do what comes to hand with a correct
and natural dignity, and with humanity,
independence and justice...
— Marcus Aurelius

Ichiban means "number one" in Japanese and serendipity is defined as an aptitude for making desirable discoveries by accident.

On Friday, great good fortune came my way. Noda-san, President of the world-famous Okura Hotel, rang me at my plush suite at the YMCA. He asked me to come to his office at 11:00 a.m.

Mr. Noda offered me a job as a hotel advisor and English teacher at his world-class hotel. And what would I get in return? For eight hours a day, sometimes on a split shift, I would get a grand room in the hotel and all my meals free. I sure was going to miss the YMCA. My life had taken a turn from night to day. I was on my way in Tokyo.

I had come upon the best job I could possibly have gotten in Tokyo. What this meant was that I was then free to go out and teach English at companies to bring in cash. In the meantime, I would be living and eating in style. Heaven had smiled down on me once again.

It was now going to be possible to take Kazuko out for a fancy bowl of noodles. I did just that. She was impressed. I was in awe.

That very afternoon I went to all the fancy department stores in the famous Ginza area trying to line up jobs to teach English. By always laying extensive groundwork, something good would always come if it.

On Saturday, things kept moving at an exciting pace. Nagai-san, who worked for the steel export department of Okura Trading Company, took me to lunch. We discussed terms for my teaching English at his company. Hotel Okura and his company had no connection, only the name.

At 2:00 that afternoon, I met the Mitsuda family at their home. He was a medical doctor at Tokyo University. At 7:00 that evening, I met the Yamagishi family. I was always amazed at how one contact lead to another. Of course,

Clarke with students of one of his English classes for Japanese engineers.
A great comradeship developed with this group.

it seemed everyone in Japan was interested in hearing and speaking English. But no one could ever quite understand "Y'all" for some strange reason. It was just simple, pure "Texan."

On the day I moved into the Okura Hotel, it had been exactly nine months since I arrived in Japan. This was right on schedule for the plan I had set for Tokyo. Every once in a while, my plans hit the mark. It was January 9.

The hotel furnished me with two uniforms that looked like something one would be married in—in Japan. I looked rather "spiffy" in my gray and black striped pants.

My first teaching job was outside the Tokyo area. It was at the Bridgestone Tire Factory where I had eight engineers in the class. This started just three days after moving into the Okura. It took one and a half-hour by train to reach the factory.

My second teaching job was at Okura Trading Company. It also had eight men in the class, most were business graduates from Waseda University.

With only three weeks under my belt in Tokyo, all was going unbelievably well. I had teaching jobs, a famous hotel to live in, an alluring girlfriend, and many new Japanese friends. It was a blessing I didn't have a car, because I wouldn't have lived long in the kamikaze traffic.

One Sunday afternoon, Kazuko-san took me to see the Olympic Stadium, a most impressive sight. After dinner, we watched TV at the hotel. My Japanese was improving by leaps and bounds, given she couldn't speak a word of English.

What an incredible world it is. Prince Juan Carlos and Princess Sophia of Spain showed up for a stay at the Okura. I renewed my friendship with them. It had been three years since I had been assigned to assist them during their honeymoon stay at the Royal Hawaiian.

The Prince and Princess were astonished to see me at the Okura. Of course, it was a pleasure having the privilege to serve them once again. During their stay, the royal couple were received by the Emperor and Empress of Japan.

My third teaching job came when I signed up Daimaru Department Store. I was now bringing in around $1,000 U.S. a month. This was good money in those days, especially when one had no housing or food costs.

My "old friend" from the Royal Hawaiian, movie star Charlton Heston, checked into the hotel one night when I was on duty. I greeted him with, "Aloha, Mr. Heston, it's nice to see you again." He had no clue who I was until I mentioned the Royal. Then, he was warm and gracious as usual.

In line with my desire to learn about the Japanese government, I spent an afternoon in the Japanese Diet listening to Prime Minister Sato and his cabinet members make their policy speeches on the forthcoming session. On a Sunday, Kazuko accompanied me to see the election of the Chairman of the Japanese Socialist Party at their lively convention.

Yoshiko called from Okayama to give me the bad news that my passport Visa was expiring in five days. Here we go again! She said, "The man at Immigration was adamant and not even Prime Minister Sato can help you this time." Well, we'd see about that.

Win some and lose some, but hold the record. Nothing worked. I was made to believe that I held the all time record in renewing a tourist Visa in Japan. On the positive side, Tokyo Immigration gave me some extra time to leave the country to get a new visa. It took me a whole day at the Immigration and Ministry of Justice to work it out. The cheapest way, but not the most pleasant way, was to take an old, small cargo-passenger ship to Okinawa. So be it. The next day I bought my ticket and had my Alien Registration booklet renewed.

The hotel manager kindly provided me a leave of absence to go out of the country to get a new Visa. As for my job at the Okura, I'd found most of the men at the front desk staff cold to work with. I could almost taste the aloofness and feel the palpable resentment in the air. No matter, I took care of the English-speaking guests far better than they did, making many new friends from around the world.

Kazuko and I went to a movie on a Sunday. We had to stand the whole time. It was same every Sunday at every place in Tokyo—always busy and overcrowded. We spent almost every Sunday together.

As some who have been to Tokyo know, the Imperial Hotel was designed by Frank Lloyd Wright and was one of the few buildings still standing after the great earthquake. After work one day, Henry Kramer had me over for dinner at his house, also designed by Mr. Wright. It was a marvel.

Over lunch several days later with Mr. Lei, Mr. Lee, and Mr. Hsu of the Nationalist Chinese Embassy, we discussed the situation between Taiwan and Communist China. They offered to help me when the time came for me to head for that island nation.

On February 21st, I boarded the ship *Naminoue Maru*. It looked the worse for wear and a smaller ship than I would have preferred. Fortunately, no storms were on the horizon.

At 4:30 in the afternoon, the small 2,500-ton, cargo-passenger ship sailed from Harumi Pier. *With a little luck, we will make it to Okinawa*, I prayed. The sun was setting in its usual red-colored glow.

As Tokyo disappeared from sight, I thought, *What one must go through to renew a visa*. Of course, being low on money I had no choice in the matter. The entry in my diary that evening was quite shaky due to me bunking on the floor with over fifty Japanese. The ship was pitching and rolling like there was no tomorrow. *Those seasickness pills better work, or there is going to be trouble on the high seas*, I worried.

We slept with the lights on all night. Sleeping two inches to my right was a grandmother. Two inches to my left was an attractive college girl. The small room we were crammed into had no portholes. People were lying shoulder-to-shoulder; foot-to-foot; the air was stale; and the snoring out of this world. We ate our meals where we slept, a bowl of rice and bowl of soup. And these were the first class accommodations. I pitied those in second class! I wrote in my diary, as the ship pitched up and down in the high seas, "These are, undoubtedly, the worst conditions I've ever experienced on a ship. If I just had some rosary beads and a bottle of whiskey." Again, I was proving to be no sailor.

Luckily, no one spoke English or wanted to practice it. I was in no condition to talk. The next morning we arrived at the port of Kagoshima at the southern tip of Japan. *Blessed land!* I rejoiced. I could hardly walk on my sea legs.

Hirata-san was there to greet me at the dock. I had met her on an earlier trip overland to that city. She spoke not a word of English, so my Japanese was getting another good workout.

We went to her little house on a hillside and had tea with her sweet old mother. After three hours of welcome shore leave, it was back to the slave ship.

Another rough night! I turned at least four shades of green. *If I could endure this voyage, I could endure almost anything*, was my only semi-positive thought. We docked at Naha, Okinawa at noon. I felt only half alive.

Any place would have been exciting and beautiful after that voyage. After getting my visa, I walked the town, had a square meal for a change, and exchanged some money on the black market, which was common there. My second "shore leave" lasted five blessed hours before boarding the *Queen Kong* once again. *God, spare me!* I prayed.

It was another "rocking" night! At Kagoshima, Hirata-san was again waiting for me. We had a lovely dinner at her home and then went dancing. After a hot bath in the wooden tub, I slept like a baby. The world had righted itself once again.

I wasn't about to "ride the waves" back to Tokyo. I got up at 6:00 in the morning to have breakfast with pretty Hirata before catching a train to Kumamoto. Such kindness from her and her mother was deeply appreciated. After exploring Kumamoto, I boarded another train and arrived in Fukuoka at 6:30 that evening. I walked the town, had dinner, and caught the 9:55. That was when my troubles began!

The train was jammed with people standing packed like sardines right up to the doors in the vestibules. I lacked only 300 yen, about $1 U.S., being able to buy a reserved seat in first class, so I started dodging conductors.

After three hours of dodging and continually being caught sitting in first class coaches, I finally borrowed the small amount of money needed from two high school students. I had met them while we were dodging conductors together. From 2:00—6:30 in the morning, I slept peacefully in my first class seat. Those conductors really did their job. Just like everything in Japan, they were highly organized.

It was March 1 when I arrived back in Tokyo. The next day I started back on my usual hotel shift, 8:00—12:00 noon and 8:00—12:00 midnight.

The second major plane crash at the Tokyo airport within a month occurred on the night of March 4. John, one of our frequent and well-liked guests, was among the victims. It hit me hard, as I had said goodbye to him that evening. It showed me just how important it is to live every single day—for it can end in a flash.

With my best friend Murai-san at a Zen temple.

CHAPTER 36

The Setting of the Rising Sun

*People travel to wonder at the height of the
mountains, at the huge waves of the seas,
at the long course of the rivers, at the vast
compass of the ocean, at the circular motion of
the stars, and yet they pass themselves without
wondering.*

— St. Augustine

*I*t had been eleven months since I'd arrived in this special land of geishas, samurai legends, Zen, cherry blossoms, and the martial arts—and ultra efficiency. It was time to begin closing the book on Japan and opening a new one on *who knew what* kinds of adventures.

This had been a period in my life that opened up a way of living and thinking that was totally different from anything I had ever known. There had been a great deal of adjusting on my part. With uncertainty and soul searching being a part of being human, I'd had more than my share in this sometime bewildering country.

There were still some interesting people to meet and greet before sailing into the sunset. I had lunch with Hans Baerwald, a distinguished American political scientist who was in the process of making a study of the Japanese Diet. He had served in the Government Section in General MacArthur's Supreme Command Allied Powers during America's occupation of Japan. Baerwald wrote the definitive book on the purge of Japanese wartime leaders titled *The Japanese Leaders Under the Occupation.*

One evening while working at the front desk, an attractive young woman appeared before me. Naturally, I asked her where she was from. Her name was Marta and she was the daughter of the Argentine Ambassador to India. After a pleasant conversation, she said, "Clarke, be sure and look me up when you get to India." I told her I sure would. This was truly an international world for a young Texan working in Tokyo.

As my days in Japan were coming to an end, I had lunch at the Foreign

Correspondent's Club with the Japan Manager for Carrier Corporation, the company my dad worked for; visited the Tokyo stock exchange; was the guest of Rafael Zaera, a counselor at the Spanish Embassy, at the bi-monthly Toastmasters meeting; had a two hour talk one evening with Senór Ayerza from Argentina who had met with Japan's Finance Minister that day; struck up a friendship at the front desk with Pedro Almada, whose father was a general in Mexico; got to be friends with John Pickup from London (with that name he would fit in well in Texas); and so it went, meeting interesting and important people.

My list of worldwide contacts was growing by leaps and bounds. I didn't have much money but I was rich in friends and influential contacts. That was invaluable when I arrived a stranger in strange lands.

On April 2, I packed up my things at the Okura Hotel and said Sayonara to my Japanese friends there, along with sweet Kazuko. Shunsaku Nakajima, the friend who greeted me at the Tokyo train station when I first arrived, again helped me out. We took a train to the station near his home. I was a guest in his family's home once again. Just the week before, I had gotten him a job as a room boy at the hotel.

Mr. Lei at the Chinese (Taiwan) Embassy helped me secure my visa in record time. Even better, he arranged my passage "On a Slow Boat to China." Actually, it was a banana boat set to sail on April 29.

After getting my visa, I was interviewed by a reporter from the Mai-nichi newspaper. On April 19th, an article and my picture appeared in the newspaper. It was titled, "Marco Polo from Texas." I liked that title.

There was time for a bit more sightseeing after finishing up at the Okura. On April 4, my faithful friend, Shunsaku, saw me off at Tokyo Station. One hour later, I was in Kamakura, home to the Great Buddha.

The great bronze statue was cast in 1252 and was originally located in a large temple hall. The temple buildings were washed away by a tsunami tidal wave at the end of the 15th century, and since then the Buddha has stood in the open air.

My life of traveling was never without challenges but there were times that things hit right. By train and bus, I journeyed to the famous resort area of Hakone. Kimura-san, manager of the Hakone Hotel, gave me a "comp" room. It never hurt to ask. He had one of his employees give me a tour around town.

From Hakone, it was by bus to Japan's most famous resort, Atami. I had little money in my pocket and a small, old, beat-up suitcase. I checked at several hotels to see if I could pull off another "comp" room, being a hotelman myself. No one seemed impressed. It must have been my blue jeans and tennis shoes.

I walked the streets and at the fourth hotel my luck changed as I walked into Atami's newest and best hotel. Thirty minutes later, I occupied the best suite in the city with a view of everything. It just goes to show the value of never giving up. Roughing it was fun, especially when I had a luxurious place to sleep.

For the third night in a row in Nagoya, I was able to get a free room. With such good fortune, I decided to splurge. After a relaxing Turkish bath, a Japanese doll, clad only in panties and a bra, massaged my back by walking on it. I had always wanted to try that. Once was enough. My back hasn't been the same since.

Arriving in Okayama, I received a warm welcome from my Japanese family. It was April 9, my one year anniversary in that intriguing, and sometime frustrating, country. That evening I composed a letter to Mr. Koo, General Manager of the new President Hotel in Taiwan, setting forth the terms I hoped to work under in Taipei, as if the job were already mine. In two weeks, I would set sail for that island nation.

A week later, I got a letter from Mr. Koo telling me I could start to work at the hotel as soon as I arrived. It was like manna from heaven.

My big aluminum trunk went by truck to Kobe where it would be put on my ship to Free China (Taiwan). I mailed home a box with books and other items, and packed the rest of my belongings in two suitcases to take with me. It would not be long before I would need a pack mule to make my way around.

Of all days, the day I was supposed to leave Okayama for the last time, a nationwide strike by the railway workers was called. I knew they planned it just to spite me. Luckily, I got on one of the few trains running. Yoshiko, great friend that she was, accompanied me to Kobe to assist with any last minute disasters.

And there were disasters. Together she and I accomplished small miracles in the short four hours after the train pulled into Kobe Station. To start with, we got off one station too early. Then the hotel couldn't find her reservation. When we called the shipping company, the clerk said, "The ship has been delayed from today (April 27) until May 13." Terrific, my visa was expiring that very day. To make matters worse, it started raining non-stop.

I had to arrange for another ship immediately. There went my discount on the ticket that had been arranged. We went to three places before finding the right place to buy a ticket. That's when I found out I couldn't go to Taiwan without a cholera shot. *I'm sure to get cholera now*, I thought. In fact, I was sure I then held the world record for the number of cholera shots. It was so absurd it had become a joke.

I had to literally talk my way onto the only ship sailing. It was so full, they gave me a couch in the smoking room. The other ten passengers on the banana boat were heavy smokers. I considered buying a gas mask.

With grim determination, Yoshiko and I plowed ahead against all obstacles. I got my passport stamped with an extension visa. There was one bright spot in the gloom, however, Hashimoto-san at the Oriental Hotel gave me a free room. Being a hotelman-of-sorts was still coming in handy.

At 6:00 in the evening on April 29, waving a fond farewell to Yoshiko, my banana boat sailed for China. Without her kind help, I would never have made it. We still keep in touch after these many years and she and her son have visited us in Texas.

Lafcadio Hearn, the great scholar of Japan in the 19th century, wrote in his *Japanese Letters*, "What an education the Orient is! How it opens a man's eyes and mind about his own country, about conventionalisms of a hundred sorts—about false ideals and idealisms—about ethical questions."

CHAPTER 37

On a Slow Boat to China

*The strength of Confucianism is its confidence
in truth, in the validity of moral values, and
in the dignity of man.*

— Anonymous

*L*uckily, at the last minute, a space opened up in a cabin on the M/V Atai, a Taiwanese banana boat. My roommate was Mr. Lo, a Shanghai-born Chinese. He could speak and understand English fairly well, my Chinese being almost non-existent at the time.

It was smooth sailing the next day and I stayed mostly on deck, as far away from the smoking room as possible. At nine in the evening, Wan, the third mate, gave me a lesson on the positions of certain stars and how they are used in navigation.

The bright moonlight reflected on the calm sea, the ship cutting billows of white spray, and this made for an enchanting sight. Especially since I wasn't seasick—for a change.

At mealtimes, the two girls on my right spoke Japanese, the others spoke Chinese, and Lo and I spoke English. The Chinese food served aboard was surprisingly tasty.

Liang, the second mate, explained the chart and navigational instruments to me in Japanese. Japan ruled Taiwan for almost fifty years, so many of the Taiwanese could speak the language.

On May 3, we docked at Kaohsiung, three hours behind schedule. Kaohsiung was the major southern port of Taiwan. Here I went again! It was a day to remember because of the difficulties encountered. I wouldn't have known what to do if things went smoothly.

The authorities wouldn't let me disembark because I had no ticket out of Taiwan. "Why hadn't someone told me this?" I asked the man in charge. I bought a ticket for Japan to pacify him, even though it seriously depleted the meager funds I possessed.

They said they would send for a ticket right away. After I'd waited three hours, I lost my temper, "I'm going to call President Chiang Kai-Shek for delaying me like this." The ticket soon arrived. I'm sure Chiang would have gotten right on it.

By that time, it was too late to catch a train to Taipei, which was on the far northern part of the island. As I strolled around town that evening, I found half of the U.S. Navy on leave there. *Tomorrow has got to be better*, I speculated.

Better day? It was perfect! I embarked on a scenic six-hour train ride to Taipei. A special hotel limousine was waiting to pick me up at the station. This was too good to be true. Mr. Koo, the General Manager of the beautiful new President Hotel, had a spacious room waiting for me. "I was in like Flynn," as the saying goes.

God, what a fright! On the third night after I arrived, I was sitting at the desk in my room writing in my diary. All of a sudden, the hotel started moving left and right. I opened my door. Guests were running out into the hallway in their nightclothes screaming. There was one guy in his jockey underwear. I quickly darted back into the room and stood with my hands on the door jams of the bathroom door. If I was going down, it would be holding on for dear life.

After several minutes, the earthquake subsided with the hotel still standing. *Welcome to Taiwan*! I said to myself. No one can know a more helpless feeling than being on the ninth floor during such a quake. Once in a lifetime is enough, not knowing whether you will live or die.

What a deal I had at the hotel, except for the earthquakes. For working four hours a day at the front desk, helping to train staff and setting an example of how to take care of guests, I received my room and meals free. Teaching English would provide cash flow.

My name cards arrived, so I was official. It is absolutely necessary to have name cards in the Orient. Without them, you're a nobody. I was now a semi-broke somebody.

When I started studying the history of Taiwan, I discovered some interesting facts. Its modern history goes back 400 years, to the day when the first Western ship passed by the island. Jan Van Linschoten, a Dutch navigator on a Portuguese ship, exclaimed "Ilha Formosa" which meant beautiful island. The name Formosa stuck.

In 1895, the Japanese defeated the Manchu Chinese Imperial troops in the Sino-Japanese War. In the Treaty of Shimonoseki, China ceded Taiwan to Japan "forever."

The Japanese occupation was harsh. When World War II ended in 1945, the Allied powers agreed that Chiang Kai-Shek's troops would temporarily occupy Taiwan. In 1949, Chiang lost the war on mainland China and fled to Taiwan. Formosa/Taiwan became the Republic of China.

H. Wong from Hong Kong introduced me to the Peitou Hot Springs resort one Sunday afternoon. It had been designed and built by the Japanese during their occupation. It was known as a paradise for men. It was one hotel after another full of beautiful Chinese women, delivered by motorcycles on a moment's notice. I had never seen anything like it in my life.

Modeled after the baths at Izusan in Japan, it became the largest hot spring facility in Southeast Asia. One of the Japanese buildings, built in 1921, became a rest house during World War II for the kamikaze squadron before they launched off in their planes to crash into American ships.

I settled into a happy, exciting, and comfortable life in Taiwan. I turned 28 years old there and had been on the adventure trail for almost five years. My plan was to continue adventuring for another five years.

At the May Day Celebration, Chiang Kai-Shek was inaugurated for his fourth term as president. Over 200,000 people were assembled in front of the Presidential Office Building to cheer him when he appeared on the balcony. I had been reading about Chiang and seeing him in "movietone news" since I was a small boy. It was somewhat of a historic moment for me.

I began teaching English to a Mrs. Lu. It was an interesting challenge. I was using Japanese to teach her English, because it was the only language we had in common. The pay made it worth the effort.

As I was shaving one morning, the hotel began rocking again. It was my second earthquake. *This isn't anytime to be shaving*, I feared. Nothing else seemed important when the very earth was trembling nine floors below one's feet. I threw my razor down, grabbed on to the door jam, and started praying.

Once again, the hotel did not collapse, but I was starting to have my doubts about what would happen with the next "big" one.

While working at the front desk one morning, I answered the phone and heard, "This is the Pan American Airways stewardess in 312," the feminine voice said, "My suitcase has been lost and I don't have anything to wear." This could prove very interesting. "How can I help you," I answered. "Do you have anything I can wear?" she said. "Well, let me check," I replied. She also wanted to move to another room because of the loud repair work going on near her room.

I rode to the rescue with a key for a quiet room and one of my cotton Japanese kimonos. This blond beauty came out of her room wearing my kimono, barefooted, a pillow in one hand, and her purse and shoes in the other. We proceeded down the length of the 3rd floor corridor, up the back stairs to the fourth floor, and into her new room.

Fortunately, no guests saw us, or they would have wondered what in high heaven I was up to. That is how I came to know Desiree from Paris. I got back my perfumed kimono that night. There is no business like the hotel business!

My two months in Taiwan were drawing to a close. I had notched another "first class hotel" on my working experience belt and had gotten to know the history and people of "Free China."

The Front Office and Reservations Staff threw a fun going away party for me. I had become friends with them all. And Mr. Koo, the General Manager, had treated me like a prince. What a delightful time and experience it had been.

C.B. Chen at China Travel Service arranged my sailing date for June 30. Early that morning, I had a farewell breakfast with Mr. Koo. He arranged for the hotel limo to deliver me to the sea terminal at Keelung on the northern tip of Taiwan.

CHAPTER 38

The World of the King and I

*In the universe, there are things that are
known, and things that are unknown, and in
between, there are doors.*
— William *Blake*

As I stepped out of the hotel's black limo at the Keelung Sea Terminal, it was as if mass hysteria had ignited. Hundreds of people were yelling, pushing, talking, and going in all directions. *Could this be a Chinese fire drill?* I wondered. If it wasn't, it was a darn good representation of one. Never had I seen such chaos. My first thought was, *Had my boat sunk at the dock?*

The problem was everyone was trying to get through customs inspection at once I quickly learned. Bob, an American angel, appeared from nowhere and offered to help me, since he had already been cleared through customs. Doing it myself would have been like going through a Marine Corps obstacle course. I thanked Bob profusely for his assistance.

Before moving on to Thailand, I was returning to Hong Kong first. At 2:30 in the afternoon, we sailed for the Fragrant Harbor. The date was July 1. On the morning of July 3, the ship arrived at the opening to the harbor.

It was 7:30 that morning, when my passport was returned to me by a Customs Officer. It was pure chaos, again, getting off the ship. *What is going on?* I wondered. I had to carry my two suitcases and a big trunk off by myself. This was the fun part of traveling, but it did tend to keep one in shape.

I called my friend Fred Aw who was expecting me. He drove down to the docks to pick me up. Off we went to his spacious, luxurious apartment overlooking Repulse Bay. We jumped into our swimsuits and headed for the beach.

That evening, Fred and I were joined by Tina, his Chinese movie star girlfriend, for dinner at the plush Repulse Bay Hotel. It was almost as if I had come home again to that sparkling city of oriental enchantment.

How do I get to Thailand? was the big question then facing me.

Meanwhile, back at Fred's place, he introduced me to Alice, an alluring Chinese girl who lived in the same high-rise condos. Not only was she good-looking, but some kind of rich. She invited me to go water skiing with her at Repulse Bay the next day.

As we were sitting on the speedboat getting ready to ski, I saw a Chinese girl about fourteen years of age yelling for help thirty yards away. She was starting to slip under the water when I got to her. Saving her was my good deed for the day.

At that very time, danger was lurking far out to sea. Typhoons were a constant threat in Hong Kong and Lola was to hit with full force several days later.

I was thankful Lola hadn't hit when I was on the high seas. She hit full force as I was attending a Toastmasters dinner at the Mandarin Hotel overlooking the harbor. I had no choice but to spend the night in the hotel. There was one compensation—I got the room free.

Twelve days after coming back to Hong Kong, I bought a ship ticket for Bangkok. It set me back $78 U.S. Of course, I had no contacts or job lined up in Thailand but it was time to roll the dice once again.

I wrote letters to the owners of two hotels in Bangkok. Over lunch, Major Stanley, Director of the Hong Tourist Association, kindly gave me an impressive "To Whom It May Concern" recommendation letter, and told me to look up a Mrs. Swan. In addition, I started making telephone calls to line up any and all contacts possible.

My passenger-cargo ship was delayed twice. To pass the time, I finished reading *Great Lives, Great Deeds*.

It was July 28 when we sailed out of the harbor on the *Hai Hing*. I'd never seen a calmer sea. The Good Lord was watching over me, as two typhoons had passed through Hong Kong in the last several weeks. I was not in the mood to be deathly seasick again.

I was up at seven in the morning to welcome the sunrise and then absorbed a gorgeous sunset into my soul that evening. Ah, the pleasures of sailing under such splendid conditions! Then came the full moon to illuminate our nightly course.

Our soft-spoken Norwegian captain had never seen such a big eater as me. On land, I was on a tight budget. On the ship, meals were included. I ate as if there were no tomorrow.

On July 30, we spent all day steaming within sight of the coast of South Vietnam. Although it looked peaceful, a war was fiercely raging through the length and breadth of the country.

The target date I had set to arrive in Bangkok was August 1st. Barring any unforeseen problems, I would arrive in the Land of Smiles right on schedule. That evening the ship laid anchor in the Gulf of Thailand at the entrance of the river that would take us to Bangkok. We had been at sea four days. I was restless and anxious to get back on land. I was still no sailor.

I had $7 U.S. in my pocket and $133 U.S. being sent by check from Hong Kong. I had no hint of a job, no friends, and no place to stay. One must always have hope.

We lay at anchor all the next day so to keep myself occupied, I checked the shelves in the ship's small library, got all the books I could find on Thailand and set to reading.

In 1238, two Thai chieftains rebelled against Khmer (Cambodia) domination and established the first independent Thai kingdom at Ayutthaya. In 1767, Burmese invaders destroyed this capital. This angered the Thais tremendously and they quickly threw the Burmese out. Since that time, the Thais have never been conquered or controlled by any other country. They are still fiercely independent.

The Kingdom of Thailand was known as Siam until 1939. Bhumibol was crowned king in 1950 and Thais now revere his son, King Bhumibol, as a semi-deity.

We ended up sitting out in the Gulf for five days. Eighteen ships were now lined up waiting on the Bangkok Bar. Thank goodness for books. I started reading *The Rise and Fall of the Third Reich,* and lost all track of time.

The problem had been a strike by dockworkers. On the sixth day, we headed up river. It took three hours to reach Bangkok's docks. From there it would be a half-hour's car ride to the city itself. At nine the next morning, I got a free ride to the YMCA, my home away from home. It had no walls but did have mosquito nets over the bunks. One of the giant mosquitoes tried to make off with my suitcase. And I thought we had big mosquitoes in Texas.

I had enough money in my pocket for two nights' lodging at the Y, a little bus fare, and some bowls of rice. The $133 check I had mailed to a local bank better had arrived, or it was going to be "starvation city."

First thing, I took a bus to the Rama Hotel. I waited two hours to see the General Manager, Mr. Handl. I had no time to waste, but plenty of time to wait when it came to getting a job.

Even though Mr. Handl had no job available, he generously provided me with a truck and a driver to pick my trunk up from the ship. When we got back, I was introduced to Tritip Telen, the owner of the hotel. Mr. Telen suggested I go meet several other important people.

After opening up a checking account at the bank with the grand sum of $133, I went to the Tourist Organization of Thailand Office where I met General Chalermchai, The Director. "Clarke, we may be able to use you as a part-time teacher in our hotel training school and I will have someone check on hotel jobs for you," he said.

Next, I was off to meet the General Manager of the new Siam Intercontinental Hotel. No luck there. My feelings that day were fluctuating between hope and discouragement. The owner of the Imperial Hotel seemed to have some interest, but the owner of the President Hotel gave me no hope at all. At my last stop of the day, the Asia Hotel, the manager said, "Sorry, we don't hire broke Texans," or words similar to that effect.

In one day, I had made some excellent contacts. *There just had to be a hotel in Bangkok desperate to put my hotel and people skills to work*, I thought to myself. One might have said I was desperate.

The next morning, I decided to give Mrs. Swan a call. Major Stanley in Hong Kong had given me her name. I called. Mrs. Swan, an American, said, "Why don't you come out to the house this morning. I'd love to meet and visit with you." She told me which bus to take and I was on my way.

As I stepped off the bus, I searched for the right street number on Larn Luang Road. The number I was looking for was across the street, but that was one of the royal palaces. *No way*, I thought, *Mrs. Swan hadn't mentioned she lived on the royal palace grounds*. Sure enough, she did. There is nothing like starting at the top.

The guard at the open, giant iron-gate had a rifle slung over his shoulder. I said humbly, "Does Mrs. Swan live here?" He shook his head yes and pointed me down a specific driveway that curved to the left.

The grounds were beautifully manicured with lots of towering trees. I came to a large two-story house and knocked on the door. A Thai servant girl greeted me with a warm smile. Mrs. Swan graciously welcomed me into her Thai-style house. I came to find out it had been used as a study for one of the kings of Thailand.

This grand, white-haired lady had lived in Bangkok for a number of years. She had become friends with some of the royal family, eventually moving into that setting of subdued splendor.

After hearing my story of travel and the state of my funds, almost nil, Mrs.

At home in Bangkok on palace grounds—
once the study of a Thai King.

Swan said, "I have lots of extra room in this grand house and you are welcome to stay here until you find a job, Clarke." Never had I had a more glorious offer. *Do the King and Queen ever drop by for coffee?* I wondered.

Just about that time, some of the royal family dropped by. It was Ying and two of her young children. I later came to learn that Ying would have been Queen of Thailand, had her royal fiancée not been assassinated at the age of 22 under peculiar circumstances. More friends and royal relatives showed up for dinner. What a way to begin my life in Siam!

I moved from the YMCA to the palace grounds the very next day. Strange as it seemed, a new hotel was just about to open across the street. My first thought was, *I'll go over and apply for anything I can get—bellman, front desk clerk, dishwasher, or whatever.*

This was one of those acute times in my life when the next week or so could turn out either very good or very bad. I went to the front desk of the Rajasupamitra (R.S.) Hotel and asked to see the manager. I was soon escorted to the owner's office. Mr. Wong, who spoke no English, was of Chinese descent. The rumor was that he had made his fortune in gold smuggling and decided to build the hotel to cash in on American soldiers coming from Vietnam in droves.

Mr. Wong's assistant, who had the look of a Chinese triad mafia guy, spoke some English. After he heard I was an experienced hotel man, he went to get the Thai partner in the operation. Clearly, they were desperate.

Kun Prachuab was a kind man who spoke perfect English. We hit it off immediately. He asked me where I was staying. "At the palace," I said. This seemed to take him aback. "You mean across the street?" he asked.

"Yes, sir." He must have thought, *This guy is either a liar deluxe or he knows the king.* Actually, I told him how I came to know Mrs. Swan.

"I would like to meet her," he said.

"Sure," I answered back.

The next thing I knew, I was signing a contract to officially become the Manager of the newest hotel in Bangkok. I was given a penthouse suite to live in that overlooked the entire city. In ten days' time, I had literally gone from rags to riches. It was like a dream, as once more serendipity came through.

My passport visa had been due to expire a week later. All was well. With a high salary, a penthouse suite, all my meals and drinks free, and laundry and dry cleaning thrown in for good measure, I was more than set to relish Bangkok to its full.

All I needed to do was get the hotel officially opened and fill it up. No sweat! I hardly knew anyone in the Thai capital, had no clue how I would accomplish this mission, and on top of that had to get the staff properly trained, but I was ready for the challenge. This was going to be a real trip.

To celebrate my first day on the job, I invited Udomlock for dinner at the hotel, now that I could afford dinner. She was the Thai model-dancer-movie star I had dated in Hong Kong.

My next key contact, a Filipino, was General Vargas, the Commander of SEATO. It was akin to NATO in Europe, the Southeast Asia Treaty Organization (SEATO) was based in Thailand. The former First Lady of the Philippines' daughter, Terisita, had married General Vargas' son. Frankie and Terisita had told me to be sure and meet the general when I got to Thailand. He was most cordial and later wrote me a nice letter of recommendation.

I hoped the General would put up a visiting brigade in the hotel. I needed to attack on all fronts to win the room occupancy battle and bring the hotel into the black.

In the meantime, Mrs. Swan took me to a dinner to honor the Thai Foreign Minister. I was able to give my card to a number of prominent people and make some new friends. It didn't hurt that the President of the United States (LBJ) was a Texan.

Before the official opening of the hotel, I organized cocktails and dinner for all the travel agents, hotelmen, and airline people. I greeted and talked to every single one of them.

Two hotel men befriended me. Bernd Chrengel, from Germany, was the Assistant Manager of the Manohra Hotel and Darrell Konine, an American, was the Sales Manager of the Rama Hotel. Between them, they gave me sound guidance on procedures and steering through the hotel pitfalls in Bangkok.

Two days later, the hotel officially opened for business. We had one guest.

The beauty and grace of Thai classical dancers is something to behold.

CHAPTER 39

Living the Bangkok Life—King, President and All

*He was a romantic, a born traveler with the
indispensable gift of curiosity.*
— from *Jose Rizal*

Susie, a reporter with the Bangkok Post newspaper, and two of her girlfriends invited me to go to Pataya Beach after work one Friday. It was located several hours south of Bangkok.

She told me, "Pataya is a beautiful, secluded beach with a few small quaint hotels and cottages." I was ready for some relaxation after the recent hectic activity at the hotel. We arrived at eight in the evening. After a steak and lobster dinner, we were off to dance at Balbo's Bar.

Having been in Thailand for three weeks, I had had only one date. This sojourn to the beach could not be classified as a date but being with three pretty girls sure made it a pleasant weekend.

Back in Bangkok I began visiting businesses, U.S. Agencies, airline counters at the airport, and travel agencies to promote the hotel. However, "trouble in river city" flared up about this time. Pramuan, the leader of the Thai-Chinese inner circle in the hotel, was jealous of my having become the manager. It was a position he had thought he would fill, being the right-hand man to the Chinese co-owner. He had hired a number of his cronies in different positions, which didn't bode well.

Pramuan didn't have a clue about the hotel business. We had a direct confrontation in front of the staff at the front desk over a matter of policy. This guy looked and acted like Mr. Moto in one of the James Bond movies, so much so that it gave me a chill. If there was such a thing as a Thai Mafia, he had to be one of the leaders. This was more than a confrontation; it had a sinister aspect to it. But I was able to weather the storm, which was good, because I had royalty to attend to.

The former Queen of Thailand, the Queen Mother, was the guest of honor at Kun Prachuab's 35th wedding anniversary celebration that was hosted at the hotel.

There were over fifty distinguished Thai couples waiting in the hotel lobby for the Queen Mother to arrive. The men were in tuxes and the women in dazzling evening gowns. It was an awesome sight.

As the Queen Mother entered the lobby, every single person prostrated himself or herself on the floor in complete subservience to her presence. It was a scene right out of *The King and I*. I stood in amazement off in the wings. The couples did exactly the same thing when she departed the hotel. I couldn't imagine this happening any other place in the world.

Although I was able to hold things off with Pramuan until after the royal celebration, the big showdown finally came. He was undercutting everything I was trying to do. I met with Kun Prachuab. "Either they get rid of him or I would resign," I emphasized. Mr. Prachuab was a gentleman and a diplomat who well understood Pramuan would be worthless as a hotel manager. He put a stop to Pramuan's destructive meddling, even though I suspected I then had a contract put out on my life. This was a deep-seated feeling.

It was like day and night with the hotel staff the next day. The attitude of the staff who had been giving me a hard time, Pramuan's buddies, became one of cooperation. They apparently got the word, *Work as a team or you're gone.*

At the very last minute, the day my tourist visa was to expire, Mr. Prachuab guaranteed my stay. Saved once again in the nick of time, I owed this man great respect and gratitude, because he had battled for me from day one. Of course, he was a true Thai and that was the difference.

Jad, a Thai woman with the most beautiful eyes I'd ever seen, came to the hotel one evening and introduced herself. It wasn't only her eyes—it was everything. "Bernd told me to drop by and meet you," she said. I was almost at a loss for words in the presence of her stunning beauty. Bernd was my German friend who worked at another hotel. "Would you, er, ah, uh, care to have a drink?" I mumbled. "Oh, yes, that would be nice," Jad replied. Sparks were flying all over the place.

The Board of Investment had approved my visa. I was in the money, the hotel was starting to fill, and Pramuan had been put in his place, or so I thought.

Over the past month, I had met and become friends with a number of Thai Army officers. The Thai military has always been a powerful influence behind the scenes in the country. In 1957, in fact, a military coup led by Field Marshall Tharnarat overthrew Pibul and made General Kittekachorn the Premier.

If Pramuan directly threatened me, I could always call on my military buddies for backup. I subtly passed the word around so that the "evil one," as I called him, would get the word. I had actually been invited into the inner circle of the military "Young Turks" at the Turf Club (horseracing track). I believe my background as a Marine helped form the special bond that developed between us. *Bring it on, Pramuan, it will be your mafia against the military,* I imagined.

One evening some of the young Turks and I ended up checking out six different nightclubs, one being the "Sorry About That" Club. Somchye, one of the young Turks, and I had become especially good friends. Whenever I needed help or advice, he was always there.

As fate would have it, several days later, one of the girls at the reception desk called me over to the desk. She quietly whispered, even though no one else was in sight, "Be careful every time you go out of the hotel. Pramuan and his gang may try to harm you." So, it was confirmed, I was definitely in danger.

One evening, the Young Turks invited me to a birthday party at the Turf Club. I let Somchye know about the dire warning I had received. He said, "Some of my friends and I may need to pay a call on Mr. Moto soon." At least I wasn't in this by myself and all these guys were veteran jungle fighters or "snake eaters," as they were called. And there was no doubt Pramuan was a snake. Their experience included fighting the communist guerrillas in northeast Thailand.

To break the tension, Bernd, who was dating Pussy (of all names), Jad and I took off for Pataya Beach. Pussy must have been named after Pussy Galore from one of the James Bond books. We stayed at a rustic, two-story beach cottage with six bedrooms. Life was good, or so we thought.

Shortly after we returned to Bangkok, Bernd was fired from the Manohra Hotel. The problem for us foreigners in Asia was a cultural gap, which often caused misunderstandings. My misunderstanding with Pramuan was likely to turn out to be a deadly one if I didn't take special precautions. That was why I decided to carry a bowie knife and a .45 caliber pistol with me at all times, or at least I thought about it.

Every week, Mrs. Swan had me over for dinner with her extended Thai family. They threw a big birthday party for Bunny, one of Ying's little girls. The kids all called me Uncle Clarke. It was a joy to be a part of this loving family.

As a model at a Thai temple for a travel magazine.

Mr. Diskul, who was part of this group, and his family took me with them to visit the Royal Summer Palace one hour north of the city. He was the grandson of one of the Thai Kings. It was a privilege and honor to be in such royal company. They explained the history as we walked the palace grounds past monks in saffron robes.

The summer palace of the kings of Thailand dates back to the 1600s. Today, it is infrequently used, and then mostly for state occasions. The "signature piece" is an elegant Thai-style pavilion in the middle of a pond, with the rather daunting title of "The divine seat of personal freedom," which said it all.

Bob Udick, Editor of Bangkok World Newspaper, took me as his guest to the Foreign Correspondents Club meeting at the Rajah Hotel. Bob had become a friend and kept me up to date on what was happening in Thailand and the world. The war in Vietnam was always near the top of the list. I was also getting reports straight from the battlefield from military men on R & R (rest and recuperation) staying at the hotel.

Bangkok flooded on the night of September 16. The city is criss-crossed by canals called "klongs." Heavy rains were always a danger. Add to that, those mean mosquitoes bred in the klongs. No matter what else, it was hot and muggy most of the time in this city of temples.

Rumors were flying that I would be fired. Pramuan needed his mouth washed out with soap. With such rumors spreading through the hotel, I booked 47 rooms for TWA's Inaugural Flight to Thailand. That quashed the rumors dead in their tracks.

As I took a tour of the Grand Palace, I met Dr. and Mrs. El-Kayem from Beirut. They invited me to dinner and to see Thai dancing at the Rama Hotel. We became instant friends. I would stay with them in Beirut at a later date.

Beautiful Udomlock and I went out for dinner and dancing. It was late at night when I left her apartment on the fifth floor. I was on my way down in the elevator when it came to an abrupt halt and the lights went out. It had to be Mr. Moto at work. *The plot was thickening,* I speculated.

Being in such a spot gave me a frightening feeling. Near panic was closer to the truth. *Had Pramuan or his henchmen followed me?* I wondered. I had been warned. The only thing I could do was start singing, *Texas, My Texas.* That was enough to wake up the dead or scare away the bad guys!

After considerable banging, cussing, and singing, the lights went on and the elevator continued to the ground floor. There was Pramuan and two of his thugs waiting for me with clubs. No, it was only the short, old night watchmen in his sarong. He apologized in Thai for turning off the power.

But trouble with Pramuan was still brewing. For the first time in my life, I felt like someone wanted to do me bodily harm. His henchmen included the hotel storekeeper, Virit, a big Thai fellow who left Air America to work at the hotel. Air America was the CIA operation in Laos. That meant this guy was more than one tough customer.

Good news came the next day when I got a call from the Tourist Organization of Thailand. They wanted me to teach English, on the side, to hotel trainees. It was another opportunity to work with the Thai people and make extra money in the process.

Fate intervened on October 13, in a good way. I had planned to go out that evening but decided to stay in my room and read.

At 8:20 p.m. the phone rang and the clerk from the front desk said, "There are three men from Washington, D.C. and two men from the U.S. Embassy here to see you." My first thought was, *My gosh, what had I done? Am I in trouble?*

I quickly put on a suit and went down to the lobby. Mr. O'Brien and Mr. Zeller were with the United States Information Service based at the U.S. Embassy in Thailand. Mr. Hand, the leader of the party, Mr. Waters, and Mr. Chadwick were a part of President Lyndon Johnson's advance team for his forthcoming state visit to Asia.

"Clarke, we're here to explore the possibility of holding the news conferences for the President's visit at your hotel, plus reserving all of your rooms," Mr. Hand explained. *Fantastic!* I thought. Kun Prajuab, the Thai who owned half of the hotel, would be amazed and delighted with this blockbuster news. I knew I was!

The group decided to have dinner in the hotel's dinner room. I furnished all the drinks. It was my first glimpse into presidential power as the group discussed the ins and outs of the coming visit. It would be the first time a U.S. President visited mainland Asia—while still President. Eisenhower had been prevented from coming in 1960 when the Zengakuren Japanese Communist students instigated huge riots. I sat and listened quietly to top-level political conversation that took place around the table. Being a Texan made a difference in the trust factor to those gentlemen—because LBJ and several of them were Texans.

The next day, the three advance men came around again for a closer look at the hotel's facilities. After giving them a complete tour, I introduced them to my chief defender and supporter, Kun Prachuab. He was ecstatic about the turn of events. Our hotel would become White House headquarters for the world for a few short days.

It was day three since the deal had been set. I spent the afternoon at USIS Headquarters discussing the presidential party arrangements with Mr. O'Brien and his staff.

On day five, the entire key staff working on President Johnson's State Visit came to the hotel for lunch to discuss the minutest of details. It appeared that I was going to be fairly well known around Bangkok after this landmark visit. Before all the activity got underway, I was only known by the dry cleaner down the street and my Thai barber.

Thailand and the U.S. were strong allies. That was one of the key reasons for the presidential visit. Thailand had signed a technical and economic aid agreement in 1950 with the U.S. and had sent troops to support the U.N. action in Korea. Since that time, the country had received military grants from the U.S. and was the seat of the Southeast Asia Treaty Organization from 1954 to 1977. As this visit was getting ready to take place, Thailand had troops in Vietnam and its army was fighting communist guerrillas in the northeast jungles of their country.

About this time, I attended the American Chamber of Commerce luncheon. I happened to be seated by the First Secretary of the Russian Embassy. That was the position most time filled by a KGB agent. I was very careful not to reveal any details of the upcoming presidential visit. Of course, the U.S. and Russia were involved in a Cold War that was a life and death struggle for the hearts and minds of the peoples of the world.

I'm sure Sergei thought I was a CIA operative. Boy, did I have him fooled! As two would-be spies, we danced around all kinds of interesting subjects. *How did he come to be sitting next to me?* I wondered.

Are you James Bond or who? In one week's time, I was told by women that I looked like James Bond, actor Rod Taylor, Pat Boone, and Rock Hudson. It was beyond me. I was supposedly a man of many faces.

At 11:00 one evening, Ray Weiss, Foreign Editor for NBC News, checked in. Having just come from filming President Johnson in New Zealand, he looked wrung out. Ray was the first to arrive to cover the upcoming visit.

I spent that next day working with Bob Roadarmel on rooming assignments for White House staff members. On October 26th, some of the press corps and camera crews started arriving. I made friends with the CBS camera crew when I checked them in. They in turn invited me to go with them to film the dress rehearsal of Thai dancing to be given in honor of President and Mrs. Johnson.

The Big Day arrived! The White House and international Press Corps members arrived—200 strong. Among them was Dan Rather from Texas. Some of the most well known journalists, TV commentators, and correspondents in the world were sharing my home. I had been instrumental in putting the hotel on the world map. It was more than exciting! The eyes and ears of the world were focused on my little world.

I was involved in every phase of the organization and operation of that massive undertaking, from the laying of telephone lines to planning the menus. Fortunately, there were only a few minor hitches from start to finish.

As I stood in front of the Royal Stand with TV cameramen, photographers, and reporters, the president's helicopter landed 100 yards away on the Royal Plaza in front of the Parliament Building. The King and Queen greeted

President Johnson as he stepped out of the helicopter. They were then driven to the Stand where they stood at attention for the playing of the national anthems. It was a perfect, sunny day for this historic event.

The next day, I went along with Ray Weiss of NBC to Chulalongkorn University to see the President receive an honorary doctorate in political science. He had come a long way from Southwest Texas State Teachers College in San Marcos, Texas.

From the University to Government House, I rode in the stake truck with a group of reporters. This truck was in front of the President's car wherever he went. I had high hopes that rubbing elbows with all the reporters would ensure that my writing skills would take a dramatic turn for the better. My goal was to someday write a book on my travel adventures.

Princess Prim and Mrs. Swan came to the hotel to have lunch with me. They could not believe it was all happening in front of their very eyes. Neither could I. Mrs. Swan had kindly taken me in three months before when I was a broke guy with no job and no prospects. Bless her.

I later saw Secretary of State Dean Rusk at the Royal Hotel and talked with Jack Valenti and Bill Moyers, who were on LBJ's staff. The unique opportunity of the day came when Paul Noto of CBS let me go along with him to the official Royal Palace residence. I was his light man as he filmed the President, Lady Bird, the King, and Queen from ten feet away. I only dropped the light once. Me nervous? Never.

The President and his entourage took off for Malaysia the next morning. I had become a seasoned veteran of a presidential state visit. After all, we Texans have to stick together.

CHAPTER 40

A Saga of Romance and Soul Searching

*In that world, you'll be able to rise in the
morning with the spirit you had known
in your childhood: the spirit of eagerness,
adventure and certainty which comes from
dealing with a rational universe.*

— Ayn Rand

Right after the presidential visit, I got a form letter giving me one month's notice before I had to leave the country because my passport visa had just expired. Here we go again. I had thought I was set.

Buddha was with me in this Buddhist Land. The Board of Investment, through the Director of the Tourist Organization of Thailand, sent a letter to the Immigration Department so that my visa could be extended for thirty days.

My visa was actually cleared through December 31. On Halloween, the hotel gave me my one-month's notice, the date when my contract would be up. I sure would miss my nemesis, the man who was scary enough without a mask, Pramuan. I still feared for my safety every time I left the hotel. *He would someday get his just deserts*, I figured.

Thinking ahead, on November 3, I sent a letter to Mr. Bonde, Manager of the Cavalieri Hilton in Rome, about going to work for him. It was a long shot, since he had no idea about me whatsoever, but one had to start somewhere. As always, I laid as much groundwork as possible.

My savings looked good for a change. I had $1,500 U.S. in the bank—a fortune for me. I hoped it was enough to eventually get me to Rome. Of course, once again my traveling would be by hitchhiking, third-class trains, ancient buses, walking, riverboats, old planes, camels, and horse-drawn wooden carts—across some rugged, dangerous territory with some of the highest mountains and hottest deserts that existed on earth.

I wanted to go to Pataya Beach and, if necessary, would go by myself. I rode down in Nipa Lodge's hotel bus for free. Kurt, the German manager, kindly gave me a free room. Then, I ran into some friends from Bangkok. The next thing I knew, I was out water skiing.

At 7:00 the next morning, I hit the beach. The beach was usually deserted until around 10:00 a.m., so I had it all to myself. I was lying in the sand, half-asleep, when I heard a splashing sound. It was a vision. I could not believe my eyes. I had been laying there on the beach, minding my own business, in total peace. It was what many men dream about happening to them, and I definitely wasn't dreaming.

Standing ten feet in front of me was a perfect "10." She was wearing nothing but white panties, standing in crystal clear water up to her ankles—a statuesque Thai girl with classic beauty and proportions. She gave me a flashing smile revealing perfect white teeth. *No, I've got to be dreaming*, I told myself. She then turned around, walked into the water up to her thighs, and dived in. It was apparent that she had deliberately made the splashing noises to get my attention. She certainly got it!

She turned, the water up to her perfectly shaped breasts, her eyes inviting me to come to her. That was all the invitation I needed. I scrambled up, ran and dived in. I came up two feet in front of her. It was just the two of us. No one else existed in the world.

Usa could not speak a word of English and my Thai was super limited. Somehow, we understood each other perfectly. We left the water and sat on the beach, her shapely, wet body glistening in the sunlight. In about fifteen minutes, Usa indicated she needed to go.

She walked along the beach the thirty yards to where her shorts and t-shirt laid on the sand. *If only I could speak Thai*, I thought. As she got dressed, she looked at me several times, giving me a shy smile each time. As she disappeared over the sand, it all seemed but a dream.

Back in Bangkok, Mr. Anderson, manager for TWA in Thailand, had decided, with my assistance, to use our hotel for TWA's Inaugural Flights—a real coup.

When the day came, we checked in a U.S. Senator, nine congressmen, company presidents, and newspaper publishers and editors from throughout the U.S. After getting all the dignitaries off to their rooms, I invited all the TWA managers and organizers for a drink. All went well with the visit.

Kun Pranom, our travel agent at the hotel, gave a party at his home for me. Twelve people came. Among them was Sri (pronounced see) for short. Sri was 5'7" and had long, black, silky hair down to her waist, moved with a grace lovely to behold, and was one of Thailand's best Thai classical dancers, and an actress as well. The attraction between us was mutual and from that evening forward we got together almost every day.

Three days later, Sri and I went to a restaurant in her convertible, not far from the hotel. She parked on the street a half a block away, fortunately under a streetlight.

After leaving the restaurant, as I went to open the door for Sri, I noticed a poisonous "Gila Monster," on the front seat. Alert! This was clearly Pramuan's work. I got a big stick and shooed the deadly reptile out of the car. We surely had been followed and the warnings had been true.

A friend had referred Mike Jalla, from the Kuchin State of Burma, to me. I invited him to lunch at the hotel. I was considering checking out Burma before I left Asia for India and the Middle East. For three hours, I sat spellbound as he explained the situation in Burma, a country right next door to Thailand. The military dictatorship is still a brutal disgrace in that country.

I learned that Ne Win had staged a military coup in 1962, four years before and basically took away all freedoms, discarded the Constitution, and established a Revolutionary Council, made up of military leaders who ruled by decree. They imposed a policy of international isolation.

Pro-Chinese Communist rebels were active in the northern part of Burma, where from 1967 on, they received aid from Communist China. This was all happening just as I was getting ready to head for Burma.

Ten months before Mike and I had lunch together, he had escaped from Rangoon a marked man, taking four months to cross over the mountains and make his way through dense and dangerous jungles to Thailand. His minority group was being brutally oppressed and he hoped to return someday to help restore freedom. It was my first time to meet a true rebel who had risked his life to fight another day.

As an American, I realized how easy it was to take for granted all of the freedoms we have. Years later, as many of the countries I visited in my youth continue to struggle with conflict and strife, I continue to be grateful for the liberties and freedoms we have in America. Freedom is a precious commodity.

On November 30, my contract with the hotel came to an end. It had been an interesting ride. I was ready to step back into real adventure, with all its inherent dangers and thrills. By 8:00 that evening, I had moved all my things over to Mrs. Swan's house. Since my old room was occupied, I took up residence in the servant's quarters, which had no windows and was full of mosquitoes. It was back again to rags from riches, from the penthouse to peanuts. No matter, I was much the same whether I had everything or nothing. Life was meant to be lived to its fullest, whatever the circumstances.

The next afternoon, I had lunch with three friends from the Foreign Broadcasting Information Service located at the U.S. Embassy. In the evening, I attended a Russian reception at the Trade Fair at the invitation of the First Secretary of their Embassy. He was a nice guy and a smooth operator, but most likely a KGB agent looking for any and all information he could extract from me. I was on my guard.

I talked to many of the Russians at their trade pavilion. Although they were cordial and talkative, I'll bet every one of them was highly skilled in espionage, Thailand being a key ally of the U.S. While today our enemies are terrorists operating within various borders, after World War II our greatest threat was from the "Red Menace"—Communism. Russia was the standard bearer of communism and by the 1960s their oppression had spread from Eastern Europe in Southeast Asia. While I could joke about spies, the truth of the communist threat was a reality around the globe.

When I returned to my "palace" headquarters at 11:00 that night, I found Mr. Dorsey Tran talking with Mrs. Swan. Dorsey was a Church of Christ missionary in Northern Thailand. He offered to take me up to Chengmai with him the following week.

Several days later, General Vargas of the Philippines, Secretary General of SEATO, who headed up allied military forces in Southeast Asia, called and invited me to dinner at his home. The KGB would have been interested in that, and most likely surprised.

With all the troubles in the world, sporting events represented "what could be." Only three years earlier in 1964, Tokyo hosted the Olympic Summer games. But I was able to witness another prestigious event as I attended the opening ceremony of the Fifth Asian Games. It was my first time to attend a multi-national games event of any kind. While Thailand was at peace, other countries in the region were in turmoil. The Vietnam War raged with no end in sight. Cambodia tried to challenge the Asian Games movement by organizing "The Games of New Emerging Forces" just before the launch of the Fifth Asian Games. However, the love of sports prevailed and the Games were started and concluded with great success. Fourteen sports comprised 143 events. It was a splendid spectacle.

Campaigning at a hill tribe village on the Thai-Burma border. I won the election.

Since leaving the hotel, I had been making my plans for travel through dangerous Laos and Cambodia—communist guerrillas were operating in both countries. Also, I was considering how to make my way from Burma to Beirut, and then to Jerusalem and Israel.

But first, there was a side trip to take. One fine morning, Uthai and I pulled out at 5:30 in his jeep and headed for Chengmai near the Burmese border. It took 15 hours of almost straight driving over the roughest, dustiest roads I had ever seen. It was like being put through a pulverizing machine. I felt as if I had been stirred, shaken, and turned upside down by the time we got to that lovely city.

We pulled into Chengmai close to 9:00 that night. Ken Rideout and Ola Traw from the Church of Christ came to pick me up. I was covered head-to-toe in dust and looked like a ghost. I never appreciated a bath so much.

Ken led seven of us, including two Aussies, on a hike up the highest mountain in the area the next day. Near the top we came to a famous Buddhist temple covered in gold leaf. It was glowing in the sunlight; a magnificent sight to behold.

We then pushed on to the top of the mountain. There we came upon a Mao Tribe village. The men were all smoking bamboo water pipes filled with opium. Ken explained, "The men smoke and the women do all the work."

The day following, Ken, one other guy, and I took off on three motorcycles to tour Chengmai. The university there was as modern in design as any I had ever seen. At four in the afternoon, I boarded the train for Bangkok.

Trying to sleep in the seat on that train, with all the noise and lights on through the night, was a challenge and a trial. We pulled into Bangkok station twenty hours later. It took me an hour to stand up straight.

It was preparation time. I got my passport visa at the Embassy of India, talked with a counselor at the Italian Embassy, and visited with Mr. Greenwood at the British Information Service. While I was preparing for the next leg of my trip, at the same time, I was in the midst of deep soul-searching. In the past year I had been in four countries: Japan, Taiwan, Hong Kong and Thailand, but I was beginning to question what direction I should take? Did I want to settle down? I was starting to have doubts after five years on the adventure road. How would I get from Burma to Beirut? I prayed for God's guidance, as there was some dangerous territory ahead to think about, too.

On New Year's Eve, Sri and I attended a party at Vudapan's home. She wore a green, low-cut dress made of Thai silk. Ravishing! It was a grand start to the New Year.

CHAPTER 41

Into the Jaws of Danger

*Security is mostly a superstition. It does not
exist in nature, nor do the children of men as
a whole experience it. Avoiding danger is no
safer in the long run than outright exposure.
Life is either a daring adventure, or nothing.*

— Helen Keller

Since I had no income coming in, I put myself on a strict budget. For breakfast, it was two cups of hot Ovaltine and I had one meal in the evening, limited to $1 U.S. (20 Thai baht) or less. It was a marvelous way to shed the extra pounds I had put on living high on the hog. I could get a bowl of soup with noodles for 15 cents.

My adventure plan was in total flux. I called shipping companies about passage to Malaya and my friend Gotu at Air India was working on finding me a family to stay with in India. Also, I went to the rundown hotel where all broke students and hitchhikers stayed when they came to Bangkok (i.e., those who have little money.)

At the "Hitchhiker's Hotel," as it was called, there was a scene reminiscent of strange characters coming and going. Never had I gained so much information at one time on how to travel cheaply. It changed my whole itinerary. Meeting some of the characters there brought home how soft and satisfied I had become.

After learning how little money these traveling wanderers lived on, I made up my mind to hitchhike north through Thailand, try to make it through war-torn Laos alive, and explore the famous temple ruins of Angkor Wat in the jungles of Cambodia. It was time to be daring and maybe a bit crazy. My life hung in the balance, as it turned out, literally.

Thailand had no diplomatic relations with Cambodia at the time, so the only way to explore the fabulous ruins of Angkor Wat was to make it alive through communist guerilla territory in what was "The Secret War" raging in the southern mountains and jungles of Laos. Many had not made it through. Mel Gibson's movie, *Air America*, depicts the reality of that time.

A newspaper article entitled *In Laos, a 30-year Communist lock*, dated December 2, 2005, stated, "The U.S. backed government had finally succumbed to Communist Pathet Lao guerrillas and their North Vietnamese allies. America and its allies had dropped nearly two million tons of bombs on Laos to stem the advance of the Communist forces." The people of Laos still live under total Communist subjugation today. The presence of Red China and North Korea is a constant reminder, even in 2008 of communism's threat.

Nonetheless, I headed to the U.S. Embassy to talk to Mr. Spurgin about the situation in Laos. He and I had become friends during President Johnson's visit. He advised me that it would be more than dangerous to attempt to go through that war-torn country overland.

At the Indonesian Embassy, I secured a visa for Cambodia, the only place one could be obtained. Next, I checked in with my friend Prisha at the Thai Immigration office to get a re-entry Visa. I was loaded for bear or battle, as the case may be. *My Marine Corps training may come in handy on this little venture,* I thought.

Meanwhile, back at the "Hitchhiker's Hotel," I learned from Sean, an Irish lad, who had just returned alive and in one piece, the latest on the situation and terrain in Laos and Cambodia. It didn't sound good. "The poorer and dirtier you look in Cambodia, the more the people will help you," he commented. What encouraging news!

Off I went to get my Visa at the Laotian Embassy. I called Mr. Hines at USAID, the U.S. Agency for International Development, and asked him to let my friends, Bill and Sheila Faulkner at USAID in Vientiane, Laos, know I was headed their way.

I bid Sri a fond farewell over dinner, not knowing if I would make it back to Bangkok alive. She cried and said, "I will pray to Buddha for you. Please come back alive."

At 7:00 the next morning, I set off hitchhiking on the highway near Don Muang Airport. I was back on the adventure road. The first ride I got was with a middle-aged Thai man in a rather old car. As we were perking along at 50 mph, a truck sped past us. In an instant, the windshield shattered totally, sending glass all over the car and us. I was off to an explosive start. We stopped and picked the glass out of the car.

Luckily, the flying glass was in tiny pieces. If it had come off in large, jagged pieces, we could have died on the spot. Because I had on my sunglasses, my eyes were protected. All I suffered were a number of small cuts on my face and bare arms.

I decided right then and there, I would check everyone's windshield before getting in any other vehicles. I'd also check their tires, brakes, engine, gas tank, and radiator. We sped on along with a wind of 50 mph in our faces. Who needed air conditioning? When he came to his turn on the narrow two-lane highway, I got out and put my thumb up. Vehicles were few and far between.

On the second fabulous ride, an hour later, a dilapidated dump truck driven by a ruddy-faced old driver, who spoke fairly good English, came my way. As we started to enter the jungle, he said, "We don't want to have an accident or stop for any reason from here on. Tigers, deadly snakes, and wild elephants call this territory home." I was all for not dallying. Twelve miles down the road, the dump truck started smoking, as the engine skipped every other beat until it just flat died. This was my opportunity to see tigers and elephants for the first time in a live setting. I was simply overjoyed!

I stayed close to the truck as I kept my eyes peeled for any threats. Along came a 1958 Ford fifteen minutes later. The young Thai man stopped and I hopped in. Twenty miles down the road—the radiator cap blew. The car took on the appearance of a geyser erupting at Yellowstone Park. We kept going for it through a cloud of steam. *So much for my car inspection plan,* I thought

It was as if I jinxed every vehicle I climbed in and it was only noon. By the grace of God and with assistance of Buddha, I reached the town of Korat at one o'clock.

After a lunch of noodles, it was back to the road. The truck driver that picked me up was the spitting image of the wild Mexican outlaw Pancho Villa. The incredibly sleepy fellow somehow got us to Khonkaen by sunset. For a while, his snoring bothered me.

With just my backpack, I approached an ancient Buddhist temple. One of the monks took me in, got me fed, and kindly showed me a place to sleep. The mosquitoes were so big they were biting the soles of my feet.

After a bowl of rice for breakfast, I walked the two miles to the highway and within five minutes, a man driving a beat up truck offered me a ride. It wasn't smoking and the engine wasn't coughing. It was almost too much to hope for. Three miles down the road—we had a flat. I was batting a thousand.

We reached the northern border town of Nongkhai on the banks of the mighty Mekong River at 11:30 that morning. A man at Thai Immigration stamped my passport. The ferry, a narrow wooden boat seating eight people, plied its way across the muddy Mekong. It cost me about five cents U.S.

On the riverbank of Laos, there were only a few small houses and shops. The immigration official didn't even check out my health card, just my passport. I just knew he was going to say, *You look like you need a cholera shot.* By a miracle, he waved me through.

I started walking up the dusty road that led 22 kilometers into the capital of Laos, Vientiane. I soon hitched a ride in a truck that was smoking like a chimney. It seemed like it was on its last cylinder as we reached the outskirts.

After getting directions, I walked into the USAID office. Bill Faulkner had been expecting me but had had no idea when I might show up. Neither had I.

Bill, Sheila, and I had become friends two years earlier in Hong Kong. After all American government workers had been kicked out of Cambodia, they were reassigned to USAID in Laos.

The Faulkners put me up at their house. That night a Marine colonel came over for drinks after dinner. He went into detail how badly things were going for the Royal Laotian Forces fighting against the North Vietnamese army and communist guerrillas in southern Laos. Right where I was headed!

It was cold in Vientiane at night. A jacket and warm clothes were a must. All I had was light clothing, so I bought a cheap wool blanket to put around

A Swiss adventurer and Clarke on Laotian riverbank getting ready to board the Mekong River Queen—*not as nice as the* African Queen.

me. With my dark tan, I could have passed as an Indian in one of the old Western movies, but it kept me warm.

I spent the following day searching for transportation to make it through Laos to Cambodia. I was going to explore the famous ruins of Angkor Wat, come hell or high water, and I was to get a bit of both. Plane fares were too expensive, boats were not regular, and I was informed the buses were like wagon trains—and there was a chance they would get shot up along the way.

I ran into Bruno, a Canadian adventurer I had met in Bangkok. He was going to go by a local "wood and tin" riverboat, so I thought, *Why not?*

At the American Embassy, I talked with Mr. McGuire, the security officer, about traveling through Laos and Cambodia. He said, "As far as Pakse, it is relatively safe, but from there on down through southern Laos, anything could happen. The communist guerrillas and North Vietnamese Army are everywhere." He went on to explain, "That is, if your boat is not shot out of the water on your way to Pakse. For an American, it is especially risky and dangerous." This gave me pause.

I decided I would go as far as Pakse and check out the situation. With great doubts as to what kind of reception I would get as an American at the Cambodian Embassy, I walked in to apply for a visa. Surprisingly, I was treated with politeness, although our two countries had no diplomatic relations. "Your visa will be ready tomorrow," said the young male clerk.

Bill took me on a tour of the nightlife in this capital city of 60,000 people. It consisted of the White Rose Bar. While Bill drank, I danced. *Live and be happy, for tomorrow you may die*, had become my philosophy. I remember when the famous movie star Errol Flynn's son, Sean, who was also a star, went into Cambodia on a motorcycle. He was never heard from again and his body never found. A famous name made no difference in this extremely dangerous area of the world.

Here I go again, I thought. Bill and Sheila were very "shot" conscious. I went to get some of the numerous shots they recommended, but I refused to get a cholera shot, unless it was at the point of a bayonet. They gave me malaria pills to take once a week. The drug they insisted I should take daily without fail was tetracycline capsules. Supposedly, it was a wonder drug that would knock out a number of diseases if it didn't kill one first. The shots made me feverish.

Bill decided I needed to travel to the Mekong riverbank in style and with decided to have some fun with me. He dressed up in a black chauffeur's coat and cap and opened the back door of his vintage 1950 Rolls Royce limousine for me. He had bought it from a diplomat who needed to unload it fast.

As the big, shiny limo slowly pulled up to the dusty area where the riverboats docked, everyone's head turned in curiosity to see what dignitary was about to grace their presence. My chauffer came to a stop, quickly got out, and with a great show of deference, bowed at the waist as I regally emerged. I'm sure everyone was thinking, *Who is this character in blue jeans, t-shirt, and tennis shoes?* He must be loaded. Who were they expecting, the British High Commissioner?

Bruno waved to me from the deck of the Mekong Queen. There were eight other similar boats tied up along the bank. Humphrey Bogart's boat in the movie *African Queen* was a yacht compared to this boat. Actually, this "Queen" was two wooden boats tied together. They were each about sixty feet long and built about the same time Christopher Columbus sailed to America. I was not sure if it would make it away from the embankment without sinking.

In my backpack, besides several changes of hiking shorts and other clothing items, I had canned goods, fruit, and French bread and my gray and white striped wool blanket to keep me warm during the cold nights.

Bill and I shook hands. I thanked him for his and Sheila's gracious hospitality and let him know I would never forget his tour de force in delivering me to my "luxury liner" in such grand style. *Never before and never again would anyone arrive on that muddy river embankment like I did*, I speculated.

Straughan crossing the Mekong with his dedicated and nonchalant troops.

CHAPTER 42
A Tale of Tigers and Guerrillas

I can do all things in him who strengthens me.
— Philippians 4:13

There were four other Caucasians on the *Mekong Queen* besides myself and a Laotian family of seven. The four were basically broke guys, like myself, so they kidded me unmercifully on my fancy mode of arrival at the riverbank. One Canadian, one Swiss, one German, one Australian, and I were the foreign contingent aboard. The Swiss was a boilermaker, the German, a discouraged ex-concert violinist, the Australian was an autoworker, and the Canadian a jack-of-all-trades—and me, an itinerant hotelman/adventurer.

We pulled away from the bank a little after noon, two hours late. The crew consisted of five Laotians. Two of them befriended me and adopted me, even though they only spoke Laotian and a smidgen of French. French got us through.

When I was growing up, there was a cartoon strip entitled, "Mutt and Jeff." Mutt was tall and aggressive and Jeff was short and docile, so I called my new friends Mutt and Jeff, since their Laotian names were almost impossible to pronounce. They fit the cartoon characters to a tee.

The Mekong is a fascinating river. It is the 12th longest in the world. Approximately half the river's length is in China, where it is called *Lancang* in Chinese, meaning "turbulent river." The river divides Laos and Thailand before a stretch passes through Laos alone. Gorges and rapids characterize the Lao stretch.

In the region above Khone Falls near the Cambodian border, endangered dolphins can be watched. According to researchers, the river houses more species of giant fish than any world river. One systematic taxonomic study has identified 456 species. The migratory *Giant Catfish Pangasianodon Gigas* is believed to migrate over a thousand kilometers each year.

As we started downstream, I spotted the Mekong dragons. These are balls of light that are observable from time to time rising from the water's surface in the stretch of the river near Vientiane. These are sometimes referred to as the Naga fireballs. *Now I have seen it all*, I said to myself.

223

The cargo consisted of cardboard boxes filled with cigarettes, a small Japanese car, sacks of rice, motorcycles, coils of steel wire, and soap, among other things. Each person had to find his or her own place to sleep at night. Being cold at night, I went into the closed cargo section and slept on cardboard boxes, fully clothed with my light blanket pulled over me. I still got cold.

The boat didn't travel on the river between sunset and sunrise, but would tie up in an inlet or at a small village on a tributary. If someone wanted to warm or cook food for breakfast or dinner, there was a small wood stove on the back deck. I would whip out my trusty can opener and have a can of whatever looked good at the moment. Mutt and Jeff always offered me a little of what they had. Everyone sat on the deck to eat because, for some strange reason, the deck chairs had disappeared.

I was up at the crack of dawn with some of the crew that first morning. The river was beautiful in the red and golden light of sunrise. As we began the day's journey down the Mekong, the mountains were so prominent and the wind so cold, it was as if we were going down a river in the Canadian Rockies rather than in the tropics. A short stop at Pokane gave us a chance for a hot bowl of noodle soup.

At about 3:00 that afternoon, the water was so choppy and the wind so strong against us, the boat was making little headway. The captain tied up on the bank on the Thai side. He had been keeping close to that side because the communist guerrillas were shooting boats out of the water if they got too close to their operations on the Laotian side of the Mekong.

At the top of the steeply sloped bank sat a small thatched-roof house. Looking down on us was a peasant farmer in sarong with a rifle slung over his shoulder. Apparently, the *Mekong Queen* had tied up at this place before. Mutt and Jeff immediately motioned me to follow them down a jungle path. Everyone else started up the embankment toward the farmer or scout or soldier or whatever he was.

I had no idea where Mutt was leading us in that deep, dark jungle. It was a scene right out of an old Tarzan movie I had watched as a kid. The foliage stood like walls on either side of the path and the canopy cut out most of the light from above. Never mind that I had heard stories of cobras, tigers, wild elephants, deadly spiders and other assorted varmints that roamed these jungles. *Mutt must know what he's doing*, I guessed. I would never guess again after that episode.

Deeper and deeper we ventured. Thirty minutes later, we entered a clearing where several natives were sitting on the ground pounding rice. There was some talk between them and Mutt before we three proceeded deeper and deeper into the dark jungle.

Twenty minutes later, another clearing appeared where I observed several huts on stilts. In the middle of the clearing, an old man was sitting on a straw mat, working with bamboo. I could hear voices coming from one of the huts.

Mutt asked the old man something to which he shook his head yes. Pay dirt! But what was the surprise? Mutt looked overjoyed. *Was he looking for a woman*? I wondered. Jeff looked stoic about it all. I was full of bubbling curiosity of what had literally driven us through that deep, dark jungle. It held a powerful sway over Mutt.

The old man went up the bamboo steps of a hut with Mutt following closely behind. Jeff and I sat down on the ground to wait. Fifteen minutes later Mutt stuck his head out of the door and motioned for me to join him. *What on earth is going on behind that bamboo door*? I thought as I rose to my feet.

As I entered, there sat Mutt cross-legged across from the old man. He looked as if he was in fairyland. The old man was stuffing opium into a bamboo water pipe. Once done, he handed it across to Mutt, who lit it up.

Mutt took several big drags on the pipe and then offered it to me. Well, I had never even smoked but to appear hospitable I acted as if I was taking a drag off the pipe—*but I didn't inhale.*

After several more huge drags, Mutt was ready for anything. It took Jeff and I ten minutes to get him back down to the ground. He was "smashed," to put it mildly. Now we had to somehow get him back through the jungle to the boat. He was like a butterfly wandering here and there off the jungle path. It took everything Jeff and I had to keep him moving forward as night was approaching.

As we exited out of the jungle darkness into the light of dusk, the crew and my fellow foreign mates came rushing down the embankment yelling. "Didn't you know a man-eating tiger has already eaten six people around here?" they shouted. My heart sank and my legs felt as if they were going to go out from under me.

Thanks, Mutt, I thought. *If the tiger had gotten us, you wouldn't have felt a thing.* Going into the jungle, I was last in line on the narrow path. Tigers always prefer to grab the morsel in the rear. I came out extremely lucky on that opium-foraging expedition. Sometimes one can take trust too far.

The wind had died down, so we proceeded down the Mighty Mekong. That night I found a place to sleep on boxes filled with cigarettes. At dawn, I had a can of chili and a can of pears for breakfast. Mutt and Jeff shared their tea with me. Mutt appeared to have slept off his opium escapade.

As the sun was setting, the boat motored into the small jungle town of Thakhek. We tied up on the bank of a small tributary. I asked some of the local people, "Do any Americans live here?" They pointed to a small wood house located half a block away along the dirt street. There I found several Americans who worked for USAID.

These folks informed me that only forty kilometers to the east was one of the largest training and staging areas for the communist guerrillas and Pathet Lao troops. I was closer than I wanted to be to the lion's den, especially after the tiger incident. No one there was really safe if push came to shove.

Dennis, an International Volunteer Service worker, and his wife, Pam, put me up in a spare room in the IVS complex. I was overjoyed I had a real bed to sleep in. That any Americans would choose to live in such a place, given the imminent dangers, was amazing to me. The Secret War in Laos was at its zenith, exploding in all directions.

I walked back to the "queen of the river" at 7:30 the next morning. It was being unloaded by coolies running boxes across a plank set between the boat and dusty riverbank.

Two hours running time down river, at almost exactly noon, a thundering sound occurred. A tremendous head wind ripped off a part of the tin roof covering the barge tied to the side of the boat. A razor-sharp tin sheet sailed just above the heads of the people on the top deck. A foot lower and heads would have rolled. Being below deck, I thought we had hit a rock.

Rushing up topside, I found part of the tin roof had jackknifed on to the roof of the boat. We tied up on the bank and cleared the mess away. At least we didn't have five headless people on our hands.

An hour later we were on our way again, minus one roof. At sunset, we reached our final destination downriver, Savanakhet. Much of the town's architecture was French Colonial, as it had been an important place during the colonial era.

When I arrived there, it was a dangerous place. Not far from the town, North Vietnamese troops had built a network of trails through the jungles. Along those trails, they transported troops and provisions to the war zones in South Vietnam. It was known as the Ho Chi Minh Trail. The trail was within

Laos and was being saturation bombed with 900 sorties a day. I heard bombs going off throughout the night. It appeared I might not only have to dodge deadly communist troops and guerrillas, but bombs, too.

The "luxury" tour downriver had lasted four days. I'd miss my friends Mutt and Jeff, but not necessarily the tiger trail, and, fortunately, our boat hadn't been shot out of the water.

Dong with USAID put me up for the night. I was told he was ex-Viet Cong. But who really knew if he was ex or not in the volatile situation that existed. Nevertheless, I trusted him, as I really had no choice. Over dinner at a small French restaurant, we discussed the evolving cataclysm I was about to advance into.

I boarded a local bus the next morning. It looked like an old school bus, probably French-built, with the door on the right side towards the back. The regular fare was 400 Kip but I bargained it down to 300 Kip.

The bus bounced along the road, stopping every so often to take on and let off Laotian native passengers.

Halfway through the trip to Pakse, I got up on top of the bus with all the bags, rice, and chickens. I thought this was the perfect place to observe the beautiful countryside. It was like riding a bucking bronco, no less. The view was 100% better than from inside the bus. Of course, I was a 100% better target for the guerrillas in the jungle along the way.

I was hoping they would say, "Look at that crazy Frenchman on top of the bus. No American would be dumb enough to expose himself like that." That was my hope. After all, I was on vacation and didn't want to miss any of the sights.

As the bus rolled into Pakse, I was covered in four inches of red dust. No one would have recognized me. I saw several fellow adventurers I had met in Vientianne walking along the side of the road. They gave me the bad news. "Clarke, for the first time in two years, a local bus going further south was machine-gunned from both sides of the jungle road, and every man, woman and child was killed," they explained.

They pointed out the bus, which was off in a vacant field where it had been towed. Bullet holes an inch apart covered the entire bus. No one could have lived through such murderous fire. And this had happened only two days before my grand entrance into this total war situation. *No more riding on top of buses for me*, I decided.

Killing all those innocent Laotians was a tactic of the communist guerrillas to say, *We control everything and this is what will happen to you if you don't obey our every whim.* Pure evil was the only way to describe such sub-human beings. They went on later to murder over two million innocent Cambodians in the same way—teachers, doctors, nurses, business people, high school graduates and anyone with education.

The warnings I had been hearing all along the way took on frightening aspects. *How was I going to make it through to Cambodia given this living nightmare,* I thought to myself. The day after the bus had been shot up, a Royal Laotian Army patrol of 20 men was ambushed and killed near the same area.

At the International Volunteer Service House, I was greeted with cold courtesy. Apparently, many bums and beatnik types had imposed on their hospitality one too many times. For fifty cents I got a place to sleep and a hot shower. The shower was like pure heaven. It took me an hour to wash all the dust off.

After talking to as many people as I could, I reached the only conclusion available to me. Between Pakse and the Cambodian border, the situation was grim. At USAID and IVS headquarters, I got only warnings of how great the risk was going down by road. The river was too low to navigate in that January timeframe, so going by boat was out. Someone told me I might check with the Air America guys, actually CIA, out at the small airport. One of their pilots said, "Clarke, we wish we could help you out and fly you to Cambodia, but things are in total chaos right now." So by plane was out.

So it came down to "do or die." I had come that far and I was determined to make it to the famous temple ruins of Angkor Wat. There was no way I was going to turn back at this point. So I strapped on two pistols, grabbed a sack of grenades, put belts of ammo across my chest, and slung a 50-caliber machine gun over my shoulder. That was what I felt like doing, but at least having a B.A.R. like I carried in the Marine Corps would have sufficed.

The village town of Pakse was swarming with Royal Laotian troops. They were moving in every direction, as helicopters and troop transport planes were taking off. I decided to take decisive action. I washed my dirty clothes.

I soon learned that the jungle road south was open once again. Open season on peasant buses was more like it. "Any time there was trouble," I was told, "the Army blocks the road off."

When I went to bed that night, I was wavering on whether to chance the first bus through in the morning. I had met a French gentleman that afternoon. He had been a French officer at Dien Bin Phu when the Communists overran it. "I am going south on the bus in the morning if you would like to accompany me," he said. "My Laotian wife and I live in Cambodia. Since I'm known to the communist guerrillas, coming to Pakse often on business, they may think you are French, too, being with me." If ever I had had a better offer, I couldn't remember it. At least it might save me if the guerrillas boarded the bus instead of machine-gunning it. I decided to roll the dice.

After a breakfast of coffee and croissant, I boarded the bus with the former French major. We walked up toward the front and sat in about the middle of the bus on the left side. He took the window seat. His English was good and my French only fair. To be on the safe side, we conversed in French, so as not to blow my cover completely. Several miles out we came to a Royal Laotian Army checkpoint.

Twenty miles or so down the jungle road all seemed well until the driver slowed down to a crawl. The bus driver appeared to be scared out of his wits. As I leaned into the aisle and looked out the front window of the bus, I could see nearly a dozen men in black pajamas standing on each of the road in the dark jungle shadows. I swallowed hard.

The bus driver slowed down to a snail's pace, hands tightly gripping the wheel. At least they hadn't opened fire without warning. As the bus came to a stop where they stood, two of the guerrillas got on at the one door at the back. They didn't say a word but just apparently looked to see who was on board. My breathing nearly stopped while I kept my eyes glued straight ahead.

After several minutes, they got off and the bus started moving slowly forward. I was told that if they decided to ask for identification, as an American I would have been taken off the bus and shot by the side of the road. My guardian angel was with me on that heart-stopping day.

But we still weren't totally out of the woods. Being machine-gunned or running over a land mine were still possibilities on that journey through hell. The Major may have been the difference, since he was not considered a combatant but a familiar face.

I'll never forget the small, young Royal Laotian soldier that sat directly across the aisle from me. Next to him, by the window, was his wife holding their baby. As we rumbled down the dark jungle road, I saw him take the top off a little round straw basket. Sitting on top of the rice inside the basket was a hand grenade. He took it out and laid it on the seat between them. He took a handful of rice and gave it to his wife, got himself a handful, put the grenade back, and put the top back on. He had been ready to go down fighting!

Thank the Lord we arrived in Khinak in one piece. The bus company couldn't have afforded to lose another bus. In Khinak, the Major rented a jeep and I rode the 80 kilometers to Stung Treng with him. Although it was 60 kilometers into Cambodia, Stung Treng was where the Immigration Station was located.

Approaching the river at sunset, I could see Stung Treng along the opposite bank of the Mekong River. A small ferry got us to the other side. A neat row of two-story French-style buildings lined the broad avenue along the river.

After going through Immigration, I walked to the Buddhist Temple. The monks were hospitable and friendly, as always. Several of them could speak a little English, inviting me to have tea and share their dinner. I slept on the straw matting of the temple floor, which was raised ten feet off the ground. It got a bit chilly with just my thin blanket for cover. Once asleep, I slept soundly. At last, Cambodia—alive!

CHAPTER 43
A Wonder of the World—Stupefying Angkor Wat

*It is not how far a man travels that counts as
how intensively he does so.*
— Henry David Thoreau

When I was a kid, I thrilled at watching Bing Crosby and Bob Hope in their "Road" movies, like *The Road to Singapore*, starring with glamorous Dorothy Lamour as the love interest. I was following in their footsteps. Perhaps it was those movies that subconsciously had something to do with me going down so many roads in all parts of the world.

"The Road to Angkor Wat" was one of the roads they never took, but then not many people have. The temple, built around 1140 A.D., was about as remote as it gets.

I awoke at the Buddhist temple in Stung Treng as the sun peeked over the horizon. Walking the few short blocks into town, I met a local schoolteacher. He told me the restaurant at the market was the best place to eat.

While I was busy eating, the waiter said something to me in Cambodian to get my attention. As I looked up at him, he pointed to all the people in the market. Everyone was standing at attention, as their national anthem was being played over the radio and piped through speakers. I sprang to my feet instantly. *No use risking getting shot by the good guys for a lack of etiquette,* I quickly concluded.

At the edge of town where the jungle takes over, I stationed myself to hitch a ride. It was 7:30 in the morning. Soon I saw two ladies walking back from the market with bananas they hadn't sold. I tried to buy some using my poor French. Not understanding a thing I said, they gave me a small bunch of bananas and went off laughing, good-naturedly. This was the start of a series of kindnesses I received from Cambodians that day.

After three hours of waiting and no cars, I set out walking the jungle road. It was 141 kilometers to Kratie in oppressive heat. Several miles down the road, two young women came along on a bike. The one on the back was

231

holding a baby. They stopped, the young mother got off with her baby and said, in French, "You look too fatigued walking so far with your backpack balanced on your head. Come to our house and have something to eat and rest." She let me know a bus would probably be along in about an hour.

At her family's thatch-roofed house, they fed me a nice meal. When I told the young mother I was very low on money, she pulled out a wad of bills from the top of her blouse and held them out to me. I thought I would cry. Never had I experienced such concern and kindness. I was learning the Cambodians are wonderful human beings.

I politely refused the money and expressed my deepest thanks for her unbelievable kindness and hospitality. I told her not to worry, that I was strong, and liked to walk. She seemed reluctant for me to start walking again but bid me farewell. I shall never forget that angel lady.

Three miles farther down the road, I was enveloped in the deepest of jungles. Remembering what I had been told several weeks prior about tigers, I was prepared to set a new record in the 100-yard dash. The jungle sounds, and there were many, caused me to ask myself, *Straughan, do you have any idea why you have ventured into this garden spot without a Tommy gun or at least a knife? If the tigers don't get me first, there are always the Khmer Rouge Communist guerrillas hanging around*, I concluded. Just then I heard the sound of an engine in the distance.

The small white Fiat shot passed me like a flash leaving me with a drooping thumb. But 100 yards down the road, the car stopped. A guy got out and waved at me to join him. I took off running. At least I would be safe from the tigers.

Theng spoke English. He had studied business in Canada and New Mexico. *My, are these Cambodians kind*, I thought. I had expected the opposite, since our countries had no diplomatic relations. Theng had literally saved the day and maybe my life. Not to mention lots of miles of walking in sweltering heat.

Thanking Theng for rescuing me from the dangers of the jungle, I boarded a double-decker riverboat at the town of Kratie. Sitting down on a wooden bench by some Cambodians, one of them motioned if he could have one of my bananas. I motioned for him to help himself.

A few minutes later, as I was reading, he tapped me on the shoulder and pointed down the deck to let me know some fellow had taken all my bananas. I looked and then pointed at him. Sure enough, he was playing a joke on me. We laughed and became fast friends, neither being able to speak the other's language.

I love the Cambodian people. On a Mekong riverboat, with new friends, headed for the capital of Phnom Phen.

The steamboat-looking conveyance set out for the Cambodian capital of Phnom Phen at 3:00 that afternoon. I was on board barefoot, wearing Bermuda shorts and a t-shirt. Until I went to sleep on the deck that night, I was shown many kindnesses by the people aboard. In fact, I now knew that these were some of the sweetest people on earth.

When the fare collector came by, he wouldn't take my money. That's when I discovered my new friend had paid my fare. In awhile, he motioned for me to follow him to the lower deck. There were three of his friends sitting on the deck getting ready to eat and drink. I was invited to join them.

Back on the top deck, I made friends with Popom, a university student who spoke enough English to get us by. He informed me that the Angkor Wat temple is the epitome of the high classical style of Khmer architecture. In fact, the temple is the symbol of Cambodia, appearing on its national flag.

By dinnertime, I had made friends with a teacher. We conversed in French. He invited me to share a meal with him and his young family.

As it got late, my friend Popom offered me a place to sleep on his king size mat, since I was without a mat. It sure beat sleeping on the raw deck.

I truly felt like an honored guest in that gentle land. It was tonic to my soul because I never expected such treatment.

A soft, pink sunrise welcomed us to Phnom Penh. How clean, neat, and well painted everything was. Other attractive features were the elegant tree-lined boulevards. It was almost like I was in France, seeing formal gardens that flourished with fragrant flowers.

After bidding my new friends a fond farewell, I changed some money as soon as I landed on shore. The rate was 32 reals to $1 U.S.

I set off walking to find a place to stay. Coming across a French-style sidewalk cafe, a bistro, I decided to have some breakfast and do some people watching. With my hunger satisfied, I set out to find a Buddhist temple.

After thirty minutes of walking and following orange robes, I spotted a temple in the distance. As I entered the grounds, I found a group of monks chatting. Two of them spoke a bit of English. Tatch-Suong took me under his wing, showing me where I could sleep and bathe. And was I in desperate need of a bath!

The bath was a trough out in the open. I used a small pan to dip out the water. Standing there in front of Buddha and the world in my jockey shorts, a group of children found me a fascinating study.

After taking a picture with "my fellow monks," I set out to explore. From 11:00 in the morning until 4:00 that afternoon, I walked all the way around the edge of the city. Soon after I had started off, a boy of about 12 years old started following me at 20 paces or so. When I turned around and waved at him, he'd stop. It was clear he was shy and he'd say nothing. To this day, I'm not sure why he latched onto me. I ended up taking a picture of him in front of the Royal Palace.

Ironically, at that time, Phnom Penh was as lovely and peaceful as any city I had ever seen. The takeover of the country by Communist guerrillas was already in progress during that January of 1967. It started with an attack on royal government officials in the province of Battambang.

Disturbing stories of Khmer Rouge guerrilla atrocities began to surface over the next eight years. Teachers, civil servants, and educated people were selectively murdered, including women and children by those sub-human communists.

The Khmer Rouge and North Vietnamese Army initiated an offensive to capture the Cambodian capital on January 1, 1975. Their units entered Phnom Penh on April 17, 1975. It's estimated that they then began to brutally murder nearly two million innocent people over the next four years, lest anyone ever forget. Pol Pot can be ranked right up there with the miscreants Hitler, Mao, and Stalin. It was genocide at its worst.

Cambodia was established as the Funan Empire in the first century AD. In the fourth century, an Indian Brahmin extended his rule over Funan, introducing Hindu customs. In the sixth century, Khmers overran Funan. With the rise of the Khmer Empire, Cambodia became dominant in Southeast Asia. Of course, Angkor, the capital of this empire, was one of the world's great architectural achievements.

When I finished walking around Phnom Penh, I returned to my temple home. Monk Tatch-Suong and I talked for an hour over a cup of tea. At 6:00 that evening, I walked back into town to have a dinner of rice covered with cabbage and pork. It set me back 8 reals or 13 cents in U.S. money. Afterwards, I decided to investigate the nightlife; I poked my head into six bars. It was sedate. After exchanging $5 U.S. on the flourishing black market, I called it a day. I was exhausted from all the walking in the high humidity under a hot sun.

The next morning, I was up at 6:00. After the monks finished eating, I ate my breakfast, as was the custom. It was time to hit the road for exotic Angkor, the place I had literally risked my life to come see.

By 7:00, I was walking along a narrow two-lane paved road, hoping to catch a quick ride. I had walked three miles before a young Cambodian couple picked me up. They took me as far as the ferry and helped me get a ride from there. That leg of the journey to Siem Reap was with a fellow driving an open-air, government administration jeep. The weather was perfect. Fortunately, no guerrillas chose to ambush us.

Nestled between rice paddies stretched along the Siem Reap River, the small town of Siem Reap serves as the gateway to the millennium-old temple ruins of the Khmer Empire. The legendary Angkor Wat temple's architectural significance and visual impact puts it in a class with the ruins of Machu Pichu and the Taj Majal.

It was mid-afternoon when I walked onto the grounds of the Buddhist temple in Siem Reap. I was given a room to share with Albert, a South Vietnamese traveler. He was friendly, about 30 years old, and on the pudgy side. We hit it off right away.

After walking around the town to get the lay of the land, I got a bowl of noodles at a small sidewalk cafe. I observed very few foreigners in the area, and no wonder. War was raging in all directions, below the surface, and guerrillas

Before the great main temple of Angkor.

were laying ambushes and kidnapping and killing people on the roads. It was lovely to be in such peaceful surroundings, at least for the time being.

Back at my temple home as night fell, I asked a monk, in French, where I could take a bath. He got me a long bamboo pole with a hook on one end and a wooden bucket with a looping wire to carry it by. I was now armed for one of the most harrowing baths I would ever take.

Marching out to the middle of the compound under a full moon, I found the well. It was about six feet in diameter and made of rough stones cemented together. It rose three feet off the ground. I could see the moonlight reflecting off the water some fifteen feet below. I expertly lowered the bucket hooked onto the pole.

When the bucket touched the water, it came off the hook. I did everything I could to snag the bucket wire to absolutely no avail. Fortunately, there was not a soul in sight watching this foreigner in his jockey shorts fishing for a bucket. Well, there was no way I could return to the temple without the bucket. *I must retrieve it or drown trying*, I decided. So, over the side of the well I went, clinging gingerly to the slippery rocks inside the well. Inch-by-inch down I went, almost losing my grip several times.

At the bottom, I retrieved the rebellious bucket and hooked the wire over my right arm. Buddha was with me as I made it back to the top of the well after fifteen minutes of valiant struggle. To heck with a bath! It must be said, "There is an art to lowering a bucket into a deep well and coming up with water."

I collapsed on my mat-bed exhausted, dreaming all night of that elusive bucket. *Maybe I could find a monk in the morning to do the honors for me. No one had ever worked harder or deserved a bath more*, were my last thoughts before drifting into sleep.

Albert and I rented bikes the next morning. We set out at 8:00 to tour the famous temple ruins. The road from town to Angkor is straight as an arrow for six kilometers. The outer wall encloses a space of 203 acres. Forests, rendering some temples almost invisible because they were overgrown with vegetation, covered most of the area.

The inner walls of the main temple bear a series of bas-reliefs, depicting large-scale scenes. One expert called these "the greatest known linear arrangement of stone carving." On the southern gallery, 32 hells and 37 heavens of Hindu mythology are carved on the walls.

On the eastern gallery is one of the most celebrated scenes, the churning of the Sea of Milk, showing the serpent Vasuki churning the sea. The northern

*On top of a 900-year-old Angkor temple ruin celebrating having made
it alive through the Viet Cong jungles.*

gallery shows Krisha's victory over Bana, and the western gallery shows the
battle of Lanka.

By lunchtime, we had gotten hungry but had forgotten to bring food with
us. Being out in the jungle, we spotted several houses. One of the boys there
went up a tree and got us two coconuts. We drank the sweet milk before
cutting them in half to eat the coconut meat. Refreshed, we continued our
explorations through the widespread ruins in luxuriant jungle settings.

We arrived back at the temple at sunset. I paid a monk to draw my bath.
After a meal of rice and vegetables, I hit the mat.

There was one problem at the temple. The roosters had no idea when the
sun was going to come up, so at 3:00 in the morning, they would let go with
everything they had. Their favorite spot to bed down was right under my
window.

The next day Albert and I explored the rest of the ruins we could get to.
Some were so covered up by jungle growth we gave up trying to see them.
Some of those same ruins were shown in the movie *Tomb Raider*.

On a hill not far away from the main temple stood a magnificent pyramid-
like temple that was 900-plus years old. It was on the only hill within miles.
Albert was too tired to climb it, so up I went.

As I reached the narrow top, I carefully stood up on the edges of the crumbling rock, a deep hole between my feet disappearing into the center of the temple. It was akin to standing on the edges of a huge crumbling chimney. I yelled at Albert to take a picture quick before I crashed through to the temple floor. It was an amazing picture; my arms raised in a victory sign at having made it to Angkor alive.

From this exalted vantage point, I was treated to an amazing view from the center of the Angkor ruins. It was mine alone! In truth, I felt it was one of those great moments in life that is rarely experienced. The only soul in sight was Albert, appearing as but a speck on the jungle floor. The peace, the sky, the jungle, the quietness, the ancient temple below my feet, all blended to give me an exhilarating and powerful feeling of life itself and the God who created it.

As we rode our bicycles back into the temple grounds, everything was tinted with the moon's silver light. Mission accomplished. I had lived the dream of experiencing Angkor, in my mind one of the wonders of the world.

The next morning, Albert set off on a bus for Phnom Penh and I started hitchhiking to the Thai border. My first ride got me 50 kilometers down a jungle road to a country road junction.

After an hour of waiting and no cars, I started walking, praying no guerrillas were in the area. Soon a local bus came along and the driver insisted I ride free. It was me along with chickens, pigs, and peasants riding merrily along.

At a little past noon, the bus rolled into the village of Sisophon. Off I went walking once again. The road was dusty, the weather sultry, and of the few old cars and trucks that passed by, none chose to give me a ride. Five hours of walking and resting found me down and discouraged. Of course, I was in about as remote a region as you could find on Earth. Just pure jungle and no houses!

At last a bus came along. It rolled into Poipet at sunset. The chickens on the bus floor found the hot, dusty ride as uncomfortable as I did, no doubt, but it sure beat walking in the hot, jungle wilderness.

A Swedish man on the bus and I walked across the border bridge into Thailand and spent the night at a small temple, Wat Ana Phnom. I gave a sigh of relief as I once again touched Thai soil. Cambodia had looked peaceful on the surface but no one was really safe at any time in those days. Sad. Over the next ten years or so, many foreigners in Cambodia would disappear and never be heard from again.

Bless Buddhist monks everywhere for their great goodness and kindness. The struggle between good and evil was extraordinarily clear in Cambodia.

CHAPTER 44
Tales of Burma and India

Wandering re-establishes the original
harmony which once existed between man
and the universe.
— Anatole France

*T*hat following morning, as I walked the long dirt road from the temple out to the narrow two-lane highway, my thoughts were on what adventures lay ahead. But first, I had to make it back to Bangkok.

After only a half-hour wait, along came two Thai-Chinese cookie salesmen in a Mercedes microbus. They told me to hop in the back doors and take a seat on one of the round cookie tins, each two-feet tall. I was getting good at riding on containers! They kindly told me to help myself to some cookies. Well, there was nothing I liked better than cookies and having had no sweets in weeks, I dug in.

The salesmen stopped at a number of small towns to peddle cookies. Of course, thanks to me, their supply had been cut nearly in half along the way. A cookie monster was loose in the back of the van.

By the time we reached Bangkok, I never wanted to see a cookie again in my life. I was reminded of the French proverb that goes, "He who keeps eating after his stomach is full digs his grave with his teeth."

My three-week adventure through Laos and Cambodia had cost me the grand sum of $29 U.S. I would venture to say not many could've made it on that amount of money.

It was back to my servant quarter's room at Mrs. Swan's house. At least three pounds of dust came off when I took a shower. I trimmed my incipient beard that had become ragged around the edges.

I began making an outline of all I wrote in special journals during my Laotian-Cambodian adventure. With luck, I could sell the story to a newspaper. Bob Udick of *Bangkok World* expressed an interest.

Vim with the Tourist Organization of Thailand gave me a wonderful letter of recommendation to carry with me wherever I went from then on. I had worked closely with TOT during President Johnson's visit and had taught English at their hotel training school.

At the Red Cross Hospital, I checked to see what shots I needed for the countries coming up. "You're in good shape," the nurse said—little did she know. I knew that every country I would cross into would always be the same—*You've had only 73 cholera shots, you need another one.* I was sure to die of cholera shots sooner or later.

On a Tuesday, I booked a flight on Union of Burma Airways to Rangoon for the following Monday. My ticket would take me through to Calcutta. Since Burma was controlled by a military dictatorship, they allowed foreigners to stay only 24 hours in the country.

A new chapter in my life was about to open after six months in Thailand. I had a lovely dinner with Mrs. Swan, Ying, and her children. I thanked them for their exceptional kindnesses and hospitality to me.

Mr. Anderson, the TWA manager in Bangkok, told me he would air freight my aluminum trunk to Rome at no cost. Wow! Otherwise, it would have cost me a small fortune to ship it. Now all I needed was a larger backpack to journey across the highest mountains and hottest deserts ahead.

Through TOT (Tourist Organization of Thailand), I became a model for a Sunset Magazine ad. Patti was the girl model they had selected. In the over 100 pictures taken by three photographers, there were the temples, 1,000 pigeons, and us. Our picture at a temple, no doubt, appeared in many parts of the world.

Sawad and Chanit arranged for a limousine to take me to the airport and gave me a flower lei to put around my neck. Sri gave me a long, goodbye kiss, as I boarded the plane late that afternoon. I was tempted not to leave.

Farewell to Thailand, Burma, here I come! The Burmese Airways Viscount plane took only 90 minutes to reach Rangoon. As the plane was landing, I noticed soldiers with machine guns posted at numerous emplacements along both sides of the runaway.

It looked like they had been expecting me. A friendly greeting and message it was not. *Welcome to Dictatorial Burma*, I reflected.

I was put up in a venerable British hotel complete with a ceiling fan. The hotel setting was right out of a 1930s movie.

Bob, an Australian bloke, and I toured the city in a trishaw. One of my first impressions was that everyone was wearing the national dress, a sarong-type affair.

The city had a cosmopolitan feel, with Indian temples and mosques rising between the 19th century buildings. Barefoot Buddhist monks dressed in burgundy robes wandered the streets at dawn and sunset, carrying food bowls. At Sule Paya Square, there was a 46-meter high, 2,000-year-old stupa, a dome-shaped monument to Buddha.

The most impressive of all the temples in Rangoon was the Shwedagon Pagoda with its 100-meter-tall, gold-plated stupa, a marvel to behold. This Buddhist area within the city features 82 buildings, 8,000 gold slabs, 5,000 diamonds and over 2,000 semi precious stones. It was breathtaking. Rangoon was like a city that time forgot.

That pleasant evening, Bob and I went to the National Flag Day Fair. Our timing was excellent. There was music, merriment, food, booths covering several square blocks of the park, and people dressed in their most colorful clothes.

My prayer was that Burma once again would know freedom and peace for its gentle people. The ruling military junta has kept Nobel Peace Prize winner Aung San Suu Kyi a prisoner in Rangoon on and off. She was held from 1989 to 1995, and again from 2000 to 2002. She was again arrested and placed behind bars in May 2003. She was moved from prison back into house arrest in late 2003 and has been held there ever since. I never take my American freedoms for granted. Political oppression still prevails in Burma (Myanmar), probably worse than it has ever been. How precious is freedom!

It was up at 5:00 the next morning to catch an early flight to Calcutta. The plane was delayed from taking off for four hours. As I waited in the terminal, I could see the soldiers with their machine guns lining the runway.

The Black Hole of Calcutta! I had heard this story since I was a boy and I was expecting the worst. However, it didn't appear that way to me at all. Somewhere along the line, Calcutta was dubbed the City of Joy.

The Black Hole actually refers to the Indian leader of Bengal imprisoning 146 British prisoners of war in an airless dungeon. The next morning, when the door was opened, it was claimed that 123 of the prisoners had died.

I was excited to be in India. Mahatma Gandhi was one of my heroes. And just to think, Gandhi had been inspired by reading Henry David Thoreau's *Walden Pond*.

From the airport, I went straight to the Government Tourist Office with other young travelers from the plane. That's where we got information on Calcutta and cheap places to stay.

I had one contact. It was Mr. Paddar, an Indian travel agent I had met in Thailand. I headed for the Orient Express Company office hoping to catch him in. Mr. Paddar was out but I met his manager when I walked into their office at 1:00 that afternoon. If it hadn't been for this new friend, K.K. Sharma, no telling what my reception and situation would have been in Calcutta. One contact or one friend can make all the difference when arriving in a new country on a shoestring, especially one as kind as Sharma. Fate!

Sharma treated me royally from the first minute I met him. It was as if we had been lifelong friends. He took me to a worker's hotel where I had to pay only 70 cents U.S. a night.

I wasn't looking for such luxury, but once in a while I was willing to splurge. My second floor room was about 6' x 8' with a window that had no glass or screen, only wooden shutters, and a screechy ceiling fan on the high ceiling. The window overlooked the teeming narrow street that had cows wandering about. I felt right at home. The bath was a dungeon-like affair with high ceilings, no window or light, 12' x 12', and a faucet in one wall. This had to be the infamous black hole.

That evening I read up on Calcutta. The British opened a trading base in the area in 1687. In 1696, Old Ft. William was established and that was the origin of the city. It was situated on the Hooghly River and is India's chief port.

It's interesting to note that Calcuttans are sports fanatics. Two of the biggest sports arenas in the world are located there.

With my first good sleep in three nights, I was ready for my first full day in India. P.D., a young boy who was an all-around worker at the hotel, brought me two fried eggs, two pieces of toast and a cup of tea for breakfast. It was an excellent start.

With a bucket loaned to me by Satish, who worked at the government social security office, I washed my dirty clothes and then myself.

My first task was to see if I could find work among the 10,000,000 souls there. After I went door knocking, I met with Mr. Green in the afternoon. He was the General Manager of the Grand Hotel. Unfortunately, my language skills in Hindi and Bengali were not quite up to par. To soothe things over, Sharma kindly took me with him to have dinner with an Indian family he was close to.

The very next day, Sharma took me to see the horse races at the elaborate racetrack. Afterward we went to Trincas Restaurant to talk, observe people, and I danced with several attractive Indian girls sitting near our table.

That evening, Dogra led us to the Ramakrishna Mission to hear a swami's lecture. The swami was wrapped in white cotton robes and had a shaved head. His main message, *Treat each man as a subject and not an object. Man is the end and not the means.* That was well put.

I had met Dogra, a most likeable fellow, at the worker's hotel. He actually lived there. He became my friend and guide in that fascinating city. As is done in some parts of the East and Middle East among men friends, he would grab and hold my hand while walking down the street. Needless to say, I hoped I wouldn't run into any of my Texas friends. But this was the custom of friendship among men in India. I was willing to adapt to the customs wherever I ventured, up to a point. When in Rome, after all…

One lovely morning, I stopped by to ask Mr. Bhowmik, the "worker's hotel" manager, a question. Then and there he invited me to go to his village with him. We caught the 1:35 train and arrived in Similegare at 4:00 that afternoon.

Walking along the dirt road between rice fields, I knew this was a part of India I had been anxious to see and experience. Houses made of mud were covered with roofs of red tile over a bamboo framework. Small plots of land were being plowed with water buffaloes and everyone was barefooted. There was no electricity; only hand pump wells were in evidence.

As I viewed these sights, my thought was, it probably wasn't much different 100 years ago. When we reached Mr. Bhowmik's home, we got on bicycles and toured a wide area. Along the way, we met with some of the village leaders for tea and conversation.

Mr. Bhowmik's home was simple but comfortable and well ordered. The Indian Government had given him his small plot of land he came from Pakistan as a refugee.

I woke up the next morning at the crack of dawn without the assistance of any roosters. I had slept well on a flat board bed covered by a mosquito net.

My host's parents lived in a separate small house. I found them very kind but they spoke no English.

After a breakfast of boiled eggs, bread, bananas and tea, we once again rode bicycles so I could see new sights. I saw how bricks were made, weaving on hand looms, an irrigation system, some small shops, a Kali temple, and had tea with the members of a once wealthy, land-owning family. The latter had been relegated to living in what I would call a huge, rundown, feudal home.

By bus, train and taxi, we made it back to the hotel in Calcutta at sundown. I was richer for having experienced how the "other half" lives. *Quite well, considering the poverty of so many in this gigantic city*, I thought.

There was no hope of finding work in Calcutta, so I spent a day on a sightseeing bus tour. It is always an excellent way to get a taste of a huge city that has interesting landmarks. When we stopped for lunch, an Indian university student, Kanu, invited me to have lunch with him. I was always able to learn something from everyone I met.

Calcutta was a kaleidoscope of activity for me, which included saturating myself in the history of British India at the Victoria Memorial; going with Sharma to a restaurant to listen to Indian music; meeting an Indian gentleman at the Consulate of Nepal, and ending up in a long discussion on events in the world; chatting with several American fellows at the Salvation Army Hostel, and the list went on and on.

One afternoon as I was leaving the Grand Hotel, a 17-year-old Indian boy by the name of Chico accosted me. This young character became my shopping guide. He helped me order a rucksack to be made.

After one week in Calcutta, I had only spent $15 U.S., which I'd exchanged into Indian rupees. I got a lot of mileage out of every dollar. Practice makes perfect.

Somen, with the National Christian Relief Council, took me by jeep to see two of the villages that this organization had settled with refugees from East Pakistan. Over 1,000 families had been settled in three villages some 20 miles outside of Calcutta. As we were walking through one of the villages, I helped a little girl, not much bigger than her bucket, pump water from a well.

The time had come to head to Nepal by train. Sharma helped me to get a reserved seat in third class by offering a one-rupee bribe to the conductor. I was to learn that third class was one step up from a cattle car. It was February 28.

Dozens of barefooted porters, carrying huge loads on their heads, were going in every direction, shoving their way through the bubbling mass of humanity. This was going to be a challenge.

As Sharma and I stood in awe on the platform, we saw six Indian men pick up a friend and ram him head first through an open train window. The poor fellow went in halfway. When they let him go, he popped back out.

The fun began. Sharma showed me which rail car to get on. And I thought Japanese trains were crowded. This scene took the cake. I fought my way aboard, then through the mob to the middle of the rail car. I had my rucksack on top of my head, not to be outdone by the porters. This was when I was informed after 20 minutes of battle my "reserved" seat was in the next car. A shoehorn would've come in handy.

Fresh air was non-existent. *Where is a cholera shot when you need one?* I wondered. Slowly I inched, lurched and banged my way through the narrow aisle. Thirty more minutes of all-out effort got me to my "reserved" seat, a wooden bench where three could comfortably sit on each other's laps. It was beyond absurd. People of all ages were still pushing, yelling, and fighting for seats. I collapsed into my reserved seat. If this was the reserved section, I shuddered at the thought of what the unreserved section must have been like. I vowed to never ride an Indian train again—if there was any possible way to avoid it.

*With my friend Gupta at our boarding house
in Calcutta.*

CHAPTER 45

Lost in the Himalayas, Far from Katmandu

It is in the compelling zest of high adventure and of victory, and in creative action, that man finds his supreme joys.

— Antoine de Saint-Exupery

As the sun came up on March 1, I was sitting on a wooden bench on the train platform at Samstipur. I had traveled about four fifths of the way from Calcutta to the Nepalese border.

Being in between trains, I wrote about the events of the day before in my daily journal. It had been one of the most uncomfortable, noisy, and cramped days of my life. While I wrote, I had two cups of tea to boost my spirits.

The train for Rauxal pulled out at 7:30 that evening. I was in the first-class coach. I bit the bullet. It cost me all of $3 U.S. more than a third class fare. To me, it was worth a thousand dollars in peace and tranquility.

During the nine-hour journey, I was the only person who rode all the way. Sixty or seventy people must have come and gone as the train steamed across India, including beggars, families, young couples, shoeshine boys, sick ones, salesmen, and babies to name but a few in the human parade.

Customs took much too long on the Indian side of the border. As dark fell, I rode in a horse cart into the nearest Nepalese town. The first so-called hotel room I walked into saw me stepping on a scurrying rat. No wonder the price was so low. The room had one light bulb hanging from the ceiling, a wooden slat for a bed, no window, and no basin. If it had had two light bulbs, I would've stayed.

I retreated out of that place as quickly as I could! At the next ratel nearby, no rats were visible as I entered the room. This hotel had a Triple A rating, so I paid up front for a rat-free room. However, during the night I was awakened by the magnified sound of a rat chewing through cardboard.

Over the drainage hole in my bare, concrete-floored room, I'd placed a piece of cardboard, using a brick to secure it in place. That little varmint was

247

doing his best to get through it. I added on three more bricks. It had become a test of wills.

Bright and early, I headed for the open market. After an hour of waiting, I caught a ride in a coal truck for 12 rupees. Lucky for me, I got a seat inside the cab. The three other people paid eight rupees each to ride on top of the coal.

For twenty miles or so, the truck moved along on a straight, narrow road on a plain. The first hills I saw were not too high, but as the truck began to climb they became successively higher. Six hours later, the mighty, and majestic Himalayas appeared out of nowhere.

It was as if we were approaching heaven. The peaks were the whitest white and as high as the sky. It took 11 hours, most of it winding upward, to reach Katmandu.

Nepal is the home of the world's highest mountain range, the Himalayas. Katmundu, its capital city, stands 4,500 feet above sea level in a fertile valley. The city lies on an ancient trade and pilgrim route from India to Tibet, China, and Mongolia. Gurkhas, who made it their capital, captured it in 1768. In the late 18th century, the British arrived on the scene and Gurkhas eventually became an outstanding fighting force in the British Army.

One thing can be clearly stated: "Not many people have the honor to arrive in the Nepalese capital in a coal truck." I got dumped off in the central area a little worse for wear. At least I hadn't turned black from coal dust like those folks that were in the back of the truck.

As I started looking for a cheap place to stay, I ran into Suresh, a fellow adventurer I'd met along the way in India. He was also looking for a place to stay. Entering the 500-year old Central Hotel, we met four exchange students from the U.S. Bob and Larry invited me to share their room at no cost. I was off and running.

It looked like I would be able to live in Katmandu on $1 a day. At that rate, I'd be able to hold out for four days—that is until I could cash a $20 travelers' check.

The next morning, I trekked down to the Tourist Information Office to learn all I could before planning out a schedule of things to see and do. This was my usual modus operandi when I arrived at a new destination.

When the exchange students left, I got a small room at the hotel for 30 cents a night, with meals costing around 15 cents each. This was my kind of place. The hotel even furnished a bucket with which to take a bath in a dungeon.

On a hilltop temple outside of Katmandu.

The hotel, probably built in the 1800s, was right in the center of the old city. Serma, the manager, was a pleasant fellow. Knowing that I was a hotel-man too, he became my advisor and guardian. In the afternoon, I explored the northern part of Katmandu. I went for another long walk after dinner, before calling it a day.

This was a fascinating spot on Earth to be. The old city looked as like it was from Biblical times. Cattle roamed the streets, women were having their ears pierced squatting in front of small shops, and people and bicycles were going in every direction.

I set off at 6:00 the next morning to hike to a temple located on a hill two miles away. As I reached the top, the sun rose. It was a chilly morning with fog covering the valley.

The temple had huge eyes painted on its spire. They were watching over a group of musicians playing enthusiastically and chanting prayers at the same time. It was an invigorating and spiritual way to start the day.

Six American beatniks checked into the hotel. Having met them at the border, I had a sit-down talk with them. From what I could gather, they were not much more than aimless wanderers. It apparently had become the fad of the day in America.

I rented a bicycle one day for 2 rupees and bicycled all over Katmandu. My goal was to see the main temples, along with parts of the city I had not seen.

In the daytime, hiking shorts and a short sleeve shirt were comfortable, but at night a jacket or sweater was necessary. I had come at a good time of the year.

It must be said, the general filth and dirt there was appalling. Hygienically, it was almost a cesspool in many parts of the city. Why the government hadn't launched a clean up campaign was beyond me.

Each day I was in the capital area, I'd see several marriage processions moving slowly down the streets behind a beat up brass band. The band members would always be in brightly colored but tattered parade uniforms. For all I knew, it might have been the same band in each joyous case.

I had developed a terrible cold and was feeling bad. It was partly due to not eating proper foods, getting cold at night, and not getting enough sleep. Of course, the filth, beyond reasonable limits, may have had something to do with it. A cholera shot would fix me right up.

One beautiful morning, I set out to hike to Nagarkot. For food I put three boiled eggs, cheese, a loaf of brown bread, a package of cookies, water, and a thermos of tea in my backpack.

The first nine miles, I went to Bhagdon by bus, the end of the line. I started hiking the path across some terraced rice fields. As I got higher, I started wandering off the path to explore beautiful vistas.

The folks at the tourist office told me it would take about three hours to hike to the way-station cabin in the mountains after I got off the bus. No problem, I had plenty of time to go off the beaten path and make it there by sunset—famous last words.

I later found out the three hours was the time it took a native, who knows the trails perfectly, going at full speed without rest to reach the one small camper's cabin at Nagarkot. Unfortunately for me, the few natives I met along the way, who spoke little English, did not provide reliable directions. I was having a wonderful time wandering in all directions as I spotted astounding vistas. Before I realized it, the sun was going down. I hurriedly got back to the main trail and continued trekking upward. With no moon, it grew totally dark by 7:00. I had no flashlight but could make out the trail at least up to thirty yards ahead of me in the forested mountains.

I stopped to eat and drink something several times. The air was starting to thin as I trekked ever upward; I was beginning to tire after hiking all day long.

By 2:00 that morning, I was out of food and water, exhausted, and knew I must have taken a wrong trail. There were no lights in sight. There were

Hiking in the Himalayas—a true expert on how to get lost there.

steep drop offs to the left of the trail and less and less vegetation. It was windy and cold.

Then it happened. I heard footsteps well behind me and off to the right of the trail. I froze and looked around. All I could see was dark shadows, boulders, and rock outcrops. The footsteps had stopped. My immediate thought was, *this is Abominable Snowman territory and I was going to be the first one to ever meet him in person*!

I started up the trail again, praying for deliverance—again, the sound of footsteps. *Ok, Straughan, now you've done it*, I shuddered. I stopped, it stopped! I started, it started! In total exhaustion, knowing I was going nowhere, completely lost, I summoned up my courage, turned around, picked up two big rocks, and began stumbling back the way I had come. *If the Yeti wants me, he can have me*, I concluded. I was too tired to care.

I heard no more footsteps. Maybe the legendary wild man of the Himalayas just didn't like me trespassing on his homeland. Folklore indicates these ape-like creatures have actually existed since ancient times. I was glad he and I had come to an understanding.

As the sun peeked over Mt. Everest in the distance, I stumbled onto the cabin where I was supposed to have spent the night. The caretaker went to sleep at sunset, so I had missed it completely in the dark. I enjoyed the resplendent

251

sunrise over Mount Everest. The mighty Himalayan peaks gradually were absorbed into the morning haze and were no more.

I collapsed into one of the cabin's bunk beds. Water had never tasted so sweet or a bed so soft! I slept until noon and then started back down the trail. It took me three hours, going downhill, to reach Bhagdon. From there it was back to Katmandu by bus.

I was in bad shape. Every joint and muscle was sore and aching, my throat raw, a bad cold had turned to chest congestion, and then to see all the filth and dirt again was almost too much to take. After eating, I went straight to bed and slept straight through till the next morning.

I had booked a flight to Simra near the Nepalese Border with India. The Royal Nepal Airlines flight was one I would never forget. When I got to the small airfield, there sat an old DC-3 of World War II vintage. I sat down in one of the frayed seats. I could see what appeared to be the copilot in the cockpit.

Twenty minutes after we were supposed to have taken off, the pilot came abroad at the door in the back. As he stumbled up the aisle, appearing to be four sheets to the wind, he had on a vintage aviator's cap, goggles and all. Around his neck and waving half way down his back was a bright red silk scarf. *He looked good but was he in any condition to fly the plane?* I haltingly wondered.

The pilot's shaky voice came over the loud speaker, "We couldn't find the radio officer, but he usually shows up sooner or later." Terrific! He showed up 15 minutes later. The cockpit door closed. We were in God's hands, as the plane banked over the rugged peaks below—with me working my Buddhist prayer beads for all I was worth.

At Simra, we sat in the bus for 45 minutes before getting on the road to Burgins. Then a trishaw got me to the Rauxal Train Station, five miles from Burgins. A Mr. Mahajan and his family took me under their kind wing at the station. After a three-hour wait, we boarded the train at 8:00 in the evening. At 10:00, we changed trains, getting into a jammed third-class rail car. I was on the road again in total discomfort, but what a lovely way to get to rub elbows with the masses.

CHAPTER 46

The Jewel of India

One should count each day a separate life.

— Seneca

The train arrived at the Ganges River at daybreak. Over 500 people got off and boarded a huge river steamer. *Shades of Mark Twain on the Mississippi*, I mused.

The Ganges River starts in an ice cave on the southern slopes of the Himalayas. It has enjoyed a position of reverence for millennia among India's Hindus, by whom it is worshiped in its personified form as the Goddess Ganga. Above all, it is the river of India.

After two hours on the riverboat, we reached Patna. With the hospitable Mahajan family, I went by horse and buggy to the train station. I decided to skip Banares and go straight to New Delhi. Once again traveling by myself, I boarded an express train. Luckily, I was able to get a seat in a third class sleeper, which wasn't quite so crowded.

I met a helpful fellow by the name of Saberwal and we each had a tray of food for dinner. As I only had a seat and no sleeping berth, I started looking for a place to lie down. Just as I was getting comfortably settled on a rack in a small luggage area at the end of the rail car, the obnoxious conductor came along. He made me vacate my chosen bed. Seeing no other alternative, I put my trusty backpack between two seats, creating a body-size flat surface, and went off into much needed snatches of sleep between stations.

The train rolled into the Delhi Station at mid-morning. I was worn to a frazzle and on the point of starvation. Saberwal headed through the throngs of people with me trying to keep up.

Catching a scooter cab to his friend's office, we then went on to his apartment building. After a dip bath, I caught a bus to the Ashoka Hotel. The mail I was expecting had not arrived. I always gave a prestigious hotel as a forwarding address to make sure my mail would be safe.

Saberwal had basically adopted me to insure I got off to a good start in New Delhi, India's capital. I was most grateful for his kindness. It was but one more example of the basic goodness of people.

When we returned to his apartment, I found that the room I was to sleep in had been commandeered for a wedding the next morning. My two new friends were out. To go without sweet sleep for another night, especially with such a dreadful cold, was a thought I could not bear.

I left them a gracious thank you note, grabbed my bags, and headed for the YMCA. Hot water, a clean room, and a soft bed! It had been two weeks since I had enjoyed such luxuries.

I attended the Free Church service on Sunday. It was an inspiring and strengthening service. I prayed for Divine Guidance as I began my stay in New Delhi. So far, God had been with me every step of the way.

My money situation was fair, as long as I did not run into any catastrophes. I changed $10 U.S. into rupees, leaving me a $10 bill out of the $66 I had when I left Bangkok. I still had $550 in travelers' checks to cover the next several months, as I would make my way overland to far off Rome, one step at a time, one cent at a time.

A young couple I had to come to know in Bangkok, Mick and Patti, had suggested I look up an Indian family they had gotten to know in New Delhi. Shiv and Om Bahadur turned out to be one of the nicest and most interesting couples it had been my pleasure to meet in my wanderings.

The Bahadurs invited me to come stay with their family. I went back to the YMCA, got my backpack, and headed to their comfortable home. Ravi, 19, their nephew, came out to greet me on my second arrival. He was a math student at New Delhi University.

Anyone meeting and knowing this family could not fail to come away from India with a grateful heart and a good impression. Shiv, a police officer, was married to Om. They had two sons, Hersh, 12, and Ashoka, 11. Living with them were Om's two sisters, her brother, and Ravi. For the next week, I ate and slept well, due to the unbelievable kindness of the Bahadurs. They had a lovely garden where I would sit reading in the mornings, surrounded by beautiful red, purple, orange, white, and yellow flowers. They were like a balm to my soul—and my terrible cold was slightly better.

Many evenings we sat around in discussion, as I was treated to the fascinating history and tales of India. New Delhi has a vibrant history. It has been the "capital of seven empires" and has over 60,000 recognized monuments. The first city of Delhi is believed to have been founded around 5000 B.C.

Delhi is a cosmopolitan city due to the multi-ethnic and multi-cultural presence of the vast Indian bureaucracy and political system, as well as the expanding economic base. From an international perspective, there were more than 160 embassies located there.

Several days later after my arrival, Oliver Streeton, an Aussie, and I went to the Pakistan Embassy together. At first, I was told I would have to wait three weeks for a visa. Undeterred, I saw Mr. Arshad, the High Commissioner, "Clarke, I will try to have your visa for you in a week." I thanked him kindly. Never take no for an answer until they shoot you—determination and persistence are essential keys to any success.

I went to see one of Delhi's most impressive sights, the Red Fort: a standing testimony to the magnificent power and pomp of the Mogul emperors. Its construction was completed in 1648 and derives its name from the huge walls of red sandstone that characterize the eight sides of the fort—a massive, magnificent structure.

Ravi drove me to the Iranian Embassy where I applied for a visa. From there, he took me to the railway station. I was about to test my luck, once again.

Richard Halliburton, the famous young American adventurer of the 1920s, dodged train conductors to ride free across India. *Now it was my turn to give it a try. If he could do it, I could do it. Couldn't I?* I wondered.

I casually walked in through the station exit gate where the attendant seemed to be absent. Was I devilish or what? Maybe it was just plain stupidity. I located a seat in the third class sleeping coach, my favorite place to be in the whole world. Just before reaching Agra, an hour and a half from Delhi, wouldn't you know it, the ticket collector asked me if I had reserved a seat. "Why, no Mr. Collector, sir and how are you this fine day?" I stuttered.

He said, "Quite fine," and continued on his appointed duties. That was close. I had expected to be dragged off the train in chains at that point.

At Agra, I shot through the gate while the attendant was looking the other way. I was then firmly convinced I was meant to be an intelligence agent.

After checking into the Tourist Bungalow, I hopped on a bus for one of the wonders of the world, the Taj Majal. It was near sunset when I first cast my amazed eyes on the jewel of India.

Long, long ago, in a land called Hindustan, a dynasty of kings reigned who built a splendid empire of beauty and grace. Among them was one known as the "King of the World." He built this poem of stone for the sake of his love. Her name was Mumtaz Mahal.

The Taj, which was begun in 1631, is the most architecturally beautiful tomb in the world. English Poet Sir Edwin Arnold described it as "the proud passions of an emperor's love wrought in living stones." It is a celebration of a woman, built in marble.

The colors of the Taj change at different hours of the day and during the seasons. Like a jewel, it sparkles when the semi-precious stones inlaid into the white marble on the mausoleum catch the glow of the moon. The Taj is pinkish in the morning, milky white in the evening, and golden when the moon shines. It is a magnificent tribute to the power of love for a woman.

The sun set as I lingered in the Mogul Gardens of the Taj. My plan, following Halliburton's feat, was to hide myself within the grounds when the gates were closed. Then, when no one was around, I'd swim in the Taj's moonlit alabaster pool, just like he had done. Then I remembered that he was apprehended, as the sun rose, and marched in front of the British superintendent. Halliburton was released with a stern rebuke.

I'll probably be marched straight to jail, I thought. I decided that might be more romance than I could stand.

After a good night's sleep in my room at the Tourist Bungalow, I returned to the Taj to spend the day reveling in that fairytale in white marble.

As night fell, I dodged conductors back to New Delhi. The train stopped for a short time in a very dark area right before reaching the station. Seeing a number of people getting off and crossing the tracks, I followed suit. When in India, do as the Indians do.

Using my feet, I reached the Bahadurs' residence around nine in the evening. A warm and friendly welcome was waiting for me. I told them of my affair with the Jewel of India.

CHAPTER 47
The Famed Khyber Pass—Descent Into Afghanistan

Our country was built by pioneers who were not afraid of failure and dreamers who were not afraid of action.

— Brooks Atkinson

With visas in hand for Pakistan, Iran, Iraq, Syria and Lebanon, things were starting to fall into place. It was to be an overland adventure through some of the highest mountains and hottest deserts in the world.

I'd never forget the great kindness the Bahadurs had shown me. They literally took me in as one of their family. I would miss each and every one of them, even Dusty their dog.

Riding third class trains again was something I didn't look forward to. One of my heroes, Mahatma Gandhi, once wrote he had to give up riding in third class because he wasn't physically strong enough to fight his way off and on to the train, and then retain a good position once he made it on. My persistent cold had weakened me to the point where I needed to stay in bed for a week.

Duty called and money was starting to run low. I had no choice but to adventure on, sick or not. I was thankful that the 9:00 p.m. train wasn't crowded at all—for some unexplainable reason. I found an empty wooden seat and settled in for the all-night journey. The train pulled into Ferosepur at 8:00 the next morning.

When I asked an Indian gentleman on the train platform for information, he was good enough to take me along with him, in a horse-and-cart taxi, to the town. Since I had a one-hour wait before the bus to the Pakistani border was to depart, I crossed the street, met, and visited with four Christian students at a church.

Back at the station, I was informed that no bus was coming—serendipity came into play once again. I boarded a wooden cart pulled by a horse whose best days had long passed. My traveling companion on that jolting, plodding, eight-mile journey was Noor. He was a friendly Afghan student on his way home from India.

Noor and I sat on the back of the cart, our legs dangling off, and talked as rain poured down on us all the way. Of course, we had no umbrella or raincoat. My cold turned into near pneumonia as the cart wended its way on the muddy road through wheat fields.

After clearing the customs checkpoint, off we went on a Pakistani bus to Lahore. For some unknown reason, it was a lengthy process checking into the YMCA when we arrived. Noor and I ate dinner at a nearby restaurant and then I went to bed exhausted and feeling terrible. I was in desperate need of medicine and rest.

The next day, Noor and I walked around exploring the city. That evening, we got on the train without buying a ticket when we found out it was leaving within five minutes. It was the most crowded train I'd ever seen—the last thing I needed.

People were hanging out the doors three and four deep. Luckily, we spotted a corridor in a second-class coach with a bit of extra floor room available. Throughout the cold night, Noor and I took turns sleeping on the narrow corridor floor.

No conductor approached during the night. If one had, we would've argued it was a fourth class space and the railroad should be paying us. The train pulled into pretty Peshawar at 9:00 in the morning. The two of us were worried, wondering how we would make it past the exit gate without a ticket. We found a side gate that had been left slightly open, and we darted through undetected.

I was just about out of Pakistani rupees. It was good to have a partner on that little adventure—and to preserve my meager funds.

Again, we horse-and-carted it, this time to the Afghan consulate where we got our visas. Abdul Saced, a rich man's son, took Noor and me under his wing when we checked into a small hotel. Abdul took us for a grand lunch. My spirits brightened a bit.

That afternoon we lazed around in the warmth of the sun on the hotel roof. Noor briefed me on Afghanistan, the Khyber Pass, and what to expect.

Peshawar sits at the base of the most historic pass in the world. For millennia, many invaders marched through the Khyber Pass. At its narrowest point, it is only about ten feet wide. It is a 33-mile passage through the awe-inspiring Hindu Kush mountain range.

The Khyber had been a major trade route for great camel caravans for centuries. The mountains on either side can be climbed in only a few places, making them perfect spots for bandit ambushes. As we were preparing to traverse the pass, we heard stories of two young American hitchhikers who had been killed and stripped, a month before, and left on the side of the road. This was enough to give us deep cause for concern.

Alexander the Great and his army marched through the pass in 326 B.C. In the A.D. 900s, Persian, Mongol, and Tarter armies forced their way through the Khyber. In an 1842 battle, 16,000 British and Indian troops were killed there. And now it was my turn to sally forth.

The story of the Khyber Pass is composed of such color and romance, such tragedy and glory, that fact appears stranger than fiction. My imagination was ready to unfold the pages of history. A member of the British force of 1919 summarized it well— "Every stone in the Khyber Pass has been soaked in blood."

It was a day to remember! The decrepit bus pulled out of Peshawar at ten in the morning with a full load of people in "reserved" seats, so there was no jostling—for a change.

The weather was cold and sunny. The bus slowly climbed into the mountains. The word passed among the passengers that a landslide had covered the road deep within the pass. Near sunset, we came upon it.

Considering landslides, this was nothing unusual. Earthquakes were relatively frequent occurrences in the area, along with avalanches and mudslides. For example, since 2000, there have been nine major earthquakes. In 2002, one of the earthquakes that shook the Hindu Kush Mountains killed hundreds of people and injured thousands.

There we were, on a high narrow mountain road, steep rock walls on the left, from whence came the landslide, and a drop-off on the road's right edge that disappeared into forever. There was no turning back.

Everyone was told to gather their belongings and make their way across the crumbling, sliding mass. All it had to do was start moving again and we would all have found our graves more than a thousand feet below.

My feet sunk eight inches or so into the shifting, jagged rock and dirt that crossed the road at a steep angle. I had *definitely* made it clear to the ticket agent in Peshawar that I wanted a "landslide free" ticket. Oh, well.

We all made it safely across. On the other side, a bus was waiting. The driver had radioed ahead of time for it to pick us up. It was dark and bone-chillingly cold when we got to Kabul. I was so glad to be alive after all the stories I'd heard of bandits, earthquakes, and, my favorite, landslides.

Looking back through the centuries, this trade and invasion route from central Asia had been one of the principal approaches of the armies of Alexander the Great, Timor, Babur, Mahmud of Ghazna, and Nadir Shad in their invasions of India. Now I can't help but wonder how many terrorists pass through the 34 tunnels and over the 92 bridges and culverts that run to the Afghan border.

As I prepared to pass across Afghanistan and Persia (Iran), all the way to Baghdad, I had no way of knowing that forty years later my fellow soldiers and Marines would be fighting a war here against an enemy we in the 1960s could not comprehend.

The sun came streaming through the big glass window in my room. It brought welcome warmth in the freezing atmosphere of the capital city of Kabul. I had found a cheap, but clean, small hotel to lay down my weary head. There was one problem; instead of water, ice came out of the shower. I took the shortest shower on record.

I explored Kabul most of the day, got a shave and a hot bath at the Spinzar Hotel, and, of course, had dinner at the Khyber Restaurant. The hot bath and hearty meal would have to last me until I got to Tehran. The one-day of rest and recuperation helped prepare me for the next three days of rough bus travel through some of the wildest and most desolate country in the world.

What really got my attention in Kabul was that I saw Russians everywhere, America's Cold War enemy. *What were they doing there?* I wondered. It became very clear to me later that they were laying the groundwork to take over Afghanistan. Back then, the communists were the threat, although they did not prevail—the enemy harbored there now, the Taliban, is even worse than the red army.

As the bus departed Kabul in the early morning, a wintry blanket fell. For two hours, there was no letup of heavy snow. It didn't matter that the driver couldn't see the road. There was hope though, because he could almost make out the hood of the bus.

My feet got so cold I couldn't feel them. Of course, the bus had no heat. This was perfect therapy for my cold, now turned to bronchitis.

Once we were out of the snow, far to the south, the scenery was truly something out of this world. We could have been on the surface of the moon by the looks and color of the terrain.

Our beat-up bus pulled into Kandahar around four in the afternoon. A fierce group of tribesmen were all around us. The term Taliban did not exist back then, but this is the area where the Taliban are the strongest in today's world.

Kandahar is Afghanistan's second largest city and a chief trade center. Alexander the Great, of all people, founded it in the fourth century B.C. India and Persia fought over the city and good old Genghis Khan sacked it in the 12th century.

It is the principal city of the fiercely independent Pashtun people. During the Soviet military occupation of 1979 to 1989, Kandahar was the site of a Soviet command. The Pashtuns did not take kindly to that situation. It was like unleashing one hundred thousand Genghis Khans who had no fear.

I was in far southern Afghanistan. I checked into something akin to a manger and slept on a straw bed. The camels around were a noisy lot, part of the caravans that trek through that dusty oasis. The room set me back 40 cents.

The next morning I explored the city without incident. At the bazaar, I bought a pair of soft green leather "Genghis Khan" pointed house shoes topped with fur.

The bus pulled out of that mecca for camels in a light rain. I had been to the end of the earth, so to speak, and survived. One never knows what will happen in Kandahar, I'd been told. The question was would I survive another bone-jarring ride and possible bandits on the road?

Sitting next to me was a big, congenial tribesman in his robe and turban. He took up three fourths of the two-person seat. I had to politely keep reminding him where the middle was, lest I be pushed off the edge. His damn rifle kept falling on me. I was more than polite through it all.

We drove across mostly flat, desert plains with long, jagged mountains showing in the far distance. We reached the city of Herat as the sun set.

Alexander made Herat one of his Alexandrias when he captured it in 330 B.C. Six hundred years later, it became a seat of Christianity. In 1221, it was captured by the Mongols and later destroyed by Genghis Khan. Around 1381, it was destroyed again, this time by Timur and his hordes. I wouldn't want to be a Heratan.

Before the Soviet invasion at the end of 1979, there was a substantial presence of Soviet advisors with their families in Herat. In ten days during March 1979, the Heratans rose up and killed 350 Soviet citizens. The Soviets then bombed the city, causing massive destruction and thousands of deaths. When I arrived, no one was attacking. All looked peaceful. Little did I know that would not last—in 1995 the city was captured by the Taliban. For the next five years, suicide bombers ravaged it.

Two Canadians I had met and I walked into the only thing one might call a hotel. We signed in for the night and went to a native restaurant for dinner. Herat resembled a frontier town of old.

Walking back to the "slumtel" along the muddy streets, I slid ankle deep into a sewage canal on the side of the street. To make matters worse, I lost my balance and fell down very gracefully, I thought, seat first into the fragrant canal. No one wanted to be near me after that. I didn't want to be near me, either.

April dawned, finding me halfway stranded in that ancient city. But there was some compensation. All in all, I found the Afghan people to be helpful and kind. It was like most any place in the world, if you show respect and a friendly attitude toward people, it is many times returned.

Breakfast time brought me three new friends—Joe, Peter, and Jane—all Aussies. Together we walked around the wide dirt streets dodging donkeys, camels, and horse-drawn carts.

Jane and I were able to secure the last two seats on the bus due to leave the next day. If we hadn't made it on that bus, it would have meant a four-day wait for the next one.

Without a doubt, Herat was the worst place I'd ever seen for arranging transportation. No wonder though, we were pretty much near the end of the world.

For lunch, I had rice, fish, and tea. Tea is all they drink in these parts—with sugar only. My roommate for that night was a personable young fellow by the name of Osman Irahami, an Afghan, on his way to study in the U.S. I wonder where he is now, given all the problems Afghanistan has suffered through.

There are some days you just never forget. There were inconveniences in profusion! It began when Osman looked out the window from his bed and said, "Guess what?" It was snowing heavily—just what I needed to push me into pneumonia, since I had been without medicine or proper care for weeks.

Those waiting for the bus huddled in the bus station, which was actually a shack. As everyone was loaded on the bus, our baggage was tossed on top, while a thick blanket of snow fell. It was a perfect picture of chaos and confusion and cold.

CHAPTER 48
Shades of the Persian Empire, Baghdad, and Scheherazade

We wonder, "Is the dream worth the price?" I say, "Yes! It is." The time when many people throw up their hands in despair, give up, and quit is the best time to "go for it."

— Anonymous

*T*he bus made its bumpy way over the unpaved road to Islam Quala at the Afghan border. It was a barren, windswept desert! Everyone huddled in the six-room cabin, around a wood-burning stove, for the five and a half hour wait for the Iranian bus.

After another splendid example of chaos, we boarded an old, old bus as night fell. When we reached the Iranian border checkpoint, we were in for a shock. Everyone was told to get off and line up in the freezing desert wind before what looked like an oversized outhouse. Nothing, not even one light, was visible in any direction on the desert's flat surface. This was the ultimate desolation in border crossings.

The word that passed along to those of us near the back of the line was that there was a cholera epidemic going on in Iran. *No problem, I couldn't get cholera if I tried,* was my last comforting thought. Then I found out differently.

When I got near the outhouse, I mean guardhouse, there was a Coleman-type lantern hanging from the ceiling and two Iranian soldiers with fixed bayonets inside. Each person, in turn, was given four huge horse pills to swallow. There was one community water bucket on the floor with a ladle in it. If we didn't have cholera already, we were sure to get it, along with the other diseases of the world. One lady refused to take the pills until one of the guards pointed a bayonet at her mouth.

It was an inky, moonless night as the bus continued on to the village town of Yusaff Abad. Six of us slept on the bus to save money.

It got light around 5:00 the next morning. I felt like I'd been put through a ringer as I stretched to wake up. Soon the driver came to tell us to have

263

our passports checked. It was so cold a polar bear would have had second thoughts about getting out into the frostbitten air.

That day was so chock full of delays and unnecessary stops that it became downright funny. It seemed like every several miles the bus would stop for some ludicrous reason.

On several occasions, soldiers with rifles slung over their shoulders would check and feel almost everything carried on the bus. What was going on? The Shah was going to be upset when I told him about these delays on the express bus.

We stopped at a restaurant for lunch. We were informed only eggs were available. Four days of nothing but eggs, and I was starting to walk like a chicken.

Finally we reached Mashad. Two hours later, it started sleeting and snowing at the same time. After having tea with two young chaps, I trudged back to our group's small hotel in a back alley. It wasn't far from the famous Golden Mosque of Iran.

It was a mad scramble to get to the bus station before 7:00 the next morning. There was no time to eat, so I chomped on some cookies and dates left over from the night before. My three fellow adventurers and I occupied the long seat across the back of the bus. No one wanted to sit there because it was the most uncomfortable place to ride on the bus.

None of the roads were paved. Having a mild case of dysentery, influenza, and cholera, I was kept in a constant state of acute uneasiness, to put it mildly. All I had been living on was native bread, eggs, tea, cookies, and dates. I sure could have used a big hamburger and chocolate shake about that time.

The bus driver finally gave up after almost 18 hours of continuous driving from 7:00 that morning until 1:00 the next morning over unpaved roads. I was so tired I didn't even know what small town we were in. I got a cheap room and collapsed into welcome and much needed sleep.

At 6:00 the next morning, we were on the road again. Shortly after 10:00, we entered Teheran. Not far from the bus station, some of us discovered a cheap hotel. It had no hot water and I was desperate for a soothing hot bath or shower.

I began searching for another cheap hotel. Soon I found one that *did* have hot water, and I soaked to my heart's content. The small extra cost was worth every cent, especially after traipsing across freezing mountains and deserts aboard "unsafe at any speed" buses.

I had one contact in this capital city. It was a Mr. Kazemi, a former Iranian Ambassador, whom I'd met aboard the ship *Chusan* three years earlier. When I called his number, his daughter answered. "My father is in Europe, but I may be able to arrange for you to meet some young people here for an exchange of ideas," she told me.

On that note, I went out and had a bowl of steaming hot beans sold by a street corner vendor. It buoyed my spirits. When you're low on money in a strange city, have no friends or family around, and the weather is gray and freezing, it doesn't take much to be appreciative of every small blessing.

I went to bed early. Since I had a worsening chest cold, I needed all the sleep I could get. I was afraid it might develop into pneumonia. It was a rough night, as I woke up chilled many times. I couldn't get warm even though I was covered with several heavy blankets.

Before setting out to explore Teheran the next morning, I washed clothes and read up on the city and the country. Persia/Iran had managed to remain independent throughout much of its history.

The Shah was the current ruler and during the Cold War he was an ally of the West. Even though everything seemed free and peaceful on the surface, there was unseen turmoil bubbling below. To me, everyone looked happy.

The Shah saw himself as heir to the kings of ancient Iran. In the very year I was there, he staged an elaborate coronation ceremony, styling himself "Shah en Shah"—King of Kings.

In 1979 a theocratic revolution, led by Ayatollah Khomeini, sent the Shah into exile. He went to the U.S., where he was treated for lymphatic cancer. Iranian militants seized the U.S. Embassy in Tehran and demanded the Shah's extradition in exchange for 50 hostages. The U.S. refused and the Shah eventually moved to Egypt, where he died.

The weather was cool and sunny for a change, as I walked all around the city. What struck me was the beauty of the Iranian girls and the kindness of those Iranians I met along the way. Every other man I met seemed to be named Mohammed.

I observed how people stood quietly in long lines waiting for buses and then got on in an orderly manner. I rode a number of buses in my explorations that day.

When I asked one Mohammed for directions, we became instant friends. He proceeded to show me many of the main sights, on foot, for the next four hours.

Since Katmandu, my debilitating cold had been dragging me farther and farther down. My three Aussie friends arrived back from Mashad in even worse condition than myself. No wonder. We'd been riding in freezing, unheated buses; had constant delays; little sleep; bad or too little food to eat; basically staying in flea-bitten, dirty hotels; and were always on the move, most times in a state of exhaustion.

It was time for me to venture on to the lands of the "Arabian Nights." Once again, I was on a rickety bus filled with pungent villagers and Hindu pilgrims. The bus finally lurched off in a cloud of smoke—Baghdad ahead.

The sun set and we rode on through the desert night. Since the bus wasn't full, I found two empty seats across from each other near the back of the bus. Stretching across the aisle, I lay down and went to sleep. The next thing I knew someone was kicking my legs hard and yelling bad words in Arabic. It was the "mean and uncivilized" bus driver.

I immediately sat up and glowered at him, but knew better than to say anything.

Stopping at small desert towns along the route, during the night and day, the bus rumbled into fabled Baghdad at sunset.

Growing up, I had been charmed by movies about Baghdad and the stories of Arabian nights. *The Book of One Thousand and One Nights* is a nucleus of intriguing tales formed from an ancient Persian book called *Hazar Afsana*, or simply, "Arabian Nights."

During the reign of the Arab Caliph in the 8th century, Baghdad had become an important cosmopolitan city. Merchants from Persia (Iran), China, India, Africa, and Europe were all found in Baghdad. It was during this time that many of these romantic stories are thought to have been collected and later compiled into a single book. Among the movies I most remembered were *Aladdin's Lamp*, *Sinbad the Sailor*, and the tale of *Ali Baba and the Forty Thieves*.

I was looking forward to the adventure and romance of it all. *Would I discover a beauty such as Scheherezade?* I dreamed. Who was Scheherezade? She was lovely of face and perfect in attributes of grace, even as saith of her in this couplet:

> She comes like fullest moon on a happy night,
> Taper of waist with shape of magic night.
> She hath an eye whose glances quell mankind,

And ruby on her cheeks reflects his light.
Whereupon she came forward swaying and coquettishly moving,
And indeed bewitched all eyes within her sight.

In the meantime, I got off the bus I'd dubbed *The Flying Carpet*. I checked into a small, fairly clean hotel across from a huge mosque. I met an Iraqi student when I went to board a city bus. He pointed out the sights as we walked around the central part of the city that fine evening. I was impressed by Baghdad's modernity.

As I went to bed that night, I desperately wished I had someone to care for me in my sickly state. My bronchitis had grown worse and I was totally weary.

The following morning I jumped on a city bus. Once downtown, I started searching for a pharmacy, urgently in need of medicine. I came upon what we back home would call a drugstore. As I entered, I spotted the pharmacy near the back of the store. The pharmacist was a kindly looking gentleman of around 50 years of age and, thankfully, spoke English. I simply said, "Sir, I believe I am close to having pneumonia. I just arrived by bus yesterday evening and I'm running low on money. I'm in desperate need of medicine of some kind to help knock out the infection I'm experiencing."

"Let me see what I can find that might help," he kindly offered.

Within five minutes, he came back and said, "Here are three different medicines that will help." He proceeded to tell me what each one would do and how often to take it. As I went to pay, he refused my money and told me to come back if I needed more. Just his great kindness lifted my spirits and wellbeing tenfold.

Never have I forgotten that great kindness in that huge foreign city. I took some of the medicine immediately. The $50 I had allotted to get me across the great deserts was now down to $10.

As I set out to walk the main streets of Baghdad, I asked three young adult fellows where I could find a place to eat. One of them, Sabah, graciously offered to take me there. This kind of thing happened to me over a dozen times from the time I set foot in that impressive desert capital and not one person would let me pay for anything. Such true generosity is hard to find on such a universal scale in most countries. It was salve for my weary body and spirit.

Sabah bought my lunch and then left me off at the building housing all the bus companies. I went into every office trying to get the lowest fare possible. I finally negotiated a low fare leaving me with only 70 cents in my pocket.

That evening, Sabah, Wadie, and Annan took me out on the town. Afterwards, we had dinner at Annan's house.

All I could afford for breakfast, at a small store, was a coke, a chocolate bar, and some aspirin. This was fine nourishment for a man fit to be in the hospital. I then headed for the bus station. I was lucky I got to see Baghdad before the scourge of Saddam Hussein.

In a cloud of dust and smoke, we were off for Damascus. No matter what the hardships, I was determined to make it from India to Beirut on $50, if it killed me. And it looked as if it might. I was down to 50 cents.

We experienced more bad roads and it was impossible for me to lie down in the bus. Driving through the night, while being jarred into absolute submission and sleeplessness, we reached Damascus as the sun peeked over the horizon. I'd had all the Damascus road that I could stand.

Since I didn't have enough money to take a bus to Beirut, I started walking down the road, weary and completely down at heart. I came upon a small teashop and went in. Sitting down at a tiny table, I ordered tea.

After about five minutes, an old gentleman with a white beard shuffled over to me. "Are you American?" he asked in faltering English. "Yes sir, I am," I replied. He told me his son was studying in America, and that it would be a good idea if I got out of Syria as soon as I could. The reason being was that the Soviets apparently controlled everything in Syria and he said, "You could be picked up as an American spy and never heard from again." I thanked the old gentleman kindly, finished my tea, went out and started hitchhiking.

It was only about ten minutes before a dump truck came along with three Arabs wearing flowing white robes in the bed of the truck. They waved for me to jump in with them. If I had had a white robe, I could have passed for Lawrence of Arabia with my blue eyes.

An hour later, our band of brothers reached the Syrian border. A half-hour wait got me a ride to the Lebanese Border. A kind old Arab man gave me a ride the last forty kilometers into Beautiful Beirut. Hallelujah! I had made it by a whisker on $50.

He dropped me off at Mrs. El Kayem's travel company. Her husband was a dentist. I had met Dr. and Mrs. El Kayem when they stayed at the hotel I managed in Bangkok. Because I'd done many things to assist them during their stay, they'd said, "Clarke, be sure and look us up when you get to Beirut."

By this time, I was close to bronchial pneumonia. Never had I been sick like this in all my travels, or in my life for that matter. Mrs. El Kayem gave me a ride to the YMCA, where I went straight to bed. Several hours later, Dr. Al Kayem showed up at the Y with a medical doctor. After a thorough exam, I was given medicine to take and told to eat well and do nothing but sleep for the next several days. I took that medicine every four hours around the clock.

Several days later, I was feeling much better. The El Kayems took me out for dinner with a group of their friends.

The next day, the good doctor took me for lunch at his parents' house. His son was studying in the U.S. and was getting ready to marry an American girl.

During one of my walks around Beirut, I met a fellow American by the name of Jim Monahan. One evening Jim and I went to the Casino of Lebanon to see the outstanding floor show, and I dropped two precious dollars gambling. I had made it here on $50 and had enough in travelers' checks to get me to Rome if I watched every penny. But before discovering Europe, I was headed to Jerusalem.

When I was in Beirut, I learned it was the region's financial and commercial hub—and as lovely a city as any in the world. About 70% of the population was Muslim and 30% was Christian.

In those heady days, Lebanon was termed the "Switzerland of the East" and Beirut the "Paris of the Middle East." However, ten years later, the PLO Arab militia started using Lebanese land to mount raids on Israel. Sadly, Lebanon then started moving toward its darkest phase in modern history.

With one week of sleep, medicine, and rest, I was my almost my healthy self again. On that Friday, I accompanied Dr. El Kayem and his niece, Jackie, to a ski lodge in the snow-covered mountains. There I met a modern day Scheherazade.

The owners of the lodge proved charming people and Josephine, a Lebanese woman of extraordinary beauty, totally captivated me. She was 24, I learned. She had long black silky hair almost to her waist. She was warm, gracious, and charming—Scheherazade had nothing on her!

While I was at the lodge, I had a feeling she might be married, although I saw no ring. On the way back to Beirut, Dr. El Kayem told me she was single. I had to see her again and the good doctor provided me with her telephone number.

Josephine was home when I called the next day. She agreed to go out with me that evening. We met in front of the Alhambra Theater. She was wearing a sleeveless, form-fitting black dress and black high heels—she looked elegant.

What a privilege it was to be with such a charming woman, especially after my hard journeys across deserts.

We went by taxi to Le Cave, the hottest club for dancing in that charming city. We danced almost continuously until 2:30 in the morning.

It was romantic evening— right out of the Arabian Nights. I bid a fond farewell to lovely Josephine, as I was scheduled to leave for Jerusalem later that morning. My timing was deplorable after meeting such a warm, intelligent beauty.

My friend Henry from Switzerland and I at Capernum on the Sea of Galilee. It was near the kibbutz where we lived and worked.

CHAPTER 49

The Holy Land, Bananas, and War

Remember, there is such a thing as good
and evil.

— Aleksandr Solzhenitsyn

*A*fter getting only one hour of sleep, I got out of bed in a trance. Frank and I were two of four passengers in a station wagon that departed Beirut for Damascus. Stopping in that oldest city on earth, we ate lunch. This trip was a far cry from my first sashay through Damascus. At around 6:00 that evening, we two sinners arrived in the holy city of Jerusalem.

Jim and me got a comfortable twin room in St. George's Hostel. I attended the Divine Worship Service at 6:30 that evening. I was in strong need of repentance and prayer, as always.

For $4 a day, I had a clean room, all meals, and hot water at all times. This was about as good as it got for me.

The following morning, I checked in at the American Embassy to get forms to fill out for entry into Israel. Next, I bought a Pilgrim's Map of the Holy Land. Included on the map were the journeys and deeds of Jesus. I then set off to follow in the footsteps of Jesus.

First, it was to the top of the Mount of Olives. Not another soul was around except a small donkey tethered to a tree. *Was this a sign?* I thought.

All the stories I had heard from childhood about Jesus riding into Jerusalem on a donkey came to life at that moment. I hunted down an old Arab gentleman to take a picture of that sweet little donkey and me for posterity.

For the next several days, I walked and studied all the religious sites, including the Stations of the Cross. Taking a bus to Bethlehem, I visited the Church of the Nativity.

At Jericho, I observed a deep archeology dig in progress, viewed the Mount of Temptation, and then spied the Dead Sea far off in the distance. My sense of adventure immediately sprang forth.

Off I went, walking the eight kilometers across the desert to reach the lowest spot on earth. The quietness and stark beauty of the scenery was

*I discovered a little donkey all by his lonesome on the Mount of Olives
in Jerusalem—Jesus riding on a donkey came to mind.*

awe-inspiring as I hiked through the rugged terrain where the Dead Sea
Scrolls had been discovered.

As I hiked, it hit me that I had been near the magnificent roof of the world
in the Himalayas not long ago and now I was approaching the basement of
the world. I dipped my hand into the water of that flat "sea." It felt as if I had
put my hand in motor oil.

My roommate during the last night in Jerusalem was Jim, a minister from
England. He accompanied me to the Mandelbaum Gate the next morning.
The gate was on the dividing line in the center of the city. Israel controlled the
western half and Jordan controlled the eastern half of Jerusalem. In-between
was a no-man's land.

On each side, barbed wire and machine guns were visible along the way. War
could have broken out at any minute as I crossed over into Israel at high noon.

With backpack firmly strapped on, I started walking through New Jerusalem, having no luck getting a ride. It was three hours later down the highway
that I caught a ride. However, during my long walk the wonderful scent of
orange blossoms enveloped me.

My ride "benefactor" dropped me off near the center of Tel Aviv.

272

Shomo, a kind fellow, helped me find a cheap hotel when I asked him about accommodations.

While strolling the streets in the evening, I was flabbergasted at the way young couples hugged each other and carried on in public. *Ain't love grand*, I thought to myself.

After grabbing a bite to eat in a small restaurant, I headed back to the hotel where I met Barry, a young fellow adventurer. He loaned me his book, *Israel on $5 a Day*. I figured I could do it on $3.

From the book, I learned about the possibility of working on a kibbutz. Kibbutz means "gathering" or "together" and is an Israeli collective community. As I learned, kibbutzim played an essential role in the creation of Israel. They are a unique Israeli experiment whose members developed a pure communal mode of living.

Of note, the kibbutzim have given Israel a wildly disproportionate share of its military leaders, intellectuals, and politicians. Though the movement never accounted for more than seven percent of the population, it did more to shape the image that foreigners have of Israel than any other institution.

On my first full day in Tel Aviv, I took off walking early. While on Dizengoff Street, I decided to sit down at a sidewalk cafe and have a beer. Along this main street, the parade of beautiful girls, most in tight-fitting sweaters, was a sight to behold.

That afternoon, I sat barefooted in the sand at the Sheraton Hotel Beach and observed the passing parade while soaking up the welcome warmth of the sun. After several months of chilling mountains and baking deserts, this was the right place at the right time.

Mr. Paz and his wife picked me up at my Triple C hotel in the early evening. I had been given his name as a good person to meet to learn about Israel. He was the editor of two Hebrew newspapers. Over dinner at an Arab restaurant in the city of Jaffa, he enlightened me on some of the trials and tribulations of Israel. The first Arab-Israeli war of 1948 had sent about 150,000 Palestinians to refugee camps in Lebanon alone. In 1958, the rising star of Egypt's Nasser threatened to absorb tiny Lebanon into a short-lived union with Syria and Egypt.

The decade after the 1956 War was the most tranquil period in Israel's history since independence. Then in 1965, two years before my arrival, Egyptian-sponsored guerrilla raids by Al Fatah first occurred and there had been shellings of Israeli settlements from the Golan Heights of Syria.

As I was traveling through Arab countries, although the people I had met were kind to me, I kept hearing comments like, "We're going to drive every man, woman, and child in Israel into the sea and kill them all." The military dictators of the Arab countries were preaching nothing but hate, unfortunately, so the average person was brainwashed from the time of birth. Never did I ever hear one word of hate for Arabs from Israelis. It was a vast contrast between the two peoples. Those sentiments would prove to be prophetic in light of today's turmoil.

By the early 1960s, both sides considered a third round of war inevitable. And I had arrived at a time when things were really heating up. Sometimes my timing wasn't the greatest.

There it was, April 30, 1967. Guerrilla incursions from Syria and Jordan were steadily mounting, as did the intensity of Israeli reprisal raids. In this very month, increased Syrian aircraft shelling of Israeli border villages provoked an Israeli fighter attack during which six Syrian MIGs were shot down. It was no wonder that that kind old gentleman in the teashop in Damascus told me I'd better move on.

Syria had recently signed a mutual defense treaty with Egypt and was beginning an extensive military buildup. I thought to myself, *Let's see now, if I'm going to get a job on a kibbutz, I might as well get one right below the Syrian guns on the Golan Heights.*

On May 1, Mr. and Mrs. Paz and John, their 13-year-old son, took me to the kibbutz of Yad Mordekhai where they visited with friends. This kibbutz was only a few miles from the Gaza Strip and a battle had occurred there during the 1948 War.

We had lunch in the large dining hall. This visit gave me some idea of what to expect if I went to work on a kibbutz.

Off I went to the Kibbutz Center in Tel Aviv the next day. I was told that I might be able to work at the famous kibbutz of Ein Gev. For me, any kibbutz would do.

That evening, a famous couple in Israel had me to their home for dinner. Mr. Rapoport was a well-known architect and his wife was the head of the Girl Scouts for the country. As always, I learned a great deal from discussions on numerous subjects.

I was back in good health, thank God. I spent a glorious day sunbathing on the beach and letting my eyes run wild, looking at the bathing beauties.

Thanks to the Paz family, I was able to get a ticket to attend a concert given by the Israel Philharmonic Orchestra. My favorite piece that evening was *Pathetique* by Tchaikowsky.

A job at the kibbutz of Maagan came through when I checked in at the kibbutz center. No one would've believed where it was—right below the Syrian guns on the Golan Heights. I was looking for romance and danger and this would provide several helpings of it.

The next morning at 9:30, I boarded a city bus that would take me out to the highway to Haifa. Hitchhiking had almost become a way of life and I was close to earning a doctorate in it—meeting all kinds of interesting people in the process.

My first ride got me to Netanya. Next came a ride with a middle-aged Arab gentleman that got me to Nazareth. I learned much from him about what it was like for Arabs living in Israel, not perfect but generally much better than in Arab countries.

From Nazareth, where Jesus grew up, I hitchhiked on to Tiberius. There was the Sea of Galilee, right before my very eyes. It had also been known as Lake Tiberias. It was Israel's largest freshwater lake, approximately thirteen miles long and eight miles wide. At 213 meters below sea level, I discovered it was the lowest freshwater lake on Earth.

The Sea of Galilee is not a sea by normal definition. It is called a sea by tradition and I had to find out why. The lake is fed by underground springs, but its main source is the Jordan River, which flows through it from north to south.

The first century historian, Flavius Josephus, was so impressed by the area that he wrote, "One may call this place the ambition of nature." With the beauty spread before me, I could see why he described it in such a way.

The gospels of Mark and Matthew describe how Jesus recruited four of his apostles from those very shores. The Sermon on the Mount was given on one of the hills overlooking the lake.

It was here in 1909 that Jewish pioneers built their first cooperative farming village. The area became the cradle of the kibbutz culture. I was about to make my new home on Kibbutz Maagan and had no idea how long I might stay.

From Tiberius, I took a bus the several miles to the kibbutz on the southern tip of the Sea of Galilee, right next to where the Jordan River flows out of the lake. It was four in the afternoon. The kibbutz greeter gave me a warm welcome and showed me to the small cabin room I would be sharing with Rod from England.

Rod was a fellow of twenty-four who had decided to see some of the world before settling down to a real job. We hit it right off. He gave me a walking tour of my new home before we had dinner in the spacious dining hall.

It was going to be a boon to have three nutritious meals a day. After dinner, I went straight to bed in anticipation of the 5:00 a.m. wake up call. It was going to be like I was back in the Marine Corps, but this time I would be working in fields with Syrian guns on the Golan Heights trained on me.

On a flatbed trailer pulled by a tractor, twelve of us were taken to the vineyards along the shore of the Sea of Galilee. I was assigned by Helka to pick grapes in a specific area.

Working alongside me was Henry from Switzerland; Lyn from Rhodesia (he was 22 and a spitting image of John the Baptist and had the personality of a comedian); Pete, David and Phil from England; two pretty Dutch girls; Mary Ann from California; and three regular kibbutz members to keep us on track. Moses, the man in charge, explained to us very clearly the proper way to trim the vines.

One interesting thing about working in those vineyards and banana fields, on the eastern short of the lake, was the fact that there were manned Israeli tanks along the way. They were dug in and camouflaged. All-out war could have thundered down on us at any moment.

At 8:00 that morning we stopped work and went to a small shack near the fields. There we ate a breakfast of hard-boiled eggs, bread, yogurt, tea and salad.

On Friday, work finished at 1:00 in the afternoon because of a Jewish Sabbath observance that was to begin at sunset. I took this time out to sunbathe down by the lake with some of my fellow kibbutzers.

At sunset, I walked over to Kibbutz Kinneret to meet the Kessler family. Mr. Rapoport especially wanted me to meet Dinah, their pretty and vivacious daughter. They easily talked me into staying for dinner and the weekly movie.

The next day Dinah invited me over for lunch. She and I hitchhiked into Tiberius where she showed me around.

In 135 A.D., I learned, the second Jewish revolt against the Romans was shut down. The Romans responded by banning all Jews from Jerusalem. The center of Jewish culture then shifted to this region, particularly to the city of Tiberius.

Dinah and I sat on a wall by the water, talking and enjoying the spectacular view in the warm sunshine. The lake was so calm it looked like a mirror.

Later we hitched a ride to the spot where the Jordan and another river join. It was a beautiful day, spent with a delightful woman, just a few years younger than me. I learned more about her, her family, and Israel.

After dinner back at the kibbutz, I visited with the Daniv family in their home. My goal was to meet each evening with a different kibbutz family to learn their story and how they came to live in that particular place.

Henry Frei, from Switzerland, and I had become fast friends. When we finished work at 3:00 each afternoon, we'd usually go for a swim in the "Sea."

Why do they call it the Sea of Galilee? I wondered. It soon dawned on me. The lake would be almost like a mirror until around 3:00 each afternoon. Then, almost like clockwork, it seemed the winds would start blowing down from Lebanon in the North and waves, sometimes three feet high, would be washing in on the southern shore. It looked and felt like an actual seashore.

Due to its low-lying position in the rift valley, surrounded by hills, the sea is prone to violent storms; hence the New Testament story about Jesus calming the storm. Indeed, the main feature seemed to be its ever-changing character.

Life was vigorous and active on the kibbutz. The time was too short each day for me to do all the things I wanted to do. I had started reading the book *Exodus* by Uris to gain a deeper insight into the culture.

I had switched over to cutting bananas in the fields at the base of the Golan Heights. Ignoring the Syrian guns above, it could still be a dangerous exercise. Every once in a while, a deadly viper would strike out as the banana stalks were being cut. Luckily, I wasn't bitten.

The weather was cool in the mornings and evenings but the afternoons were getting progressively warmer. I was getting a deep suntan from the waist up, and on my legs from my days working by the "Sea."

One afternoon after work, instead of going back to the kibbutz, Henry and I hitchhiked on down to Ein Gev. It was the last kibbutz on the eastern side of the lake toward Lebanon, and only several hundred yards from the sharply rising hills of Syria. It was sure to be one of the first kibbutzim to be overrun by the Syrian Army if war broke out. We did some exercising there under the date palms, and then went for a swim.

After dinner, I went to Moshe's home for a chat. He had helped organize the escape of Jewish children out of Hungary from 1948 to 1950 in order to free them from the oppression of Communist rule.

277

Three newcomers arrived to work with us—Simon from England, Andre from Switzerland, and John from Sweden. That evening Moshe gave us foreign workers a talk on *Nineteen Years of Israeli Independence*. This was a young country and an ancient country at the same time.

It was a small world. One evening when Dinah and I went to dinner, I ran into Margaret from Australia whom I had met in Tehran. This kind of thing happened to me throughout the world. In a way, adventurers were their own small community.

One fine Saturday morning, Henry and I set out walking, with Capernaum as our destination. Out of the thirty kilometers to get there, we got two rides for half that distance and walked the other half. I was strong, healthy, and in terrific physical shape once again.

Father Godfrey showed us around and taught us about the ancient city of Capernaum. After a bracing swim, we climbed up to the Church on the Mount of Beatitudes. In that holy sanctuary, I knelt and prayed, giving thanks to God for bringing me this far, alive, and now well.

Back at the kibbutz, we had a dance party. It was to celebrate the three of us who were having a birthday in May. I got to bed at 2:30 that morning with a 5:30 wake-up call staring me in the face.

The next day, as the last glow of the setting sun outlined the lake area, a memorial service was held in front of an obelisk built in memory of those Israelis who died fighting for freedom in the 1948 War. We had a special dinner to begin the Independence Day celebrations. Lyn, my John the Baptist friend from Rhodesia, got very high on the red and white wine that was flowing like water.

I met an attractive Israeli girl by the name of Naomi soon after the dancing had begun. Before the festivities concluded at 3:00 that morning, everyone had had pastries in four different locations around the kibbutz. It was a celebration to remember as Independence Day dawned on that May 15.

Israeli Independence was on the brink of being challenged in dramatic fashion. The newspapers were filled with war preparations by the Arab countries surrounding Israel. War could start at any minute, and it would come from all directions. Explorer F. Nansen, said, "The history of the human race is a continual struggle from darkness toward light." How sad but true!

This was not my battle. On May 16, with life hanging in the balance, I decided to head for Haifa. There I would catch a ship to a safe haven. Originally, I had planned to go to Egypt after Israel.

After packing my few things, I went all around the mess hall at breakfast saying goodbye to my friends and co-workers. Lyn, my bearded beatnik buddy, walked with me to the bus stop.

In Tiberius, I caught another bus to Nazareth, which was half way to the port of Haifa. I spent several pleasant hours in Nazareth seeing the sights associated with the childhood of Jesus.

With only five Israeli pounds left, I hitchhiked the rest of the way to Haifa. When I got there, I went straight to the police station to see if they could give me a bunk for a night or two until I could catch a ship out, preferably a battleship. The policemen were courteous and said, "Your crimes are not serious enough for us to furnish you a place to stay but you're welcome to leave your backpack here while you search for a place."

A policeman suggested I check in at the Scandinavian Seaman's Church. I told one of the brothers at the church that my great, great, great, great grandfather was a Viking. A bed was furnished to me immediately in a small one-room wooden house in back of the church.

If I hadn't had this stroke of good fortune, I'd been prepared to sit up all night at the police station to save what traveler's checks I had left. It was going to be tight making it to Rome.

Fortunately, I was able to book passage to Athens on the *T.S.S. Olympia* for the next day. All was well if the Arab Air Forces didn't sink her and all the other ships in the harbor before she sailed.

With time on my hands, I read all the English newspapers to inform myself of the headlong rush into war. It looked inevitable!

On that very day, May 16, Egyptian military ruler, Nasser, ordered a withdrawal of the UN Emergency Forces stationed on the Egyptian-Israeli border, thus removing the international buffer which had existed since 1957. Syria was increasing border clashes along the Golan Heights.

On May 22, Egypt would announce a blockade of all goods bound to and from Israel through the Straits of Tirin. The U.S. feared a major Arab-Israeli and superpower confrontation and had asked Israel to delay military action, pending a diplomatic resolution of the crisis.

I had no idea what was going to happen. The Arab Armies were massed on Israel's borders poised to strike. It did not look good for Israel and it seemed that all the cards were stacked against that tiny country.

On May 17, with war hanging in the balance, I sailed out of Haifa—just in time.

CHAPTER 50

Greece and I Spy

Yesterday is history, tomorrow is a mystery,
and today is a gift, that's why they call it
the present.

— Eleanor Roosevelt

My cabin on the ship was for eight people, but there were only three of us in it. I was the only one who spoke English but we all got along famously, each speaking in his own language, using hand signals the whole while.

I was healthy, tan, and well fed for a change. Life had become luxurious for a short time. How long it would last was uncertain but I always took it one day at a time—as a gift.

I turned 29 years old aboard ship on May 18. I had been on the world adventure trail for six years without any financial backup or support from anyone during that period. I could still be styled as somewhat of a romantic, vagabond, nomad, rover, wanderer, rambler, and wayfarer all rolled into one.

Edna, a most shapely and pretty redhead, and I sunbathed and talked most of the day, as we sailed along under sunny skies on a smooth sea. It was close to idyllic.

At around 9:00 that evening, Edna and I went on deck as the ship made its way into Piraeus, the port of Athens. I bid her a romantic farewell before walking down the gangplank. She was off to New York to be a singer/entertainer.

On the bus to Athens, I met and talked with a Brazilian couple. They steered me to the area where the cheap hotels were located. I landed in a small, spic-and-span, white boarding house hotel that cost me only 35 drachmas ($1.08 U.S.) a night. My roommate ended up being Robert Smith from New York, whom I had met in Tel Aviv.

It was good to be in a country where peace reigned, or so I thought. I quickly learned that there had been a coup d'é-tat in Greece one month before and "The Regime of the Colonels" had been installed.

On April 21, tanks had been placed in strategic positions around Athens. Small mobile units were dispatched to arrest leading politicians and authority figures. By the early morning hours, the whole of Greece was in the hands of the Colonels. The King had decided to co-operate, so everything appeared peaceful.

Robert and I went to see the sights in this "Cradle of Western Civilization." After exploring all day, we had dinner in a small taverna near the foot of the Parthenon. Great Greek music filled the place.

Without any warning, an exceptionally strong-looking Greek man, around 30, stood up several tables away. He asked his two companions to clear the small round table where they sat. Once cleared, he proceeded to pick up the table with his teeth and go into a Zorba-the-Greek dance mode.

He had one strong set of choppers! It was the best impromptu floorshow I had ever seen. I heard his teeth fell out a month later.

On my own, I went to see the spectacular "Sound and Light Show" on the Acropolis and then to a Greek Folk Dancing Show. There I met Albrecht Riester, a German fellow about my age.

Albrecht and I decided to venture through the Plaka area where most of the tavernas were located. We stuck our head into almost every one of them to see if we could spot any Greek beauties dying to meet two forlorn young men. We did not generate a spark.

Albrecht invited me to go to the beach with him the next day. We got to Varkiza Beach by bus close to noontime. We met two German guys there and ended up taking them on in horse fights in the water. I got back to Athens scraped up a bit, but in high spirits after our beach battles.

Athens, named after the goddess Athena, was the leading city in Greece during the greatest period of Greek civilization. During the "Golden Age" of Greece, roughly 500 B.C. to 300 B.C., it was the western world's leading cultural, commercial, and intellectual center. Pericles built the Parthenon and other main buildings on the Acropolis in the fifth century BC.

In this modern time, the young king, Constantine II, had wrangled with the colonels and lost. I had gotten to know Princess Sophia, one of the king's sisters, while she was on her honeymoon at the Royal Hawaiian with Prince Juan Carlos of Spain. I had hoped to drop by the palace and say howdy to the king while I was in town, but that did not come about.

As I was getting dressed one morning, I was surprised to hear a band marching by in the narrow street below my second story window. It looked like a parade was getting ready to happen. I rushed down to the street to find out it was the "Name Day" of King Constantine. This was in honor of the name he was given at baptism.

At 10:30, I joined the throngs in Constitution Square. Finding a wooden apple crate in an alley, I mounted it and gave the king a big Texas wave as he passed by in his open car.

I recognized him as I'd seen his picture on the cover of *Time Magazine* the day before—commemorating the coup. Seven months later, he launched a counter-coup that was unsuccessful and had to flee the country. It's not every day you can stand on an apple crate in an alley and wave to a king.

Later, when I entered the Greek National Tourist Building, I was greeted by a redhead with a smile that would melt ice. Ireeni answered my many questions about sightseeing in this cradle of Democracy.

Since her work was slow, we had time to visit. When she finished work, we walked up to the Acropolis and then spent four hours in delightful conversation at an outdoor restaurant. She could have been the poster girl for Greece.

Reluctantly, I said goodbye to her at 8:00 that evening. We promised to meet at noon the next day. Was I glad I had wandered into the Tourist Building, lost as usual!

I met Ireeni in front of the Olympic office in Syntagma Square. She took me to see the famous ruins of the Ancient Agora where Socrates had taught. She then treated me to a tasty Greek lunch that lasted two hours.

By that point, I was completely charmed by her warm personality. That evening, we went dancing at the Hilton's Galaxy Room. She wore her long, shining red hair straight down. It was an out-of-this-world evening for a poor adventurer like me.

After several days of touring the city, I decided to enjoy a more natural setting. I set out to hike the mountains overlooking Athens—where a number of battles had taken place down through the centuries. As I was making my way across the top of a peaceful mountain, all was right with the world. Not a soul was in sight when out of the blue, gunfire erupted from a number of directions. *This is it! I am going to be filled full of holes in placid Athens*, I thought, panicked. I hit the ground hard.

After much gunfire and shouting, only the smoke remained. I lifted my face from the dirt thankful I had not been hit by one of the flying bullets.

Several minutes later, people started emerging along the hillside. Was it the king's men, the colonel's men, the Greek Mafia, or just a group out for some friendly shooting? It was none of the above.

I had walked straight into the filming of an episode of the international TV series, *I Spy*, starring Robert Culp and Bill Cosby. In the series, they played the parts of a tennis pro and his trainer, but they were really CIA agents. *I Spy* had become television's most popular buddy show of that time.

This episode, the one I had so handily stumbled into, was titled, *Let's Kill Karlovassi*. I could have sworn it was *Let's Kill Clarke*. On that killer note, I was ready to flee Greece.

On Thursday morning, I went to say goodbye to Ireeni and thank her for her many kindnesses of introducing me to the ancient city of Athens. I told her I would keep in touch and hoped to see her in Rome. It would be my turn to show her the ruins of that ancient world.

The bus for Patras left at 1:30 in the afternoon and arrived at 6:00 that evening. On the way, I got to know Bob Gardener and Judy Johnson.

The three of us had a walk around town before having dinner at a quaint taverna. Our ship, the *M/S Appia* sailed at 10:00 p.m. *Italy, here I come*, I thought joyfully. All my life, I had dreamed of seeing Rome.

It had been ten days since I sailed from Haifa. The following story was what I was getting ready to miss in Israel. On May 30, Nasser and King Hussein signed a mutual defense pact, followed on June 4 by a defense pact between Cairo and Baghdad. Also that week, Arab states began mobilizing their troops. All hell was getting ready to break loose.

Nasser repeatedly called for a war of total destruction against Israel (drive every man, woman, and child into the sea). Arab mobilization compelled Israel to mobilize its troops, 80 percent of which were civilian reserves.

I'll never forget when I was riding in a cab in Tiberius, the driver, 46, told me he was in the reserves like everyone else. He carried his uniform, equipment, rifle, and ammo in the trunk, ready to fight at an instant's notice.

Incendiary Arab rhetoric threatening Israel's annihilation terrified Israeli society, and rightfully so. What were they to do?

During the same time, and unknown to the Israelis, the Soviet Union had been mounting a disinformation campaign to provoke Syrian troops who were prepared for battle along the Golan Heights. All I could do was pray for my friends at Kibbutz Maagan, who were literally standing at death's door.

The momentum for all-out war had been unstoppable. The then president of Iraq added these words to the mountain of provocation: "The existence of Israel is an error, which must be rectified. Our goal is clear—to wipe Israel off the map."

An Arab force of 465,000 troops, over 2,880 tanks and 810 aircraft confronted Israel. Things did not look promising, in fact, it couldn't have been bleaker for Israel!

Israeli forces had been on high alert during the three weeks of tension, which had begin on May 15, the day before I hitchhiked out of Galilee. On the morning of June 5, Israel launched a devastating surprise attack on Arab air power, destroying about 300 Egyptian, 50 Syrian, and 20 Jordanian aircraft, mostly on the ground. It virtually eliminated the Arab air forces.

The air attack was immediately followed up by ground invasions into Sinai and the Gaza strip, Jordan, and finally, Syria. Arab ground forces, lacking air support, were routed on all three fronts. The war lasted only six days, with the Israelis coming out of it totally victorious. It was a swift and stunning victory and Israel had survived total annihilation.

CHAPTER 51

All Roads Lead to Rome

The tragedy in life is not reaching your goal,
but having no goal to reach.
— Benjamin Mays

With the world still turning, after the war in the Middle East, the *M/S Appia* of the Adriatica Line glided out of the harbor of Patras, Greece with over a thousand passengers aboard. The ship's deep orange funnel featured a prominent three-dimensional Lion of Venice on it, one of the most distinctive funnels sailing anywhere.

The *Appia* was a beautiful ship with the sleek profile of a modern miniliner. She could carry 145 cars on board and make a speed of 17.5 knots on the short Italo-Greco run.

After a night of smooth sailing, the ship docked at the resort island of Corfu at 8:00 the next morning. A Japanese college student, Aoki-san, was one of those boarding. He spoke only Japanese, so we became quick friends.

It was a perfect sailing day through deep blue waters with a clear sky above. The mountains lining the coast were covered in billowy clouds. At 4:00 that afternoon, the ship docked in Brindisi, on the heel of the boot of Italy.

Brindisi has an interesting history. In 245 B.C., the Romans conquered it. In 836 A.D., it was burned by Saracen pirates and through the years was ruled by many empires.

Aoki-san and I walked to the center of town with our backpacks strapped in place. From there, we caught a bus to a youth hostel but found it was closed.

Sigi, a German girl, got to the hostel at the same time we did. The three of us, the Brindisi musketeers—a German, a Japanese, and an American—searched out a cheap place to stay for the night. We were in Italy for the first time. After a spaghetti dinner, we wandered through the streets eating ice cream cones. It was a good end to a good day.

Aoki-san and I had a cappuccino for breakfast before going our separate ways; he went to hitchhike and I caught the train to Naples. The train passed through vineyard and olive country most of the way.

Arriving at 6:00 in the evening, I checked with the government tourist office at the station. I asked, "Where is the cheapest hotel in Naples, please?" It was plain, they had already seen too many of my kind that day. The cheapest hotel was full.

I got into the number two cheapest hotel, the Astoria, for $2 U.S. a night. I was amazed to find the room was large, even a bit elegant. I must have done something right. I'd paid $1 U.S. for my room in Brindisi.

A fabulous hot bath, a big plate of spaghetti, and a short walk around downtown Napoli raised my spirits. I decided I would sleep late in the morning to enjoy this last bit of luxury while I had it.

I spent most of the day walking around this colorful Italian city of the south. One thing became clear quickly, the Italians live for the moment.

At a pier, I saw a fully clothed teenage boy jump headlong into the bay just for the fun of splashing water on his friends in a rowboat. Everyone, including the splasher, had a huge laugh out of it.

Then there were two boys on a Vespa motor scooter racing madly downhill right on the tail of a pickup truck. They were singing a rousing song in perfect harmony with the lads in the back of the truck. Just crazy!

It was an engrossing and entertaining show all day long. And, best of all, it was free.

Naples was an eye-opener, but my life in Italy was just beginning. There was no telling what lay ahead on the road to Rome.

I had traveled every kind of road imaginable over a period of four months. It was a wonder, in some ways, that I was still alive as I looked back on it. Guerrillas, tigers, an abominable snowman, tire blowouts, third class trains, earthquakes, landslides, bandits, fierce tribesmen, riding in worn out trucks, sleet and snow, mountains, deserts, mine fields, rickety buses, dodging conductors, terrorists, spies, ships, Mafia-type henchmen, and hitchhiking was just half of it. I'd spent the grand sum of $350 on that thrill-seeking escapade across a third of the world.

At last, I was on one of the real roads leading directly to Rome. Who would give me a ride? I got some unusual help in Naples. Two young children, a boy and a girl, observed my motions. Once they'd gathered it all in, they proceeded to step directly in front of me on the side of the road. They'd put out their thumbs every time a car would come by. It was funny and wonderful at the same time.

This was the kind of support I couldn't buy. We were a force of three. "Did you see that father and his two kids trying to catch a ride?" must have been the comment in some of the cars speeding by on the Autostrada at 80 m.p.h.

Even the Italian kids, it appeared, knew how to have fun and be actors in the game of life from an early age. It was truly refreshing.

It was one hour before anyone heeded our upended thumbs. As a small car came to a stop in front of us, I saw a gorgeous Italian girl of about 20 at the wheel. Sitting next to her, I came to find out, was her lovely, plump, affable, gray-haired mama, Mrs. Pagano.

I thanked my two little helpers and climbed into the small backseat with barely enough room for my backpack and me. The Paganos shared their lunch with me as we sped along the Autostrada.

When the daughter stopped to pick me up, Mrs. Pagano later told me, "I told Gina not to stop because he is probably a bandit who will beat and rob us. He's just using those kids to lure us into a trap." She had been frightened to death but they took pity on a poor, wayfaring stranger. I was blessed by their kindness.

By the time we got to Rome, they'd invited me to come stay with them anytime I got to Naples. They kindly dropped me off at the address I had for the students' organization office. There, I was given an address for a cheap pensione.

My single room was about the size of a big closet with a bathroom down the hall. Meals were furnished in the daily fee. After a hearty dinner of pasta and salad, I went out walking to get my first taste of Rome by night. The free street entertainment was superb. With the Italians, it was love at first sight for me.

The next day, I got my shaggy hair cut for the first time in over two months. If I was going to land a job, it was imperative I looked halfway business-like. I could have passed for my acquaintances, the Beatles, at that point.

I mailed a thank you letter to the Paganos, went to the airport to pick up my trunk and sea bag at TWA, and started scrambling to get job interviews. I had only 350 lire (several dollars) left in my pocket by the end of the day. *Tomorrow I must get to the bank where I will transfer my small nest egg of traveler's checks to get me started in Rome*! I told myself. I had become a financial wizard at cutting it close.

At the United States Information Services' offices, Mr. Naughton gave me some contacts to aid in my job search. Of course, my work with USIS on the U.S. President's visit to Thailand proved helpful in Rome. The job hunt had begun in earnest because I had only enough money left to hold out for a month.

I had to know some Italian to be able to find work. I signed up for classes at the Dante Alighieri School, bought a textbook, and an Italian-English dictionary.

Several days after arriving in the capital, Italy celebrated her "unity" day. From a good vantage point near the Colosseum, I watched the military parade in honor of the occasion.

There was the President, passing in an open car, and waving to the crowds. There was polite applause. Next came a large, colorful troop of horse guards strung out for more than a block. What caught my attention though was thunderous applause erupting all along the parade route behind the horses. *Who on earth could possibly be receiving such adulation?* I deliberated. Whoever it was had to be an immensely popular person.

The applause grew louder and louder, like rolling thunder. And there he was, the hero of Italy. The street sweeper was performing miracles in picking up the prodigious amount of horse manure. Only in Italy! I joined in with the rest of the crowd as they exhibited their appreciation for that esteemed

As one of the models for a travel booklet in awe-inspiring Rome.

personage. He carried the day and the manure. Giuseppi Carpuchi was keeping the roads of Rome safe and clean for its citizens. I'm sure he was decorated for his artful dedication to duty on many occasions.

Rome has been a magnet for foreigners ever since the Goths sacked the city and moved in. The civilization of ancient Rome originated in the eighth century B.C., when northern tribes migrated there to settle around the River Tiber. The weather is superb year round and palm trees lazily grow out of ancient ruins.

The magnificent monuments are a constant reminder of the greatness of this city and the wisdom its people have attained through the centuries. The Romans have literally spent millennia identifying the essential and enduring elements of life, humor being one of them.

The question now was what lay ahead for me in the "Eternal City?" Rome was the ideal city in which to learn, live, and explore its many treasures. And nowhere else are so many centuries vibrantly blended. On his first day in Rome in 1869, Henry James confided in his diary: "At last, for the first time, I live."

CHAPTER 52

Becoming Roman

I have only told the half of what I saw.

— Marco Polo

*A*s Italy's capital, Rome has a cultural and intellectual life, which is unsurpassed. But above all, Rome, the mother of cities, is hospitable. Romans live and revel in their city. I was about to do the same.

My landlady's cute and witty teenage daughter, Claudia, helped me study Italian one afternoon while supplying me with cake and Cokes. She became one of my unofficial teachers. It was a plus that she could only speak a few words of English because it forced me into Italian.

When I got back to my room in the evenings, after walking the streets to find a job, I would don my cotton Japanese kimono and fur-lined and topped, green rawhide Afghan house shoes. If anyone had dropped in to see me, I'm certain they would have been awed by my attire. I decided not to wear my turban, since it would have been too much for anyone to take in at one time.

My usual dinner consisted of spaghetti, a small salad, bread, and wine, mainly because that was all I could afford. I would add meat to the menu once I landed a job.

To meet people and condition my spirit, I began attending St. Paul's American Church. At the coffee after the service, I would always make new acquaintances.

Because there is hardly ever enough hot water at the pensione, I would frequently walk to the train station where the showers had ample blessed hot water. Sometimes it's the simple little things that mean so much when you're without them.

Getting a job was paramount, since my funds were beginning to dwindle. I pounded the pavement day after day knowing something good would happen, sooner or later, and I prayed it would be sooner. On one particular day, I cold-called on the following companies seeking a job interview: American Express, CBS, ABC, *Time Magazine*, Duca di Roma (a knitwear company), Pan American Airlines, a movie casting agency, and the Motion

Picture Export Association. I even applied to be an extra in the movie, *Romeo & Juliet*, having finished at the top of my fencing class in college.

Another day, among other people, I talked with Chuck Smith at De Laurentis Studios about working as an extra in a movie about the battle of Anzio. The movie was being made by Columbia Pictures. No luck!

That evening, I decided to attend a Toastmasters Club meeting. Having become a member of that great organization in Hong Kong, I knew I'd make some new friends there. No only did I gain friends, I came away with the cup for being the best Table Topics speaker and got a free dinner in the process.

NBC, Associated Press, *Newsweek*, Radio Free Europe, Paramount Pictures, TWA, the UN office, and the *Rome Daily American* newspaper all turned me down. My chances of getting a job were getting better. It was a game of numbers and the key was hitting the right place at the right time. I was spending $5 a day. At that rate, I'd be able to hold on another month.

One morning, I saw a small ad in the *Rome Daily American* newspaper indicating a singles social-cultural club, The Intercontinentals, was having a get-together that very evening. I thought, *Why not go*. It was a splendid move.

After knocking on doors for a job all day long, I was ready for some relaxation. What a party. There were about fifty young adult singles in attendance.

The best part of the evening was meeting an Italian girl by the name of Lisa. This was on a Saturday and she invited me to a party the next Tuesday. I drank more wine than Roman law allowed but so did most of the Romans at the party. When in Rome....

The job hunting continued. The American Chamber of Commerce, Hilton, a travel magazine, and whatever establishment I was passing by at the moment that looked promising. With no real contacts in Rome, the going was all up hill.

The next thing I knew, I had a job in hand. It was too good to be true after only two weeks in Rome. I was to be the Assistant Public Relations man for Duca di Roma. It was a fashion house located right on the fashionable Via Veneto Street.

To start, I was given a car, an expense account, and a salary of 120,000 lire a month. The tough part of the job, though, was that I would be working with eight beautiful fashion models from countries across Europe. My job was to meet people and groups to arrange fashion shows for them. All I had to do was meet some people!

The club members of "The Intercontinentals" took me into their group as one of them. Besides single, young adult Italians, many of the members worked in various embassies. It was, indeed, an international group and I was the only "Texan" among them.

The white Fiat 500 I had been furnished for my new job was a smart little bomb of a car. It was so small that when I pulled to a stop alongside a bus, the bus's wheel was as tall as the Fiat. *I hope that bus driver knows I'm here,* I prayed. Traffic in Rome wasn't much different than playing "bumper cars." The key was to dodge just at the right time or be squashed flat.

Piero, one of my co-workers, took me around to a number of hotels one afternoon in his red Fiat sports car. It was like taking a tour of Rome and sunbathing all at the same time. It was fortuitous in that I got to make some key hotel contacts and scout out the hotels all at the same time.

Almost from day one on my new job, Pino, the forgetful and woman-chasing manager, gave me a hard time. He was full of himself and exalted his importance. It gave me a good idea of what Mussolini must have been like the way Pino strutted around giving orders in all directions.

I was in love with life and Rome. What a change three short weeks had wrought. Life was definitely on the upswing.

Graced by European models at a fashion house in Rome—a great PR job while it lasted.

During my fourth week in the "Eternal City," I had an opportunity to get to know columnist Pat Nair at the *Rome Daily American,* the English newspaper. I had no inkling of it at the time, but my name would appear in the newspaper's columns a number of times in the months to come.

One fine sunny day, I joined Pino and Guattierro at our restaurant hangout on the Tiber River. They later persuaded me to go swimming with them in the Tiber. That was the first and last time I would do that. The water was as cold as ice. Julius Caesar, no doubt, had experienced the same thing.

I had become friends with all the fashion models at Duca di Roma. They joked with me about them being my harem. Not a bad idea, when I thought about it.

The fashion model part of my job was good. The boss part was bad. Pino and I had had it out for the fourth time. He was a bombastic braggart filled to the brim with insincerity, irresponsibility, and irascibility. Things were going downhill at full speed. It was time to start hunting for a backup position.

I had a date with Yvonne Camillo. I had met her and her parents aboard the ship *Castel Felice* on the trip from Sydney to Singapore. Her mother was from Australia and her father was Italian, and that union had produced a beautiful daughter.

The Camillos had recently built the Boomerang Motel on the outskirts of Rome. After Yvonne and I spent a day at Fregene Beach, we came back to the motel, had a marvelous dinner, and danced until midnight. The Boomerang would prove to be a great place for parties.

I was asked to be on the Social Events Committee of The Intercontinentals' Club. Apparently, the club was lacking the enthusiasm and spark it once had. *Well, we'll see what we can do to liven things up*, I vowed.

One of the best things to happen to me as a member of the club was becoming friends with Franco Taliana. Franco was a sincere, outgoing, kind guy. As a junior executive with Coca-Cola, he was on an upward career path.

About this time, the hammer dropped! On a Wednesday afternoon, I was informed, due to poor business, I was no longer needed at Duca di Roma. Three of the fashion models went, too. It was a glorious job while it lasted, but I was glad to be rid of Pino and his bombast.

The next morning I met with Mr. Blair from Twentieth Century Fox. He asked me to prepare a resume for him. I longed to be involved in movies one way or the other.

My next interview was with Mr. Bodenheimer at the world-famous

Excelsior Hotel right on the Via Veneto across from the U.S. Embassy. "Clarke, we may be able to put you on the front desk for our busy summer season," he said to me. It looked like I had hit at the right time and the right place after being unceremoniously dumped the previous day.

Two days later I was working at the famed Excelsior Hotel. It stands at the corner of Via Veneto and Via Boncompagni.

In the years after World War II, the Via Veneto, a one-time sleepy country road, had been transformed into a glittering byway, frequented by an international crowd and immortalized as the mythic byway of high style in Fellini's *La Dolce Vita*, the sweet life.

The Excelsior embodies the very essence of the flamboyant, fashionable boulevard that is Via Veneto, where elegantly dressed Romans, movie stars, and tourists stroll past swanky restaurants, posh shops, and inviting sidewalk cafes. It seemed there was nothing Romans liked better than sitting and talking over a beverage—usually wine or coffee.

Back in the 1950s, Via Veneto rose in fame as the hippest street in Rome, crowded with aspiring and actual movie stars, directors, and a fast-rising group of card-carrying members of the jet set.

The Excelsior opened in 1906. It was an almost instant success and over the decades evolved into one of the great hotels of the world. I was back in the hotel business and what a place to be in it! It was this hotel, standing at the apex of a triangle with the Borghese Gardens and Spanish Steps at either end, that brought the world to this crossroads of Rome.

It was Modern Rome, epitomized by the Via Veneto, with the Excelsior at its heart. I was home. I was given a small salary, a nice room to live in, and all my meals furnished. What an absolute marvelous deal. One door closes, another opens!

The Intercontinentals had a party at Focene Beach. Sixteen of us, from seven different countries, had a wonderful time. At nightfall, we built a bonfire, danced in the sand to the music from a portable record player, and told stories. My new friend, Franco gave me a ride to the hotel.

To my amazement, the Intercontinentals elected me as their new president soon after. The challenge was to get some exciting things going for the nearly 100 members.

Working at the reception desk at the Excelsior was a joy, fun, humorous, insightful, and a pain. A joy because of the Italians I was associating with, especially Bruno Kali; insightful because two German fellows, about my age, were training there and it was the perfect setting to show the differences between Italians and Germans; and painful because the Front Office Manager, "De Bado," the nickname the staff had given him, must have been the twin brother of "Pino Bombast." They were two of a kind.

During my first week of work, we had Xavier Cugat, the famous band leader, John Glenn, the astronaut, and Stanley Kramer, the famous movie producer, staying at the hotel. It was interesting and pleasurable getting to know these personages.

Being somewhat a student of human nature, it was fascinating observing the personalities of the people I was working with. The Germans were ultra-efficient. The Italians had fun and were most affable—one was quiet, one always joking, another kindly, and one easygoing.

Then there was the ever-delightful Bruno. One afternoon, a storm knocked the hotel lighting out, so Bruno decided to make the most of it. We had a brass stand that sat on the counter that looked like a cross with Reception inscribed across its front.

Bruno put the "cross" on top of the room rack located across the back of the reception desk, an area that could have easily passed for an alter. He lighted candles on both sides of it, put a white tablecloth over his shoulders' and proceeded to say Mass. It was an Italian classic! And he baptized each of us in turn using water from a jug nearby. I was spiritually lifted in that light-hearted moment.

Orson Wells checked in shortly after the lights came on. If he'd been there just a bit earlier, Bruno would have baptized him, too. It had made a hit with all those in the lobby who observed the solemn ceremony.

I had the distinct honor of showing the famous Amy Vanderbilt to her room after she checked in. Then did the same for my fellow Texan, Governor John Connolly, that evening.

Ole "De Bado" was at it again. He called me over one morning and chewed me out. His exact words were, "I don't want you being nice to guests, don't talk with them, and only give them a simple greeting." I wondered what planet he was from and how he had ever gotten his position. To me, taking good care of guests was number one priority.

Being the organizer I sometimes was, I set up a swim and dance party at the impressive Boomerang Motel for the Intercontinentals monthly party. I greeted people as they arrived around the large swimming pool. My wits deserted me when I met 20 year old, statuesque Maya from Germany.

295

A jukebox was hooked up on the pool patio at sunset. I managed to have several dances with Maya and we quickly decided we would get together the following evening. With a full moon above, the dancing went on to midnight—then everyone jumped back into the pool. It was a good start to my tenure as president.

One late afternoon, a Mrs. Hatch from Austin, Texas, arrived at the hotel to check in. She had a reservation but no rooms were left. There it was, her dream vacation, and this had to happen.

Mrs. Hatch, a schoolteacher in her early sixties, started crying. I found her a room at a hotel a block away and carried her bags there. She was most grateful for a helping hand from a fellow Texan.

If "De Bado the Mean" had been there, I know exactly what he would have said, "take her bags and put them on the street." It was getting so bad, one of my fellow desk clerks, Lorensini, had quit on three occasions because of that complete bully.

Several days later, 150 Texans checked in. It was like old home week. Among them were Mr. & Mrs. Hartman and their 26-year-old daughter, Vivian, a stewardess with American Airlines.

The Hartmans invited me to have dinner with them at Hostaria Del Orso. While we were eating, two girls approached our table. One of them said, "Would you two act as photographic models for us tomorrow?" I looked at Vivian and we both said, "Sure!" We became the models for Rome for American Express' *Travel Tour Booklet* for the world. Again, the right place at the right time!

All of a sudden, I was starting to get homesick. I'd been on the *The Royal Road to Romance,* the title of Richard Halliburton's book, for over six years. Being around my *fellow* Texans apparently had an impact on me, and I was missing my family. I was too low on money to go home just for a visit, and I knew I had to see the rest of Europe first.

On a side note, John Howard, an Australian journalist living in Rome, and I had become good friends through The Intercontinentals Club. John had interviewed and become friends with many of the most famous people in the world, and had written articles on many of them. During my stay in Rome, John hosted a number of great parties at his penthouse suite, to everyone's delight. With John there was never a dull moment.

One little story I must share. There was a most distinguished-looking gentleman with graying hair who worked at the hotel. Giovanni wore a tux looking suit with long tails and lots of gold buttons on it. His title was Porter, which meant he helped the guests with their luggage. He looked more like an Italian General who was getting ready to attend the King's Ball.

Giovanni came up to me one day when I was alone. "I've had an affair with a lady guest and I need you to help me write a love letter to her," he whispered. Shades of Cyrano de Bergerac!

Leave it to the Italians. They live life to the hilt and I love them. Naturally, I helped Giovanni compose one of the most passionate love letters ever written.

One morning at work, when I answered the phone, a sexy voice said, "This is Barbara and I am a friend of James. He told me I should give you a call to see if we could get together for a drink sometime." I immediately responded, "That would be great Barbara, how about this evening?" The deal was clinched.

I took Barbara along with me to the Intercontinentals Club meeting. She was a dazzling blonde from California. She was an actress in Italian and American movies and lived in Rome.

We got off to a roaring start by going dancing at The Madison Club until 2:00 in the morning. Then we strolled along the lively Via Veneto until we found the perfect sidewalk cafe for cocktails and conversation. I walked her home at 4:00 in the morning.

Barbara and I came back for an encore the very next evening. We went to see the thrilling *Sound and Light Show* at the Roman Forum. Afterwards, we decided we wanted to drink wine and listen to Italian songs. We found a basement nightclub, "Utopia," that had been a part of the ancient forum. With the dimly lit club almost to ourselves, we danced the night away.

On Saturday, Barbara and I jumped on a bus and went to the airport. From there, we hitchhiked the rest of the way to the beach at Focene. The beach was nearly deserted as we swam, dozed, and sunbathed through the afternoon—the kind of day one never forgets.

My last day at the Excelsior was August 31. I had set that day to finish up, so I could prepare and launch into the adventure of seeing Europe. All the staff wished me well. Working with the Italians had been a "new production and show" every single day. What a joy and fun it had been, with plenty of laughs included.

I wrote a letter to Prince Juan Carlos de Bourbon of Spain. I had hopes of visiting him and Princess Sophia when I got to Madrid. It never hurts to ask. In preparation for my hitchhiking trip around Europe, I'd been reading *Europe on $5 a Day*, as well as books on different countries I planned to visit.

One of my Italian contacts from The Intercontinentals arranged for me to meet with Father Moran at Susanna Church. I told the good Father, "I would like to stay in a monastery to experience the life of a monk and read the Bible all the way through." Father Moran promised to see what he could arrange for me while I was traveling the byways of Europe. Who knew where I would end up in Europe, or what I would get into or out of. That would be up to providence.

Wandering the ruins of Rome.

CHAPTER 53

The Enchantments of Europe

I travel for the sake of traveling to escape from myself and others. I travel to make a dream come true, quite simply, or to change skin if you like.

— Theophile Gautier

As I set out for Europe, I thought of its romanticism. The term derived ultimately from the fictional romances written during the Middle Ages, and each involved the episodic adventures of a single individual. And romanticism strongly valued exotic locations.

It was a three-and-a-half hour train trip to Florence. Being the famous hotelman I was, Roberto Bucciarelli, the Assistant Manager of the distinguished Grand Hotel, provided me with a free room to stay in. Actually, the Grand was a part of the CIGA hotel chain as was the Excelsior. We hotel guys stuck together.

Florence was so much quieter than Rome. I believe it is one of the most captivating, beautiful, and interesting cities in the world and has successfully retained its medieval feel and style.

The city, situated on the Arno River, is the capital of the region of Tuscany. Its history is as unique as the city itself and was the site of an Etruscan settlement as far back at 200 B.C. Starting in the early fifteenth century, Florence has flourished as a city of intellectual and artistic life. Many artists, such as Michelangelo, Leonardo de Vinci, and Raphael, created some of their most brilliant masterpieces there.

Unfortunately, the usually peaceful Arno River had gone on a complete rampage ten months before I arrived in the city. After receiving a third of the region's annual rainfall in just two days, the river's waters burst through just about everything in Florence. Magnificent works of art and treasured books were destroyed as the water reached heights of over 22 feet. Restoration continues to this day.

At sunset, I got a panoramic view of the whole area from Piazzale Michelangelo, high above the city. During the flood, no one had been able to get past that point.

Following the advice given in *Europe on $5 a Day*, I started my walking tours. The richness and beauty of the art in the Uffizi and Pitti Palace Galleries were beyond description. Along the way, I bought a Saint Christopher medal at one of the shops on the bridge across the river, hoping it would help protect me on my sojourn through Europe.

While walking along in the late afternoon, I met a Swiss girl. We explored together for a bit before having dinner. At the restaurant, we met Patricia Everton, from South Africa. The three of us shared travel stories and talked about the sights in Florence. It was a pleasure to have company.

Several days later, I took a train to the City of Marco Polo, Venice. Marco had set out from Venice on his perilous journeys in 1271 and arrived back home in 1295. He had gotten the jump on me by 672 years, yet I felt, in spirit, he and I had much in common.

Upon his return, Marco got involved in a war and was captured. He spent a year in a Genoese prison. Fortunately, one of his fellow prisoners was a writer of romances, named Rustichello, who prompted Marco to dictate the story of his travels. My job in Venice was to get thrown in prison with a writer of romances. It worked for Marco!

Arriving at the train station in Venice, I took a taxi boat (vaporetto) to Piazza San Marco. Most of the stately CIGA-chain hotels were located around that area. Signor Zoggia at the Grand Europa Hotel arranged a free room for me. Otherwise, I would've had to stay at a cheap, crumbling, sinking, third class hotel, given the state of my budget. Once I'd settled into my fancy hotel room, I set out to explore the "city of canals."

Venice was like no other city I had ever seen. It stretched across numerous small islands in the marshy Venetian Lagoon along the Adriatic Sea. Between the islands ran about 150 canals, mostly very narrow, crossed by some 400 bridges. I walked over 379 of them, or thereabouts.

Gondolas, the traditional means of transportation, had been superseded by small riverboats. There were many lanes and public squares, and few streets. Houses were built on piles.

There were no cars, which upset the traditional idea of a modern city. The good part about that was there was no pollution from exhaust fumes. I spent most of my time wandering the labyrinths of streets off the beaten track. In this fabled city, everything went slower.

Venice, also, got hit hard in the great flood of 1966. However, the underlying threat to the city's physical survival remains the sea. Flooding has become a regular and destructive feature of life there.

I learned that Casanova hailed from Venice. From reports that have come down to us in modern times, he was extravagant, mean, proud, honest, a liar, unstable, and quite brilliant. It might be said he was the perfect embodiment of the city at its most splendid, yet decadent peak.

There I was in that romantic city, unable to find a beautiful lady to accompany me in a gondola as I glided through the canals under a full moon. My "serendipity" had fallen flat on its face. So, it was time to move on to Milano. As long as my money held out, I took trains instead of hitchhiking.

At the Hotel Principe in Milan, the kindness of the Ciga management came through for me once again. I was given the sitting room of a suite with a rollaway bed. So far, I had been going first class on a poor man's budget.

I spent the day sightseeing the famous sights—Duomo Cathedral, La Scala Opera House, and the "Last Supper" by Leonardo de Vinci, among them. The Duomo is one of the most famous buildings in Europe. This Gothic Cathedral is the second largest Roman Catholic Cathedral. A total of 40,000 people can fit comfortably inside.

In 1867, Mark Twain had this to say about the Duomo: "What a wonder it is! So grand, so solemn, so vast! And yet so delicate, so airy, so graceful! It was a vision! A miracle! An anthem sung in stone! A poem wrought in marble!" I agree with Mark.

The next day, I was off to Switzerland, the land of the Alps. As the train rolled deeper and deeper into that unique small country, the more beautiful the scenery became.

In Lucerne, I discovered a quaint, small hotel after walking several blocks from the railway station. I asked for the cheapest single room available. Happily, I was put up in the attic in the coziest little room imaginable. From the large picture window, I had a perfect view of Lake Lucerne and the glistening white Alps beyond. I couldn't have gotten a better view in a five-star hotel.

I had lunch at the Ladies' Temperance Union restaurant. It was just me and a lot of old ladies having their tea and tarts. Actually, there were several other men there who had wandered in. The attractive young waitress made it a pleasant dining experience indeed.

That afternoon, I walked everywhere, taking in the beauty and sights. The fame of Lucerne as a tourist resort was legendary and it is often considered to be the true "Swiss" capital.

That evening, dinner was quite a contrast from my luncheon experience. It was in a tavern-looking affair filled with men who'd had way too much to drink. Without doubt, it was one of the most entertaining meals of my life. Everyone was getting up and down and patting each other on the back, shaking hands, and all the while engaged in animated conversation and uproarious laughter. Some were singing while several sat mumbling to themselves over their beer.

After dinner, I stopped by the Jesuit Church, which was filled with a blessed silence. I stayed a while to pray and thank God for keeping me safe up to that time.

My next stop was in Basel on the northern border. Henry Frei, my friend and roommate on the kibbutz in Israel, lived in Basel. Since Henry was on Army duty, his father picked me up at the train station and took me for lunch at a well-appointed restaurant overlooking the Rhine River. Mr. Frei made me feel completely at home. After a good night's rest, Mr. Frei fixed a big breakfast for us. I then spent the day walking through the city and along the Rhine. Thankfully, the weather had been cool and sunny on my journey thus far.

Basel is Switzerland's second largest city and its wealthy patrician families have nurtured a tradition of scholarship and art since the Renaissance. In fact, it has more than two-dozen museums.

When I returned to the house, Henry had arrived back from his Army camp. It was a delight to see him again since cutting bananas together on the kibbutz. Henry, his father, and I drove in their car to Zurich. Since it was Mr. Frei's sister Angela's, birthday, I joined them for a big family dinner. The family virtually adopted me.

Zurich, the most populous city of Switzerland, is famous for its financial institutions and its superb art galleries, with Lake Zurich offering opportunities for swimming, boating, sunbathing, and picnicking. Henry gave me a walking tour of this charming city.

Henry saw me off on the train that afternoon. I had given him a wonderful picture taken of us standing together in the ruins of Capernun on the Sea of Galilee.

Next stop, Munich, Germany. Angela had arranged for me to stay with her parents. The five-hour train ride was full of magnificent vistas, including mountains, lakes, and rolling fields.

Angela's elderly parents, Mr. & Mrs. Aulehner, and Daniel, Henry's brother, were at the train station to welcome me. It was true Bavarian hospitality.

That evening they took me to experience one of the largest parties in the world, Oktoberfest: an event to end all events.

Eleven huge beer tents that hold 6,000 people each, all with live bands; forty smaller beer, wine and coffee houses; over 200 carnival attractions, and 55 rides; and 6,000,000 people partying over 16 of the most fun-filled days on Earth. Oktoberfest was certainly the biggest party I had ever attended.

I will never forget an old lady; she must have been 70-something, sitting at the table next to us. When the bands were playing rousing German songs, some folks stood on the wooden benches of their table, held up their beer mugs, and sang at the tops of their voices. This old lady couldn't have been over five feet tall. Her beer mug was at least a foot tall and must have weighed ten pounds when full. She managed to stand up on the bench seat, raised her mug, began to sing, and passed out backwards across the table. She was determined not to let any fun pass her by. She was quickly revived and told she had drunk enough beer for one night. That was an exhibit of spunk at its best!

Munich is Germany's third largest city. Its motto is "The World City with a Heart." In 1806, it had become the capital of the new Kingdom of Bavaria.

Daniel had just finished up his job at the Frankfurt Intercontinental Hotel. He was taking some time off before starting a new job at the Princess Hotel in Bermuda. He and I toured Munich on bikes the next day, and then spent another fun-filled evening at Oktoberfest.

Since we had no luck picking up any girls, we wandered into a coffee shop near the train station before heading to the house. There, we met two pretty girls, Naomi and Eva, who were in their early twenties. They had not been able to find a room and were going to sit up all night.

Being the gentlemen we were, we invited them home with us. They slept on a couple of chairs in the living room. We had done our good deed for the day and in the morning they took a bus back to the station.

Frau Aulehner, 75, fixed us a huge Bavarian breakfast. Daniel set off for Basel, and I took four city buses to get me out to the Frankfurt highway.

CHAPTER 54

Once Again, The Romance of the Road

*Suppose each of us should resolve today that
not a minute henceforward should ever be
wasted. What energy there would be in our
lives! What strength!*

— Anonymous

I started hitchhiking. The rides were few and far between, and then only
for short distances. By sunset, I had only made it half way to my desired destination of Wiesbaden.

There I was, on the Autobahn, trying to hitch a ride with cars racing by at
100 mph as night fell. I believed in miracles, but I had gone beyond the brink
of good sense. So, I promptly hitched a ride down a two-lane road into the
small town of Erlangen. There I could catch a train.

While waiting on the train platform, bright colors appeared in my periph-
eral vision to the right of me. Walking toward me in a bright orange mini-
skirt, black velvet boots reaching to her knees, wearing a sheer, see-through,
lime-green blouse, and a long blonde ponytail swaying with her walk, was
Germany's top movie actress. Or so I thought, given the grace and style with
which she moved. I almost fell off the bench I was sitting on.

She sat down beside me and said in English in a lilting German accent, "Hi,
my name is Ursula." Stammering, I managed to get out, "Hi, I'm Clarke." It
just so happened it would be only the two of us in the same compartment.
*This sure was going to be more pleasant than trying to hitchhike on the Autobahn
at night*, I thought.

Ursula and I hit it off. We talked about America and Germany, and I
found out her real profession. She was a highly paid stripper in Frankfurt and
was on her way to work. It was a stimulating ride! I told her I hoped to see a
lot more of her.

The train pulled into Wiesbaden at 11:00 that night. At the prestigious
Park Hotel, one of the managers, Yohen Labriola, welcomed me. After putting my backpack in the room, Yohen took me for a drink in each of the

304

hotel's three nightclubs—I was warming up to the place fast. The family of Bernd, whom I had worked with at the Excelsior, owned this particular hotel. Bernd had kindly arranged a free room for me.

Weisbaden and Baden-Baden were both famous around the world for their spas. Sometimes referred to as the gateway to the Black Forest, Baden-Baden, a premier spa resort town, is known for its therapeutic waters. I was in need of some therapy at that point.

The following day I took a bus into Frankfurt. I spent the day walking the main city and its sights. Almost every German man I talked with told me how much money he was making. The economy was apparently doing well.

On this trip so far, I had gained weight instead of losing it. I hoped I could keep it up, as I was still a bit skinny. So far, I had been going in style for a change.

It was time for more sightseeing. I had a hearty breakfast at a small restaurant on the bank of the Rhine River. The 9:05 boat was delayed because of heavy fog. Once the fog lifted, the cruise began.

Never had I seen such a busy river. The cargo tankers and boats stretched in an almost unbroken line as far as the eye could see. I found out that along this stretch of the river, there are more castles than in any other river valley in the world.

I got off the boat at the small castle town of Bacharach, a jewel of a town. I climbed the steep steps up to the Romanesque Burg Stahleck Castle, where I was rewarded with a magnificent view. Back down in the town, I sipped wine in a quaint outdoor restaurant and watched the passing parade of people.

Bacharach is named for Bacchus, the ancient Roman god of wine. From 1300 to 1600 A.D., it was a major wine center. I did my best to support the cause in my short time there.

The Rhine had turned to gold from the setting sun as the boat docked back in Weisbaden. It had been a great day to be alive and well—and four sheets to the wind.

It was a Saturday morning when I boarded the 9:55 train to Paris. I sat next to a pleasant German girl, Fernande, who was on her way to Orleans to work as an au pair. We arrived at 5:26 in the evening.

I was counting on *Europe on $5 a Day* to get me through since I had no solid contacts in the "City of Light." I had no idea what lay in store, but I was game for whatever came my way.

I plunged from the train station down into the bustling corridors of the subway. A French University student gave me a ticket and pointed the way when I asked, "How do I go to the St. Michel station?" It was a kind act on his part and made me feel easier.

The first three cheap hotels I had selected from my trusty handbook turned out to be full. On the fourth try came success. The Hotel Central des Ecoles cost me 15 francs a night—about $7.00.

Upon checking in, I met John. He was a Sociology Major at London University. We ended up having dinner together at a self-service cafeteria and then took a walk through Montmarte.

Montmarte is a hill in the north of Paris, primarily known for the white-domed Basilica of the Sacré Coeur on its summit. It was on this hill in 1534 that Loyola and seven companions took the vows that led to the creation of the Jesuit order.

Surprisingly, Montmarte became a popular drinking area and developed into a center of freewheeling and decadent entertainment at the end of the nineteenth century. The cabaret Moulin Rouge was actually located there.

Near the Basilica, artists were still setting up their easels each day. Pablo Picasso and other impoverished artists lived there as they started out. John and I absorbed the whole atmosphere as we walked.

While having breakfast the next morning, I met Jerry Pittman from New York. He and I decided to tour the famous Louvre Museum. It took up most of the day. This was typical of how I'd meet someone and we'd team up for a day or longer.

Later I strolled by myself down the Champs-Elysee to the Arc de Triomphe. As I became tired, I got a ringside seat at an outdoor cafe, drank wine, and observed the fashion parade. Those French women certainly know how to turn heads.

Next it was off to the Eiffel Tower. There I met Mike, an Ethiopian fellow, who had been going to school in the U.S. We hit it off right away.

Mike and I were trying to figure out the subway when we met John, an American medical student studying in Paris. John kindly offered to show us around the Latin Quarter. It always helps to have an experienced guide when one is totally clueless.

Mike and I decided we would look for a twin-bed room together the next day to cut down on expenses. We found a room in the attic of a 600-year-old fourth-class hotel. The toilet had an excellent view of Paris, but it had no window glass. It sure got cold in there at night.

That evening, us two musketeers checked out the basement nightclubs.

On our way to one of them, we met Cy and Ethel on a little side street. They invited us to have a steaming bowl of famous onion soup at the venerable open-air food market. It was 3:30 in the morning, a perfect time to get something to eat in Paris.

Mike and I walked the Left Bank, saw the Notre Dame Cathedral, art galleries, museums, and ended up seeing the play *Cyrano de Bergerac* at Comedie-Francaise. Then it was time for another delicious bowl of onion soup in the early morning. I was addicted.

Mike and I were covering all the territory we could. We saw the Pantheon, Napoleon's tomb, which was more than impressive, the Right Bank, and then to Versailles.

At Versailles while having lunch, we met Maya, 17, from England. She had an interesting story to tell. She had been attending a convent school in London; however, she had such a record of devilishness, the nuns kicked her out. So naturally, her mother sent her to a French convent.

What was Maya doing at Versailles? She told the nuns she was going to visit an old lady that was starved for company. Of course, that was only an excuse to escape the convent for the afternoon. Maya was an adventurer, too.

Late that evening, I boarded the train for Madrid. I had reserved a couchette for the all night train journey to the Spanish frontier. I was in the mid-level one on the right side of the aisle; below me was a 100-year-old lady, and above, a charming young woman. On the other side of the aisle was a French Army officer, a workingman, and a rather stern woman. If it hadn't been for the old lady's snoring, I might have got some sleep. Nevertheless, I was happy to have a place to lie down, remembering my trek through India on third-class trains.

The train pulled into Irun at 7:30 that next morning. As we were changing onto the Spanish train, I met Elias Benator. He had a Moroccan passport because he was born there.

Elias' story was a fascinating one. In the fifteenth century, when Ferdinand and Isabella were persecuting the Jews in Spain, Elias' family split up and fled to different countries. Then, when the Arabs gained control of Algeria from the French, his part of the family came back to Spain.

He was in his sixth year of studying architecture at a university in Paris when we met. Elias looked to me like a gallant Spanish bullfighter—tall, handsome, soft-spoken, in excellent shape, and had an easy smile to top it all off.

The fast train from the border to Madrid was superb. Stirring Spanish music was playing as we sped over the plains. I wondered if Don Quixote had ever ventured to that area.

It was around 5:00 in the evening when we reached the capital city of Madrid. Elias and I got a twin-bed room at an ancient hotel for $3 U.S.

We met his friend, Santos, and the three of us started on a round of eating and drinking in the Old Quarter of Madrid. On Saturday nights, throngs of people took to the streets to live it up. We were right in the thick of them.

As the former capital of the Old Spanish Empire, Madrid has a great degree of cultural prominence. Following the restoration of democracy in 1975, the city has experienced an increasing role in European finances. Juan Carlos I, who it had been my proud duty to serve while he was on his honeymoon in Hawaii, has led Spain to its current position as a constitutional monarchy.

The next morning, Elias and I had breakfast at his girlfriend's house. Eva, pretty and kind, had been born to Hungarian parents in a German concentration camp in Poland. She was in her last year of interpreter's school in Geneva and hoped to go to work for the UN.

The three of us went walking through the Rastro, Madrid's Sunday flea market. They then took me to see my first bullfight. I felt very sorry for the first bull that was killed, but admired the skills of the matadors as the fights went on. We ended the evening with a typical Spanish meal in a bustling section of old Madrid and then took in a Flamenco show.

One of the quaint customs in Madrid is to clap one's hands outside a building's 100-year-old door when coming home after a certain late hour. There was usually one doorkeeper per block. He would come running with a skeleton key, a good eight inches long, to open the huge wooden door.

The next several days were spent seeing the sights. The world-famous El Prado Museum was among my favorites. It is one of the best in the world and holds more than 10,000 pieces of art, a mecca for classical art lovers. To go through El Prado is to travel through time and thought.

While I was in Madrid, the first elections in thirty years took place. It was historic. Only the head of each family and his wife could vote. All candidates had to be pro-government, or they could not stand for election. I voted twice, following an old Texas tradition, where even the dead vote whether they were eligible to vote or not.

It came time to hitchhike on.

CHAPTER 55

Don Quixote, Windmills, and Me

*If you want to fulfill your dreams, help
someone else to realize that their dreams are
not impossible.*

— Anonymous

*D*on *Quixote* was published in 1605 and it is often called the first true novel. The author, Miguel Cervantes, had an impact on literature that is comparable to Shakespeare's. It is ironic that they both died on the same day.

Don Quixote is a tale of a knight whose quest to do right sends him on idealistic journeys. His mind is blinded by dreams and he chooses to see the world not as it is, but as it should be.

Where would our world be without people whose impossible dreams coax the best not only from themselves, but from the rest of us as well?

The musical play and movie *Man of La Mancha* is based on the story of *Don Quixote.* It's most famous song is among the most soul stirring ever written: *To Dream the Impossible Dream.*

It was early morning, October 11 in Madrid. With Don Quixote in mind, I walked to the nearest subway stop with my backpack on. I got off one stop later and took the #1 bus to where the highway for Barcelona began. Five minutes later, I caught a ride with a young Spanish professor named Raphel. He got me thirty kilometers down the road.

At the town of Acala, I waited beside the road for an hour before a talkative Spanish farmer took me as far as Guadalajara. It was around noon and it was getting hot. I was in Castilla La Mancha.

It had been 400 years since Don Quixote tilted at windmills in this part of Spain. I had, in a way, been tilting at windmills since my romantic notions and travel adventures had begun. I had, figuratively speaking, been knocked off my horse at least eighteen times.

The plateau of central Spain's Castilla La Mancha region has many moods. One of them was hot. But in the mornings and evenings, there is magic as fields turn golden and rolling. It is a landscape that surrounds travelers with a solitude, and it provides a blank canvas upon which one can conjure up their fantasies. *Over there, did I see Don Quixote riding in the shimmering heat of the plains?*

The errant knight, Don Quixote, could not have arisen from any but this land across which he ranged. And now here I was ranging across it. All I needed was a horse.

I was in a land that encompassed vast plains, fairytale castles, wine, and huge windmills. I loved this *Man of La Mancha* part of Spain. Some people thought me crazy, too, trying to hitchhike through Europe. In fact, I had myself a little worried at times, to tell the truth, especially when I would be in the middle of nowhere and no one would give me a ride for hours.

The Ingenious Gentleman Don Quixote of La Mancha is often nominated as the world's greatest work of fiction. It stands in a unique position between medieval chivalric romance and modern novel. It consists of disconnected stories with little exploration of the inner life. Much like my story, which I hoped to get published someday. Of course, I had been steeped in chivalric romance as a boy, so here I was in person on the plains of La Mancha.

After a quick lunch at a small inn, I hit the road again, lance in hand. As I waited by a highway junction, a kind old gentleman by the name of Sancho came up to me. In lots of Spanish, he explained I had to walk on a bit further to catch a ride, because I wasn't in a good place to do so. My Spanish from high school saved the day.

He was right. Three hundred yards further up the road, I was able to get a ride in short order. A young Spanish couple and their darling two-year old daughter, Adela, stopped to pick me up. I couldn't speak Spanish with the parents very well, but Adela and I understood each other perfectly in baby talk.

It was around 8:00 in the evening when they let me out in Zaragoza. The city is located at a point in the valley of Ebro, Spain's most water-bearing river. It is an impressive landscape with picturesque villages and very old traditions.

Zaragosa is one of the great monumental towns in Spain. It had been founded in the first century A.D., and the Iberians, Romans, Goths, and Arabians equally left their mark on the city.

Being more than hungry, I had a bite to eat at the first restaurant I saw. I had no idea where to stay or what part of the city I was in. Food came first.

Being a time of fiesta, I found every small hotel I went to full, even the pensiones were full. My prospects for a place to sleep did not look good. The streets were alive with people, music, and lights. After over an hour of walking

At a folk festival in Zaragosa, Spain.
The little girl was quite shy.

and searching, I was weary. Walking down a small, quiet street, I saw a young Spaniard talking to a man on the steps of a house.

Thank goodness that José Valenquela spoke a little English. Soon his brother, Fernando, came up. Fernando had spent a year in Chicago, so the language barrier evaporated into thin air. They invited me to their home for dinner. Dinner in Spain is usually eaten at a late hour.

They introduced me to their cultured and friendly parents. Marianne, one of their friends at dinner, arranged a nice room at a boarding home for me. Jose, Fernando, and some of their buddies took me for drinks at Sangria, one of the nicest restaurants in Zaragosa. All's well that ends well!

Being very tired, I slept most of the next day, especially since I was coming down with a bad cold. I didn't want a repeat of what happened to me as I traveled across Arabia. In the evening, Fernando took me to see the lively folk dancing in a street alongside a huge and impressive looking church. I had begun to feel right at home in this friendly city.

As Don Quixote so often did, I charged forth once again. Fate was on my side that day. I began hitchhiking at around 9:00 in the morning. A congenial Spaniard, in a broken-down pickup, gave me my first ride after one hour of waiting on the outskirts. He got me a short ten kilometers down the road.

Another hour passed before an archeologist gave me a ride for about thirty kilometers. One more hour went by, when along came a taxi that stopped without any signaling on my part.

The taxi driver was on his way to Barcelona to pick up a fare. He said, "I will take you along for 200 pasetas." I offered him 150 pasetas and he took the deal. It was good for both of us. He dropped me twelve kilometers from the city.

Standing on a sidewalk preparing to hitch a ride, a fellow walked up and said, "I'm heading into Barcelona. Can I give you a ride?" Bless Vincente Martinez who spoke fairly good English. Having finished his work for the day, he volunteered to drive me all around the city to show me the sights. What good fortune!

After a grand tour, Vincente dropped me off at a nice pensione. I told him if he ever got to Texas, I wanted to repay his great kindness to me.

Settling in, I had dinner at a 200-year-old restaurant, at least the building appeared that old. I then proceeded to walk through the ancient narrow streets exploring all I could see.

Legend attributes that Barcelona has a Carthaginian foundation. It was called Barcino after Hamilcar Barca, father of Hannibal. About 15 B.C., Romans set it up as a Roman military camp.

While it may still be the second city of Spain, it has a charm and air that is unique and prized. And it is the most cosmopolitan and economically active city in the country.

I spent the next day exploring the city and its sights. One of the most dramatic sights was Gaudi's unfinished cathedral. Gaudi was an architect who was born in 1852 and died in 1926.

Gaudi spent 43 years working on building the cathedral. It may be another fifty years before it's completed. Nevertheless, it's an awe-inspiring sight and a symbol for Catalonia Spain.

I boarded a train for a 7:15 p.m. departure. The coach I was in was nearly empty. What a blessing, again remembering my nightmare trips on those third-class trains in India. I curled up on a seat for several hours of much needed rest.

The train arrived at the French border at 11:00 that night. While changing trains, I met Dave Armour, a fellow American. Upon boarding the French train, we found it packed. We later snuck down several cars to find a place to stretch out.

We went back to our original coach car when they disconnected other cars in Marsailles at 5:20 in the morning. We had to keep alert at all hours or we'd end up back in Paris or who knows where.

Dave and I must have set a record of some kind. We had breakfast in Cannes and sunned on the beach there for several hours; we lunched in Nice and listened to an outdoor band concert; and then we had dinner and gambled in Monte Carlo in Monaco.

I found a one-franc coin stuck in a slot machine at one of the casinos, so I pushed it on in. Out came a jackpot of eight francs. Given my deteriorating funds, that was a fortune to me. I was convinced that coin had been left there with me in mind.

Dave and I got a large twin-bed room for the amazing sum of $3.75 U.S. It had a small balcony overlooking a garden of palms. I was moving up in the magical dream world of Monte Carlo.

After we had breakfast, Dave took a train to Rome. I put my swimsuit on and headed for the beach. I expected bathing beauties to be waiting for me. No such luck that day, but the sand and sea were a relaxing balm for a weary traveler.

I did my usual exploring around, this time in a principality. In the early afternoon, I discovered that in 1215, a Genoan family laid the first stone of the castle there, which is still today the Prince's Palace where Grace Kelly once lived.

My train pulled out at 3:30 that afternoon and arrived in Genoa at 9:00 that evening. The interesting and amusing Italians in my compartment saved the day during that slow trip.

I learned that the Ciga Chain's Excelsior Hotel was directly across from the train station. *Why not give it a try*, I thought. Lo and behold, they gave me a free room. I had to be one of the luckiest guys in the world.

I ate a plate of spaghetti at a small restaurant and then went walking. "Genoa is the most winding, incoherent of cities, the most entangled topographical ravel in the world," so said Henry James. Sprawled behind the huge port is a dense and fascinating warren of medieval alleyways.

Genoa made its money at sea, through trade, colonial exploitation, and piracy. It even cold-shouldered Columbus when he sought funding for his voyages. As I walked, I found it a buzzing hive of activity.

6:22 is too blooming early in the morning to catch a train, but there was still Pisa to see—it was a two and a half-hour ride on the rails.

In Pisa, I was able to get a picture of me holding up the Leaning Tower of Pisa with one hand. That it was still standing was a miracle.

After several hours of sightseeing, I caught a train to Florence. I was in the home stretch and mightily ready for a recuperative rest.

Arriving at noon, I ate lunch at a self-service restaurant before taking a bus out to the highway to Rome. It turned out to be one of the toughest days of hitchhiking I'd ever experienced.

After two hours of waiting in the hot sun, I was baked. Finally, I got a short ride. Another half-hour of waiting earned me an even shorter ride, but by that time, I was grateful just to be moving and in the shade.

Another hour of waiting and my spirits were flagging. At last, a distinguished looking gentleman took pity on me around 5:00 that evening. I was close to having sunstroke. He drove like an experienced racecar driver, making it to Rome in a two-hour record time. It wasn't fast enough for me.

Franco welcomed me back to his apartment. After filling him in on my month of wandering Europe, I collapsed in bed. The trip had been well worth the effort, having been educational, challenging, enlightening, insightful, and the fact that I got to know so many varying personalities and cultures.

Tomorrow would be a new day and I had no clear idea what direction it might take me. There was no telling where and when serendipity might pop up.

CHAPTER 56

On Being a Monk

Try to think of your whole life as a unity,
rather than a series of unrelated fragments.
In that way, each period grows out of the last,
and you know there will be another to come.

— from *Michelangelo*

I had $300 left in the bank and (I estimated) my Australian stocks would bring in $300 when sold. It was going to cost around $600 to get me back to Texas. I was on the financial edge, but I had been there numerous times before.

It seemed the perfect time to take a vow of poverty. I was going to check out the possibilities of going to a monastery.

Right at that point, I needed clean clothes more than anything else. It was off to the laundry and then to get my semi-long hair trimmed. I kept my incipient Vandyke beard.

A week before I had set out on my European adventure, I had met a smashing English girl. There had been some chemistry there, so I called Jenny. She invited me over for tea and crumpets.

The next day, I pondered all my options, given the low state of my busted budget. *I have a great idea. I'll buy Jenny a present*, I decided. Such big decisions don't come along all that often. I gave her a necklace at dinner and we decided we'd run off to Capri soon for a romantic weekend. There was just nothing like being low on money and living extravagantly.

I went to see the Pope. Thousands of others and myself watched as he blessed the crowd in St. Peter's Square. Afterwards, I climbed the stairs to the top of the dome of St. Peter's Basilica. What a prodigious structure! It provided a marvelous view of the Vatican Gardens and Rome.

I got a letter from American Express in London. It told me to look for my "model" pictures in the Rome section of their *Europe 1968* travel booklet. I hoped that wouldn't discourage too many people from coming to Rome.

Another letter came from Ireeni in Athens. She had decided to go to Paris to try her luck as an actress. If anyone could make it, she certainly could.

Liana Palange invited me to her house for lunch. Thanks to her splendid efforts, I had been recruited into the monk kingdom. She'd made the necessary arrangements for me to stay in a monastery near Assisi. Let us pray, and I was on my way to higher realms.

At the Santa Susana Church library, I spent several hours reading up on the Camaldolese Order of monkhood. A monk's life is dedicated to embracing religion, nature, and simplicity. I was ready for some of that, but my main goal was to read the Bible all the way through.

But before becoming a monk, there was time for one last fling. I took a bus out to the Autostrada, the super highway. Two brothers, Rocco and Antonio, from Sardinia, both in the military police, gave me a lift halfway to Naples.

Next, I rode with a congenial young fellow driving a large red dump truck. For the last thirty kilometers, I rode with an Italian gentleman who worked for NATO.

This was a real switch. Five months ago, when I arrived in Italy, Mrs. Pagano and her daughter picked me up, a total stranger, on the Autostrada in Naples and delivered me to Rome. Mrs. Pagano welcomed me into her beautiful apartment around 5:00 in the evening. It looked like a palace with marble floors and large original paintings over 500 years old.

Her newly married daughter, Gina, and I had a pleasant visit together before having a superb Italian dinner with all the trimmings. Mrs. Pagano treated me as if I was a long lost son. Such kindness!

The next morning I met "Jenny with the green eyes" when she arrived by train. Then we set off by boat to the famous Isle of Capri. It was a glorious, sunny day with a calm sea running.

Capri has been a celebrated beauty spot and resort since the time of the Roman Republic. In fact, in 27 A.D., Tiberius permanently moved to Capri, running the Roman Empire from there until his death ten years later.

Jenny and I spent the weekend savoring the wonderful light and atmosphere of the island. The central piazzetta, though preserving its modest village architecture, was lined with boutiques and charming restaurants. It was indeed a weekend to remember.

Jenny headed back to Rome on Sunday evening. The next morning Mrs. Pagano had her maid pack a picnic lunch for my day at Pompeii. I was off by train.

I wandered through the ruins of that ancient and rich city. It had been buried under twenty feet of lava and ash over 2,000 years ago. I was pleased Vesuvius decided not to erupt that day.

Vesuvius has had at least 200 powerful eruptions during the past 2,000 years. Experts agree that Vesuvius' next eruption will be the greatest since 1631. There are about a million people living in the potential danger zone and it could make the eruption that covered Pompeii look like a minor catastrophe.

A typical thing happened on the train trip back to Naples. An old man sat down by an old lady, even though there were plenty of extra seats around. She moved over. After some argument, he moved. When he got off the train, the other six or seven people still left on the railcar began to discuss why he sat by her instead of where there were so many empty seats. The discussion continued for another half hour until every one had had their say. Very Italian!

Everything in Italy is up for discussion. I hesitated to mention to that vociferous vocal group that I was getting ready to enter a monastery, especially one where Dante had stayed. I'm sure they would have debated through the night whether I had any hope of redemption.

This little excursion had taken me from Rome to Naples to Capri to Pompeii to Sorrento and back to Naples. Those six days on the road had cost me the grand total of 10,000 lire or $16 U.S.

Mrs. Pagano fixed a huge dinner for me when I got "home." We had a pleasant chat after dinner and I filled her in on my adventures.

The next morning, she fixed me a hearty breakfast, kissed me on both cheeks, gave me a box of food, a bottle of wine, and wished me "happy hitchhiking." It was raining as I set off for Rome with only 350 lire left in my pocket.

I took a subway to the main station and a bus to where the Autostrada began. I got a ride almost immediately with Fernando in his red Fiat sports car. At 90 mph, we had a blowout only 10 kilometers from Rome. Thanks to God that the car did not spin out of control or roll over at that great speed. This was my fifth such harrowing experience. There had been so many occasions during my travels where my life literally hung in the balance. The Lord needed me in that monastery.

We fixed the flat and arrived in Rome in one piece. I gave Franco an update on my trip. All he could say was, "You are living the sweet life, *la dolce vita*." I had to agree with him.

Franco loaned me his book *The Italians* by Barzini. That book helped me understand why the Italians are like they are.

At 8:00 in the morning several days later, Liana Palange and her friend, Rita, picked me up at Franco's apartment. They were both attractive women.

To have such escorts to a remote monastery did seem a bit incongruous, but I couldn't ask for better traveling companions.

As we sped north, we kidded, told jokes, sang, laughed, talked of serious matters, got high on wine in Spolete, and dropped in to see the church and burial tomb of St. Francis of Assisi. The rain didn't dampen our spirits one iota on the fun and leisurely 200-kilometer journey north.

Speaking of St. Francis, one of my favorite quotes by that saint is: "Start by doing what's necessary; then do what's possible; and suddenly, you are doing the impossible." That's exactly what I did in my travels! Of course, my deep faith in God had a lot to do with it.

It was totally dark when we arrived at 5:30 that evening at the venerable Monastery of Fonte Avellana near Gubbio. To describe how venerable it is, Pope John Paul II celebrated a 1000-year anniversary mass at Fonte Avellana in 1985.

I bid Liana and Rita farewell, thanked them profusely for their kindness, and told them how much I had enjoyed the day. The good Father Pamio led me through the 1,000-year-old monastery and down a hall some twenty feet

A group of my fellow Camaldolese monks at the monastery of Fonte Avellana in the central mountains of Italy.

high and fifteen feet wide. On each side of that hall were the cells where the monks lived. Some ten cells down, he opened a huge wooden door on the right side and led me into my "new" old abode.

There were only thirteen monks left in residence, but at one time, there were over a hundred monks living in the monastery at any given time through the centuries. With me in residence, there were now thirteen and a half monks in Fonte Avellana.

Mass was held from 6:00 to 6:30 that evening in the sacred chapel located at the top of a narrow stairway. It wasn't a large chapel, but what dramatically stood out on the altar was the life-size wooden crucifix that was carved and painted by Francisco Tiraboschi in 1467, exactly 500 years before my monk-hood. In the flickering light of many candles, since no electric lights were used in the chapel, the figure of Jesus appeared totally life-like. It was as if I, myself, was at his crucifixion.

It was cold up in those mountains. Dinner was at 7:00 in a large room. Heavy wooden tables were placed in the shape of a long U, with a table across one end where Friar Priore sat as the head of the monastery. A carafe of wine sat at each place. It was the only thing that kept me from freezing to death that night.

In the Camaldolese Order, the monks do not talk unless absolutely necessary. It was just as well, because none of them spoke a word of English and my Italian was pitiful. During meals, one of the monks would stand at the open end of the U-shaped tables at a rostrum and read passages from the Holy Roman Bible.

My plan was to stay at the monastery for a month and try my best to read the entire Bible through. I had brought my King James Version along with me. I started my reading of the Old Testament that night.

Women were not allowed in the monastery, and once a month, a few chosen men might be allowed in for several hours. This was seclusion and quietness at its best. I was already feeling lonely. As Edwin Young put it, "Divine retreat."

This medieval hermitage is located on Mount Catria and is naturally isolated by the sloping hills of the Appennines that surround it. The Scriptorium is just off the main entrance. This is where the monks used to prepare their manuscripts on dried sheepskin. The crypt is the oldest room in the monastery and was originally the primary chapel.

It just so happened my cell was located directly across from the one that had been occupied by Dante. I often thought I heard his spirit walking around at night. Of course, it could have been the wind, which never stopped blowing on that mountain.

Dante, the fourteenth century writer, stayed at Fonte Avellana while exiled from Florence in 1310. He referenced the monastery in the paradise section of his *Divine Comedy* and there was a plaque on the wall outside his cell commemorating his stay. I was having a plaque forged to put outside my cell because it was a blooming miracle I was there. It just showed where prayer and providence might lead.

Dante wrote of Fonte Avellana:

> *Twixt two Italian shores are lifted high;*
> *Tall crags, and near thy home so far they rise;*
> *The thunder peels below them distantly;*
> *And where they shape their skyline humpback-wise;*
> *Is Catria; below a hermitage;*
> *Once to God's service consecrated, lies.*
>
> — *Dante*
> *Paradise, Canto XXI,*
> *Lines 106-111*

This early monastic retreat on the eastern flanks of Mount Catria stands in one of the most breathtaking settings imaginable. Its beauty is derived as much from the intentional poverty of the architecture as from the magnificence of the monastery's proportions and the extraordinary size of the entire complex. It is one of the few monasteries in the Marche area, which retains its medieval monastic form.

The Hermitage of The Holy Cross at Fonte Avellana is its full name. The place description, fonte for fountain, and avellana for hazelnut, have given their name to the hermitage. Holy Cross is the church designation. As has been noted, its origins date back to the difficult times of the first millennium after Christ.

Fonte Avellana lives on. Standing before the rocks of Mount Catria, it has been almost completely restored to its original beauty. It seems to continue to breathe faith and culture, which are the highest expressions of human civilization. In 1982, Pope John Paul II came there and elevated the church of the hermitage to the status of Minor Basilica.

The Camaldolese that inhabit Fonte Avellana is a joint order of hermits and cenobites. The order itself was founded about 1012 A.D. They then founded or reformed nearly a hundred unconnected monasteries. These monks wear a white habit, which sets them apart from other Orders, and they remain examples of austerity and monastic fervor. I was right in there pitching with them, and freezing my tail off in the process.

Everyday I went for a hike up mountains and along mountain trails. I'd never lived in a more beautiful place. Each day was an inspiration in many ways, even when we went to the chapel for Mass at 3:00 a.m. every morning.

Father Pamio and I usually had one short chat each day in Italian. I only knew about fifty words, so we ran out of steam quickly. He just wanted to make sure how I was holding up or falling down on my job as a novice monk.

At least I was spending five or six hours each day reading the Bible, even though I had given up on all the "begats" in the Old Testament. Just getting through the New Testament was going to be an accomplishment.

One of the most interesting parts of my experience was observing my thirteen fellow monks. They came in all shapes, sizes and ages, and each had his own unique personality. It was like a microcosm of the world.

The only thing that saved me from the constant cold of the monastery was the carafe of wine at dinner every evening. It acted just like anti-freeze. I would gripe in my diary about the cold every night. Somehow it made me feel warmer.

The geese below my room seemed to enjoy themselves immensely while I tried to sleep. Perhaps they were as cold as me and were letting it show. Maybe they were just trying to stay warm.

I finished reading the *Acts of the Apostles* and started on the *Book of Luke*. Little by little, I had been making my way through the New Testament.

After only one week, I decided to hang up my monkly spurs. The peace and quiet was more than I could stand. *Let's face it*, I thought, *I'm not cut out to be a monk for even a month*. All in all though, it had been an educational and spiritual adventure. My desire to experience the life of a monk had been fulfilled.

Dear Father Pamio—I had come to think of him as a true saint—saw to it that I had my usual cup of coffee and bread, although a little earlier than usual. I said goodbye to my twelve monk friends. Prior Priore took me in the car to Cagli, since he had business to attend to there.

Fifteen minutes after I started hitchhiking, a nice Italian fellow, Cicio, gave me a ride to Perugia. Since I didn't know how many rides it would take, I decided to spend what money I had left on a train ticket to Rome.

*When in Rome... from monkhood to la dolce vita—with
two secretaries and bodyguard.*

Franco was surprised to see me when I got back. He was not expecting me for two or three more weeks. I told him, "I have enough poverty as it is, I don't need the extra poverty of being a monk." Nevertheless, bless all monks for their purpose and dedication.

John Howard, my Australian photojournalist friend, asked me to lend him a helping hand. He wanted to have a special picture taken for his Christmas card.

John had borrowed two $1,000 evening dresses from Tiziani's Fashion House. He had Carla and Thelma, both models, put them on. On his outdoor terrace he laid down on a Roman bench, on his side, shirt off, and his camera hanging around his neck.

With his head propped up by elbow and hand, he had Carla feeding him grapes, Thelma behind him looking somewhat like a second mistress/bodyguard, and Sally dressed in a smart business suit at a small table with pad and pencil, as if she were taking notes. I snapped the pictures. Leave it to John to be creative.

322

Once he was satisfied with the shots, he told me to lie down in his place. I kept my suit on. It turned out to be a classic picture, showing my transition from monk to modern day swinger.

John told Pat McNair at the *Rome Daily American* newspaper about my stay at the monastery. Several days later it appeared in her column, "Lend me your Ears," that I was a retired monk. Amen!

To sum up my thoughts about my wonderful life in Italy is this quote from Gogo: "Who has been in Italy can forget all other regions. Who has been in Heaven docs not desire the Earth." It is indeed a most special place in the world.

CHAPTER 57

Arrivederci Roma, Hello Home

*All that mankind has done, thought, or been
is lying in magic preservation in the pages
of books.*

— Carlyle

*M*y adventurous odyssey of over 50,000 miles by land and sea, in sometimes inhospitable climates over 7 years, was coming to an end and I was nearly penniless— the same way I had started out—but at the same time, much richer for the experience, the knowledge and friends gained, and the good fortune of being healthy. I was in a sense a pauper once again. What was ahead of me, that was the question?

Homesickness was all that ailed me and that was soon to be cured. Having experimented and experienced living in over 30 different cultures, I was a different person than when I left the shining shores of America. *What would home be like now and how would I fit in?* I wondered.

Mark Twain said, "Travel is fatal to prejudice, bigotry, and narrow mindedness, and many of our people need it sorely on these accounts. Broad, wholesome, charitable views of men and things cannot be acquired by vegetating in one little corner of the earth all one's lifetime." I could identify with that.

One of the most important lessons I learned was that ninety five percent of the people of the world, in my estimation, are basically good and want the same things most of us want—freedom, enough to eat, a job, a place to live, good health, and the love and support of a family.

Ironically, I was preparing to start all over on a new track, with hopes of finding a good job, a place to live, and maybe the girl of my dreams. I was strongly feeling the need to settle down to somewhat of a normal life.

I was still waiting for a check from the sale of a small investment in Australian stocks to pay my expenses home. *Where is it?* I asked myself over and over. Finally, I wrote Dad to see if he could advance me the amount I needed to get me home to San Antonio. Just as at the beginning of my adventures, he came through for me right at the *end* of them.

There were many parties with my friends from the Intercontinentals Club. It was quite a contrast from the life of a monk. I took pretty Yvonne Camillo to see *Madame Butterfly*.

Bruno Kali, my good friend from the Excelsior Hotel, when he heard I had not yet seen the Sistine Chapel, said, "I must take you there and show it to you. Your visit to Italy will not be complete without that experience."

The Sistine Chapel is a chapel in the Apostolic Palace, the official residence of the Pope in Vatican City. It is rectangular and the exact size as the Temple of Solomon, as given in the Old Testament.

When we walked into the chapel, about twenty tourists were roaming around. Wooden benches were placed along the sides of each long wall. As we stood in the middle looking up, Bruno said, "Wait here." The next thing I knew, he brought a wooden bench to where I was. He placed it just right and then told me to lie down on it. I felt more than a little foolish in that most sacred place, but I did as he said. Bruno was not only a character, in his own right, but a talented artist. He proceeded to give me a blow-by-blow description of the magnificent ceiling painted by Michelangelo from 1508 to 1512.

I had just finished reading the book, *The Agony and the Ecstasy*, a biographical novel of Michelangelo. Bruno helped bring it alive for me as I lay there on my back right in the big middle of the Sistine Chapel. *Leave it to Bruno to make things special*, I thought.

My good friend, John Howard, the Australian journalist who seemed to know all the rich and famous people in the world, invited me to one last party at his penthouse suite. The guests included some of the cast of the movie *Candy*. The movie included performances by Marlon Brando, Richard Burton, James Coburn, and Ringo Starr.

And lo-and-behold, there was Ringo Starr of the Beatles! What a fabulous coincidence! When I got to know the other three Beatles in Hong Kong, Ringo had had tonsillitis. We had a good chat and I was thrilled at getting to know the fourth Beatle. I had now come full circle.

Here is what was written in the *Rome Daily American's* "Lend Me Your Ears" column about the gathering: "Ringo and Maureen Starred at the John Howard party for *London Daily Mirror's* Don Short. One of the more unaware guests stopped the show by shouting, "Hey, John. That's Ringo, isn't it? Isn't that Ringo? Hey, that is Ringo." The Beatle was with Malcom Evans, one of the group's road managers. Other partiers included London glamour photographer Hatami and Monty Fresco, both there for the *Candy* pix, Columbia Pictures man in Rome, Frances Kantor, Clarke Straughan, and a number of others." It was a great way to end my months of living as a Roman.

I put down $145 for a seat on a Charter flight to New York for December 15th. It was home for Christmas or bust. That left me with the grand total of 6,000 lire or $10 U.S.

Just in the nick of time, Dad's letter with a check in it arrived. I rejoiced, *This will get me from New York home to San Antonio*!

Franco Taliana, my best friend in Rome, and I said goodbye warmly, as I boarded the charter flight. As always, I made friends wherever I was and in whatever circumstances I found myself. My seatmate, Enrico Bartolucci, and I hit it off right away, and we would stay in touch.

Customs went smoothly in New York, even though, with a trim beard, I looked quite different from my passport photo.

All my family was there to meet me when I arrived at Home Base, Texas. My little brother, Ted, was now as tall as me. Mom was overjoyed that I had arrived home alive, hoping-upon-hope that I had gotten adventuring out of my system. Little did she know!

It was my first Christmas home after almost seven years of triumphs and vicissitudes. A new life was beginning, without means and without employment. What great adventures lay ahead!

EPILOGUE

A Story to Tell

It's kind of fun to do the impossible.

— Walt Disney

On one of my later visits to Hawaii, I happened to attend a church service where the following song/hymn was sung. I had never heard it before, but as it was being sung I got goose bumps.

It was entitled *Into the Fire* from the musical/play *The Scarlet Pimpernel*. In many ways, it epitomized my philosophy, my adventures, and the spirit of living life to the fullest, no matter what the odds. If I had a theme song, this would be it.

David walked into the valley with a stone clutched in his hand.
He was only a boy, but he knew someone must take a stand.
There will always be a valley, always mountains one must scale.
There will always be perilous waters which someone must sail!
Into valleys, into waters, into jungles, into hell,
Let us ride, let us ride home again with A Story to Tell.
Into darkness, into danger—into storms that rip the night!
Don't give in, don't give up, but give thanks for the glorious fight!
You can tremble, you can fear it, but keep your fighting spirit alive boys!
Let the shiver of it sting you! Fling into battle! Spring to your feet boys!
     Never hold back your step for a moment!
Never doubt that your courage will grow! Hold your head even higher
     and INTO THE FIRE we go!
Let the lightning strike! Let the flash of it shock you! Choke your fears away!
     Pull as tight as a wire! Let the fever spike! Let the force of it rock you!

Into mountains that surround us? Are there walls that block the way?
Knock them down, strip them back, boys, and forward into the fray!
Into terror, into valor. Charge ahead. No! Never turn!
Yes, it's INTO THE FIRE, we fly, and the devil will burn!
Someone has to face the valley! Rush in! We have to rally, and
     win, boys.

When the world is saying not to, by God, you know you've got to,
   March on, boys!
We will have our day, Sailing into the Fire!
Never hold back your step for a moment! LOOK ALIVE! Oh, your
   courage will grow!
Yes, it's higher and higher AND INTO THE FIRE WE GO.
INTO THE FIRE! Onward, Ho!

Many readers have asked, "How in the world were you able to make instant friends and have so many strangers of all walks of life go out of their way to want to help you?" My guide was simply the Golden Rule—and my faith in God. I approached every person with that in mind. If one shows respect and a friendly attitude toward others, it is generally returned many times over, even when one cannot speak the other's language.

As mentioned in Chapter 2, my Salesmanship professor at Texas A&M gave each class member a paperback copy of *How to Win Friends and Influence People.* I was a senior at the time. That little book helped change my life for the better. I recommend it as a practical guide on how to live the Golden Rule every day.

VENTURE FORTH. LIVE YOUR DREAM!

Acknowledgments

First and foremost, I want to thank my beautiful and gracious wife for her love, support, and indispensable assistance in the writing of this memoir. She is my best friend and a true Southern Belle.

No one goes through life, or a book project, without a lot of help, and I needed more than most.

My father, mother, and especially my grandfathers taught me the Golden Rule, honesty, caring, and the importance of being of service to my fellow-man—blessings for which I'm ever thankful. Also, a very warm thank you to my stepmother, Ann Monier, for her love, support, and kindness through the years. She is forever the encourager.

Donna Delvy, a long-time friend and associate, played a key role with ideas, editing, and humor on a weekly basis to help me get through the writing of the first draft of the manuscript. Thank you, Donna.

My good friends, Bruce Maness and Richard Battle, were two of my most invaluable assets in the crafting of this book. Thank you for your friendship, unflagging support, and creative ideas.

Also, thanks to my friends Dean and Ginny Mosley, Rick and Ting Reno, Doug Manger, Brian Kline, Roger Kew, Becky McFarland, Bill Ferguson, and Corrine Anderson for their ideas and support along the way.

My outstanding editor, Mindy Reed, offered superb guidance every step of the way—thank you for going above-and-beyond.

Thanks as well goes to two expert booksellers, Chris Farmer and Jo Virgil, for their guidance and encouragement through the process. They knew a real novice when they saw one.

And a special thank you to Rebecca Byrd Bretz for the outstanding cover design and her attention to the minutest creative details.

Clarke Straughan's

Romancing the Impossible

To Order the Book

Travel Treasure Publishing
6705 Hwy 290 West
Suite 502, Box 130 • Austin, Texas 78735

Yes, please send me *Romancing the Impossible!*

I enclose a check for **$19.95** plus **$3.95** for postage and handling for a total of **$23.90** For those living in Texas, add **$1.65** for sales tax for a total of **$25.55**. Make payable to Clarke Straughan.

If you would prefer to pay by credit card through PayPal,
please go to the website below.

PLEASE PRINT

Name _____

Address_____

City/State/Zip _____

Email Address _____

Please allow 2-3 weeks for delivery at the book rate.

www.TravelTreasureBooks.com